FURNITURE

TIME
LIFE
BOOKS ®

Other Publications:

MYSTERIES OF THE UNKNOWN

TIME FRAME

FIX IT YOURSELF

FITNESS, HEALTH & NUTRITION

SUCCESSFUL PARENTING

HEALTHY HOME COOKING

UNDERSTANDING COMPUTERS

LIBRARY OF NATIONS

THE ENCHANTED WORLD

THE KODAK LIBRARY OF CREATIVE PHOTOGRAPHY

GREAT MEALS IN MINUTES

THE CIVIL WAR

PLANET EARTH

COLLECTOR'S LIBRARY OF THE CIVIL WAR

THE EPIC OF FLIGHT

THE GOOD COOK

WORLD WAR II

HOME REPAIR AND IMPROVEMENT

THE OLD WEST

FURNITURE

TIME-LIFE BOOKS
ALEXANDRIA, VIRGINIA

Fix It Yourself was produced by
ST. REMY PRESS

MANAGING EDITOR	Kenneth Winchester
MANAGING ART DIRECTOR	Pierre Léveillé

Staff for *Furniture*

Series Editor	Kathleen M. Kiely
Senior Editor	Susan Bryan Reid
Art Director	Francine Lemieux
Research Editor	Elizabeth Cameron
Designer	Solange Pelland
Contributing Writers	Beverley Bennett, Margaret Caldbick, Edward Earle, Elizabeth Hart, Mitchell Herf, Michael Kleiza, Brian Parsons, Kathleen Pick, Alison Piper
Contributing Illustrators	Gérard Mariscalchi, Jacques Proulx
Technical Illustrator	Robert Paquet
Cover	Robert Monté
Index	Christine M. Jacobs
Administrator	Denise Rainville
Coordinator	Michelle Turbide
Assistant	Fiona Gilsenan
Systems Manager	Shirley Grynspan
Systems Analyst	Simon Lapierre
Studio Director	Daniel Bazinet
Photographer	Maryo Proulx

Time-Life Books Inc. is a wholly owned subsidiary of
TIME INCORPORATED

Founder	Henry R. Luce 1898-1967
Editor-in-Chief	Henry Anatole Grunwald
Chairman and Chief Executive Officer	J. Richard Munro
President and Chief Operating Officer	N. J. Nicholas Jr.
Chairman of the Executive Committee	Ralph P. Davidson
Corporate Editor	Ray Cave
Group Vice President, Books	Kelso F. Sutton
Vice President, Books	George Artandi

TIME-LIFE BOOKS INC.

EDITOR	George Constable
Executive Editor	Ellen Phillips
Director of Design	Louis Klein
Director of Editorial Resources	Phyllis K. Wise
Editorial Board	Russell B. Adams Jr., Dale M. Brown, Roberta Conlan, Thomas H. Flaherty, Lee Hassig, Donia Ann Steele, Rosalind Stubenberg, Kit van Tulleken, Henry Woodhead
Director of Photography and Research	John Conrad Weiser
PRESIDENT	Christopher T. Linen
Chief Operating Officer	John M. Fahey Jr.
Senior Vice President	James L. Mercer
Vice Presidents	Stephen L. Bair, Ralph J. Cuomo, Neal Goff, Stephen L. Goldstein, Juanita T. James, Hallett Johnson III, Carol Kaplan, Susan J. Maruyama, Robert H. Smith, Paul R. Stewart, Joseph J. Ward
Director of Production Services	Robert J. Passantino

Editorial Operations

Copy Chief	Diane Ullius
Production	Celia Beattie
Quality Control	James J. Cox (director)
Library	Louise D. Forstall
Correspondents	Elizabeth Kraemer-Singh (Bonn); Maria Vincenza Aloisi (Paris); Ann Natanson (Rome).

THE CONSULTANTS

Consulting Editor **David L. Harrison** is Managing Editor of Bibliographics Inc. in Alexandria, Virginia. He served as an editor of several Time-Life Books do-it-yourself series, including *Home Repair and Improvement*, *The Encyclopedia of Gardening* and *The Art of Sewing*.

Monte Burch has written more than 50 books on subjects such as furniture repair and cabinetmaking. He regularly contributes home improvement articles to national magazines and is a member of the National Association of Home and Workshop Writers.

Joseph Truini is Shop and Tools Editor of Popular Mechanics magazine. He specializes in how-to articles for do-it-yourselfers and has worked as a cabinetmaker, home improvement contractor and carpenter.

Irvin Wheeler teaches courses in cabinetmaking and woodworking techniques at Forsyth Technical College in Winston-Salem, North Carolina. He owned and operated Wheeler Refinishing, a furniture repair and refinishing store, for ten years.

Leonard G. Lee, special consultant for Canada, is president of Lee Valley Tools Ltd. and a woodworking hobbyist. His company sells fine woodworking tools and supplies and publishes specialized catalogues and brochures.

Library of Congress Cataloging-in-Publication Data
Furniture / the editors of Time-Life Books.
   p.   cm. – (Fix it yourself)
   Includes index.
   ISBN 0-8094-6220-6 (trade).
   ISBN 0-8094-6221-4 (lib. bdg.)
1. Furniture–Repairing. I. Time-Life Books. II. Series.
TT199.F768   1987
684.1'044–dc 19   87-25666
                                                          CIP

For information about any Time-Life Book, please write:
Reader Information
541 North Fairbanks Court
Chicago, Illinois 60611

CONTENTS

HOW TO USE THIS BOOK

Furniture is divided into three sections. The Emergency Guide on pages 8-11 provides information that can be indispensable in the event of an emergency that may arise while you are repairing furniture. Take the time to study this section *before* you need the important advice it contains.

The Repairs section—the heart of the book—is a system for troubleshooting and repairing chairs, cabinets, beds and upholstered furniture. Pictured below are four sample pages from the chapter on tables, with captions describing the various features of the book and how they work. If your table wobbles, for example, the Troubleshooting Guide will offer a number of possible causes. If the problem is a sticking mechanism on your extention table, you will be directed to page 36 for detailed, step-by-step directions for cleaning and lubricating the mechanism.

Each job has been rated by degree of difficulty and the average time it will take for a do-it-yourselfer to complete. Keep in mind that this rating is only a suggestion. Before deciding whether you should attempt a repair, first read all the instructions carefully. Then be guided by your own confidence, and the tools and time available to you. For more complex or time-consuming repairs, such as rewebbing a sofa

---

Introductory text
Describes the construction of tables, their most common problems and basic repair procedures.

Troubleshooting Guide
To use this chart, locate the symptom that most closely resembles your problem, review the possible causes in column 2, then follow the recommended procedures in column 3. Simple fixes may be explained on the chart; in most cases you will be directed to an illustrated, step-by-step repair sequence.

"Exploded" and cutaway diagrams
Locate and describe the components of the table.

TABLES

A standard, strong wood table consists of three main parts: the top, the apron and the legs. The top is attached to the apron, a horizontal wood understructure, by metal clips or by screws countersunk in pocket holes. In some simple kitchen tables, the apron is glued permanently to the top. Table legs are joined to the apron by a wood joint, either mortise-and-tenon or dowel *(page 123)*, or by a corner brace and hanger bolt *(page 120)*. On small coffee tables or end tables that don't have aprons, the legs are screwed or glued to the top. Two of the tables pictured at right have expandable tops. The drop-leaf table has one or two flaps; each is hinged to the top and supported from underneath. The extension table slides apart, allowing for the addition of one or more center leaves.

A table's surface reveals the use—and abuse—it receives. To repair scratches, nicks and stains, or to fill a minor crack, see Repairing Surfaces *(page 84)*. Fluctuations in humidity cause solid-wood table tops to swell and shrink, resulting in warpage and cracking. Cracks occur along the grain of a board or in a joint between boards. Use wood veneer, available at hardware stores and woodworking supply houses, to fill a wide split in the edge of a table top. When the split is long and

deep, first try working in glue and clamping the table top to bring the edges together. If this doesn't close the split, cut the top apart at the split and reglue the two pieces together *(page 39)*. The top should be refinished after the repair.

The stress placed on a table takes its toll at the joints connecting the legs to the apron. Wood joints come unglued and sockets cut into the leg weaken the wood, causing splits at the joint. The corner-brace joint, designed for easy disassembly, wears away the wood where the hanger bolt enters the leg. Before repairing a wobbly table, check that all screws and bolts holding it together are tight. Avoid tampering with a sound joint if possible; separate only the shaky ones, leaving joints that are firm and tight undisturbed.

Most table repairs require the simplest of workshop tools. Use a rubber mallet, which won't mar the wood, to tap pieces apart and together again. White glue or yellow wood glue will bond most joints and fill minute cracks. Pipe clamps *(page 122)* are especially useful for securing the large surface of a table top. Before applying the clamps, set the table upright, the legs resting squarely on a completely flat surface, and place a weight on the table top.

TROUBLESHOOTING GUIDE

SYMPTOM	POSSIBLE CAUSE	PROCEDURE
Table wobbly	Legs uneven	Level legs as for chair legs (p. 20) □○
	Mortise-and-tenon or dowel joint loose	Reglue joint (p. 32) ▨●
	Mortise-and-tenon or dowel joint broken	Rebuild joint (dowel, p. 124; mortise-and-tenon, p. 125) ▨●
	Split in leg at joint	Repair split (p. 33) □○
	Hanger bolt loose (corner-brace joint)	Tighten or reseat hanger bolt (p. 33) ▨●
	Pedestal leg joint loose	Reglue joint (p. 34) □○
	Pedestal leg joint broken	Rebuild dowel joint (p. 124) ▨●
Casters do not roll properly	Rollers stiff or dirty	Clean and lubricate rollers (p. 47) □○
	Rollers damaged	Replace rollers (p. 47) □○
Caster falls out of leg	Pressure against caster socket has enlarged caster hole	Replace caster (p. 47) ▨●
Scratches, cracks or gouges in finish	Wear and tear	Spot repair finish (p. 84) □○; refinish table (p. 96) ■●
Table edge split	Wood shrinkage	Fill split with veneer spline (p. 38) □○
Long, deep split in table top	Wood shrinkage; loosened glue bond	Work glue into split, then draw it together with clamps as for a chair seat (p. 24) □○; split top completely and rejoin (p. 39) ▨●
Veneer lifted or damaged	Dryness; aging adhesive	Reglue veneer (p. 93) ▨○; glue down blister (p. 93) ▨○; patch veneer (p. 94) ▨●
Extension mechanism sticks	Clogged with dirt and old lubricant	Clean and lubricate (p. 36) □○
	Sprocket out of position	Reposition sprocket (p. 36) □○
Extension table pin broken	Center leaf not properly aligned	Replace connecting pin (p. 37) □○
Drop leaf droops when raised	Pivot arm, gateleg or slider support worn	Add wedge to leaf support (p. 37) □○
	Pivot arm damaged	Replace pivot arm (p. 37) □●
Drop leaf loose	Hinge screws loose	Tighten screws; reseat screws (p. 120) □○
	Hinge damaged	Replace hinge (p. 38) □○

DEGREE OF DIFFICULTY: □ Easy ▨ Moderate ■ Complex
ESTIMATED TIME: ○ Less than 1 hour ◑ 1 to 3 hours ● Over 3 hours (*Does not include drying time*)

30

TABLES

EXTENSION TABLE

Connecting pins Hold center leaf to table top.

Removable center leaf When the two halves of the table are pulled apart, the leaf shown here is inserted between them to extend the table. In another version, the center leaf has two halves, hinged together and attached underneath the table top. This hinged center leaf can be swung up into position and unfolded when the table top is slid apart.

Top Made of solid wood boards or veneer-covered particleboard or plywood. Two-part top moves apart on an extension mechanism.

Extension mechanism Attached to the underside of the table top; made of wood or metal. Allows the table to be expanded; center leaves rest on the mechanism.

Apron Wood frame joined to the legs at the corners. Adds rigidity to the legs and overall table construction; found on sturdier tables.

Corner-brace joint The corner brace, a metal plate or a wood block, unites the leg to the apron on both sides. A hanger bolt screwed into the leg passes through the corner brace and is held with a wing nut or hex nut and washer.

Legs

PEDESTAL TABLE

Top

Legs Three or four legs, depending on the style, converge at the stem and are attached by dowel joints or, less commonly, dovetail joints.

Stem Central column of the table. Screwed to a board that is glued or screwed to the underside of the table top. A table may have one or two pedestals, depending on its size and style.

ROUND-TOP TABLE

Top Fastened to the apron with screws.

DROP-LEAF TABLE

Drop leaf Hinged flap that can be raised to extend the surface of the table.

Top

Pivot arm A drop-leaf support that swings out from the top of the apron to hold up the flap. Other common supports are the swing-out gateleg, which uses an entire leg assembly to hold up the flap, the slider, which is pulled out from underneath the table, and hinged metal brackets that lock into place when the leaf is fully raised.

Mortise-and-tenon joint Joins the leg and apron. Less common is the dowel joint (p. 123).

Apron Joined to the top with screws and to the legs with a wood joint.

31

Degree of difficulty and time
Rate the complexity of each repair, and how much time the job should take for a homeowner with average do-it-yourself skills.

Variations
Differences in style or construction are described throughout the book, particularly if a repair procedure varies from one type to another.

bottom or hand caning a chair seat, you may wish to call for professional service. You will still have saved time and money by diagnosing the problem yourself.

Most of the repairs in *Furniture* can be made with a screwdriver, a wood chisel, a hammer and a backsaw. For joining wood, you will need clamps, carpenter's glue and a solid workbench or table. You may also need power tools for some repairs. Basic carpentry tools—and the proper way to use them—are presented in the Tools & Techniques section starting on page 113. If you are a novice when it comes to furniture repair, read this section in preparation for a major job.

Furniture repair can lead to serious injury unless you take certain basic precautions. Wear safety goggles when cutting wood with a power saw, and put on a pair of work gloves to prevent cuts, especially when handling glass. If you are using strong chemicals, such as paint stripper, protect your hands with thick rubber gloves, and work in a well-ventilated area. When using most wood finishing products, wear a respirator with a vapor filter; heavy sanding requires a dust mask. Be kind to your back—work with a helper when lifting heavy pieces of furniture. Most important, follow all safety tips in the Emergency Guide and throughout the book.

Name of repair
You will be referred by the Troubleshooting Guide to the first page of a specific repair job.

Lead-ins
Bold lead-ins summarize each step or highlight the key action pictured in the illustration.

Cross-references
Direct you to important information elsewhere in the book, including access and finishing steps.

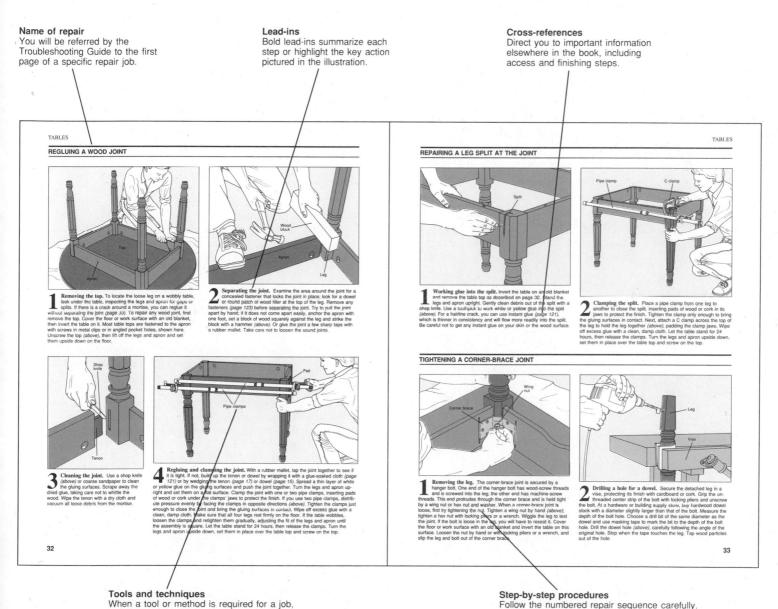

Tools and techniques
When a tool or method is required for a job, it is described within the step-by-step repair. General information on carpentry techniques, including the use of clamps, is covered in the Tools & Techniques section *(page 113).*

Step-by-step procedures
Follow the numbered repair sequence carefully. Depending on the result of each step, you may be directed to a later step, or to another part of the book, to complete the repair. Insets illustrate variations and provide close-up views of specific steps.

EMERGENCY GUIDE

Preventing problems in furniture repair. The emergency procedures in this section fall into two categories: quick clean-ups for spills on furniture, and immediate action for mishaps that may arise as you are repairing furniture.

The most important rule for cleaning up spills that can mar wood or upholstery is to act promptly *(page 10)*. Keep on hand a well-stocked household cleaning kit that includes clean, absorbent cloths and talcum powder or cornstarch to soak up stains before they set.

You can prevent most workshop mishaps by exercising the commonsense precautions presented here, but accidents may befall even the most careful worker. Sharp tools can cut skin and rough lumber can cause splinters. Many solvents, adhesives, chemical strippers and refinishing supplies contain chemicals that burn skin and eyes, and emit toxic fumes that can cause dizziness and faintness.

Spontaneous combustion is always a danger around improperly stored rags that have been used for refinishing. Cigarette ashes can cause fire to smolder in upholstered furniture and mattresses, emitting harmful toxic fumes. Deprive fire of its sneak attack by installing smoke detectors, and place fire extinguishers in strategic spots so that you can snuff a blaze before it gets the upper hand *(page 11)*.

Equip the work area with a basic first aid kit containing a mild antiseptic, adhesive bandages, sterilized gauze dressing, adhesive tape, scissors and tweezers. Make sure the work area is well lit and well ventilated. At the end of each job, put away all materials, then vacuum or wet-mop the work area to keep it free of dust and hazardous chemicals. The list of safety tips at right covers guidelines for performing repairs in this book; refer to each chapter for more specific safety information.

The Troubleshooting Guide on page 9 puts emergency procedures at your fingertips. It lists quick-action steps to take, and refers you to the procedures on pages 10 and 11 for more detailed information. Read these emergency instructions thoroughly before you need to use them, and familiarize yourself with the Tools & Techniques section *(page 113)*, which describes the safe use of tools.

When in doubt about your ability to handle an emergency, don't hesitate to call for help. Post numbers for the fire department and the poison control center near the telephone. Even in non-emergency situations, these professionals can answer questions concerning the safe use of tools and materials. Consult your fire department or local environmental agency for the correct disposal of toxic products in your community.

SAFETY TIPS

1. Before beginning any repair in this book, read the entire procedure. Familiarize yourself with the specific safety information presented in each chapter.

2. Carefully read the label on any container of paint, solvent, adhesive or refinishing product before using it. Follow the manufacturer's instructions and pay special attention to hazard warnings and storage instructions. If transferring the contents to another container, label the new container accurately.

3. Guard against electrical shock when using power tools. Plug power tools into grounded outlets only, and never cut off or bypass the third, or grounding, prong on a power tool's plug. A tool with a two-prong plug must be labeled "double insulated." Do not use any power tool in damp conditions.

4. Wear safety goggles when operating a circular saw and when using toxic substances such as chemical strippers, solvents and refinishing products.

5. Wear heavy gloves to handle broken glass and special rubber gloves to apply caustic refinishing products.

6. Wear a respirator with a dust filter when when doing dusty jobs and with an organic-vapor cartridge to protect against toxic fumes. Replace the filters regularly according to the manufacturer's instructions.

7. Do not drink alcoholic beverages while using products that produce toxic vapors—the combination can cause illness. Do not smoke while using flammable chemicals, and do not eat in the work area.

8. When working with flammable chemicals or with power tools, have on hand a fire extinguisher rated ABC or BC, and know how to use it before you begin work *(page 11)*. Install smoke detectors in your home and work area.

9. Wear long pants and a long-sleeved shirt when working with chemicals that are dangerous to the skin. Change after leaving the work area, and launder work clothes separately.

10. Ventilate the work area well when using paints, solvents, adhesives and refinishing products. If you feel faint or sick, leave the room and get fresh air *(page 11)*, then improve ventilation before continuing work.

11. Hang rags soaked in paint, solvent, adhesives or refinishing products outdoors and allow them to dry thoroughly, or store them in airtight metal or glass containers.

12. Keep tools and toxic materials out of the reach of children. If children or pets contact or ingest chemicals, call the poison control center or veterinarian at once. Store chemical products away from sources of heat (including sunlight).

13. Do not pour paints, solvents, adhesives or refinishing products down a house drain or into a septic system.

14. Post the telephone numbers of your fire department, hospital and local poison control center near the telephone.

TROUBLESHOOTING GUIDE

SYMPTOM	PROCEDURE
Fire in paint or solvent	Use ABC or BC fire extinguisher *(p. 11)*; if fire spreads, leave house and call fire department
Smoldering upholstery or mattress	Use A or ABC fire extinguisher *(p. 11)*, or soak fire with plenty of water, then cut open burned area or take furniture outside; if fire spreads, leave house and call fire department
Electrical fire in power tool	Unplug power cord; if fire continues, use ABC or BC fire extinguisher *(p. 11)*; if outlet or wall is on fire, leave house and call fire department
Cut or minor wound	Stop the bleeding *(p. 11)*; if bleeding persists or wound is deep, seek medical attention
Splinter	Use needle or tweezers, sterilized with alcohol or flame, to open skin around splinter and pull splinter out; if splinter is lodged deeply, seek medical attention
Foreign particle in eye	Do not rub eye. Remove loose particle with moistened end of clean cloth or tissue. Do not attempt to remove any particle on pupil or embedded in eye. If particle cannot be removed, cover eye with sterile gauze and consult physician immediately.
Paint, solvent, adhesive or refinishing product splashed into eye	Flush eye with water *(p. 11)* and consult physician immediately
Skin bonded with super adhesive	Dab acetone or nail polish remover on glued area and let it sit for a few minutes. Gently peel skin apart—do not pull. Repeat application if necessary. Wash area thoroughly with soap and water.
Eyelids bonded with super adhesive	Do not attempt to separate lids; consult physician immediately
Faintness, dizziness, nausea, blurred vision when working with paints, solvents, adhesives, refinishing products	Leave room immediately to get fresh air *(p. 11)*; have helper cover solvents and ventilate room; read instructions on container label and seek medical attention if necessary
Paint, solvent, adhesive or refinishing product swallowed	Call local poison control center, emergency room or physician immediately; follow emergency instructions on label and bring container with you to hospital
Spill on upholstery fabric	Blot up spill immediately without rubbing *(p. 10)*; clean fabric *(p. 66)*
Spill on wood furniture	Wipe up immediately with clean, dry cloth, working from edges to center; clean and condition wood finish *(p. 86)*
Water damage to furniture caused by flood or leak	Place wet furniture on flat surface outdoors; do not place in sunlight. Open cabinet doors and pull out drawers. Remove cushions and slip covers from upholstered furniture. A water-logged mattress should be discarded
Solvent, adhesive or refinishing product spilled in work area	If spill is small, clean up immediately *(p. 10)*; if spill is more than a quart of flammable material, or more than a gallon of any toxic material, leave house and call fire department
Power tool gives off sparks or shocks user	Unplug power cord without touching tool, or turn off power at service panel
Power cord or plug sparking or hot to touch	Turn off power at service panel, then unplug power cord, using glove or towel for insulation; call electrician to check outlet and wiring for damage

TOXIC MATERIALS IN FURNITURE AND THE WORKSHOP

The fumes emitted by solvents found in some paints, adhesives, chemical strippers and refinishing products are toxic if inhaled in concentrated amounts. To reduce the risk to your health, work outdoors if possible, positioning yourself and the furniture so that fumes will be blown away from you.

Indoors, make sure the work area is well ventilated; open all windows and aim a fan to the outside to vent fumes. Protect yourself from inhaling toxic chemicals by wearing a respirator fitted with the appropriate filter cartridges *(page 114)*. When sanding wood, wear a dust mask to avoid inhaling dust. Protect your skin from caustic or toxic substances by wearing rubber gloves rated to protect against the chemical you are using.

Plywood, particleboard, fiberboard and other manufactured wood products in furniture may contain urea formaldehyde, used as a binder and adhesive. These wood products are safe to handle, but the formaldehyde leaches into the air in a process called "outgassing," which causes indoor pollution. Over the past few years, manufacturers have reduced the use of formaldehyde in wood products. To cut the formaldehyde levels in your home and workshop, use solid wood, or particleboard made without formaldehyde. Alternatively, use exterior-grade plywood, made with a resin that is much more stable than formaldehyde. As an extra precaution, seal all unfinished wood-product surfaces with paint or polyurethane varnish.

QUICK WIPE-UPS FOR FURNITURE SPILLS

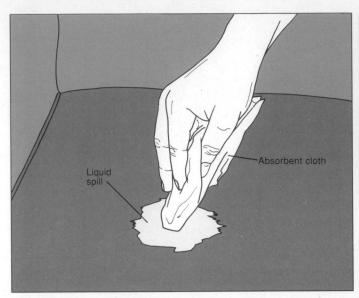
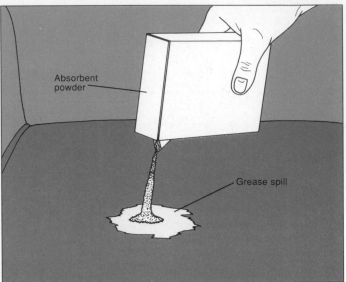

Lifting a stain from upholstery fabric. Treat spills on upholstery fabric immediately, before
they have a chance to soak into the fabric and cause permanent stains. To blot up a spilled
liquid, crumple up a clean, absorbent cloth and lightly dab the spill, absorbing the liquid into the
cloth *(above, left).* Continue blotting up the spill without rubbing until all of the liquid is absorbed.
To blot up grease or oil spills, pour an absorbent powder such as cornstarch or talcum powder
onto the spot *(above, right).* Leave the powder on the stain for one minute, or until it becomes
saturated, then carefully shake it off or use a blunt knife or a spoon to scoop it up. Repeat the
procedure, pouring on more clean powder and removing it carefully. To treat the remaining stain,
use the cleaning techniques described on page 66.

CLEANUPS IN THE WORKSHOP

SOLVENTS FOR SPILLED CHEMICALS

Material	Solvent
Latex paint or water-based wood stain	Water
Alkyd paint or oil-based wood stain	Mineral spirits or turpentine
Linseed oil or tung oil	Mineral spirits or turpentine
Varnish	Mineral spirits or turpentine
Lacquer	Mineral spirits or lacquer thinner
Shellac	Denatured alcohol
White or yellow glue	Water
Contact cement (solvent-based) Contact cement (water-based)	Mineral spirits Water
Epoxy glue	Soap and water (if not set) Acetone (if set)

Wiping up chemical spills. Work quickly to clean up chemical
spills in the work area. If the area is not already well ventilated,
open all windows and doors to the outside and turn on fans to
supplement air movement. If the spill is small, use a clean rag
dipped in the appropriate solvent *(left)* to wipe up the spill. For a
larger spill—up to a quart of flammable solvent or up to a gallon
of non-flammable toxic material—pour a generous amount of ver-
miculite or cat litter over the spill. Wait 15 minutes, or until the litter
has absorbed the spill, then use an old putty knife or a dustpan to
scoop the saturated litter into an empty disposable metal can.
Repeat the procedure until the entire spill is lifted. Scrub any
remaining traces of the spill with a clean rag or brush it off with a
scrub brush dipped in the appropriate solvent. Mop the area with
warm, soapy water, rinse it and wipe it dry with a clean rag. To
dispose of all solvent-soaked materials, place them in airtight
metal or glass containers, then call your local fire department or
environmental agency for the laws regulating the disposal of toxic
materials in your community.

   If you spill more than the amounts of hazardous chemicals
described above, do not attempt to clean them up. Open any
windows and doors that you can reach quickly and safely, turn
off electrical power and pilot lights, if possible, then leave the
house and call the fire department for advice.

EXTINGUISHING A FIRE

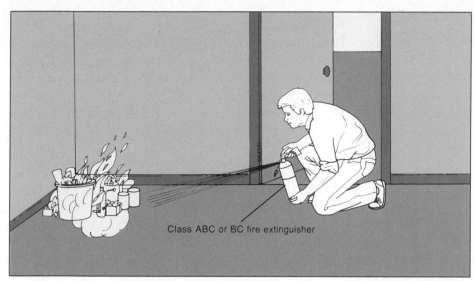

Class ABC or BC fire extinguisher

Fighting a chemical fire. Have someone call the fire department. If there are flames or smoke coming from the walls or ceiling, leave the house to call for help. To snuff a small fire in paints or solvents, in a power tool or outlet, or in a mattress or upholstery, use a dry-chemical fire extinguisher rated ABC. Note the nearest exit and position yourself 6 to 10 feet from the fire. Holding the extinguisher upright, pull the lock pin out of the handle and aim the nozzle at the base of the flames. Squeeze the handle and spray in a quick side-to-side motion until the fire is completely out. Watch for "flashback," or rekindling, and be prepared to spray again. If the fire spreads, leave the house. Dispose of any burned waste following the advice of your local fire department. Have your fire extinguisher recharged professionally after any use.

FIRST AID TREATMENTS

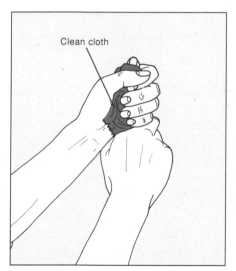

Clean cloth

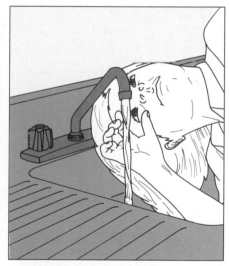

Cuts and scratches. To stop the bleeding, wrap a clean cloth around the cut and apply direct pressure with your hand, elevating the limb *(above)*. If the cloth becomes blood-soaked, add another cloth to the wound without removing the first one. Continue applying pressure, keeping the limb elevated, until the bleeding subsides. If the wound is minor, wash it with soap and water and bandage it. Seek medical attention if bleeding persists or if the wound is deep or gaping.

Toxic vapors. Exposure to toxic vapors can cause headache, dizziness, faintness, fatigue or nausea. At the first sign of any of these symptoms, leave the work area immediately and get fresh air. Remove all clothing that has been splashed by chemicals. Loosen your clothing at the waist, chest and neck. If you feel faint, sit with your head lowered between your knees *(above)*. Have someone ventilate the work area, close all containers, read instructions on the container labels and call the poison control center in your area for medical advice.

Flushing chemicals from the eye. A liquid chemical accidentally splashed in the eye must be washed out quickly. Holding the eyelids apart with your fingers, position the injured eye under a gentle flow of cool water, tilting the head to prevent the chemical from being washed into the uninjured eye *(above)*. Flush the eye for 10 minutes, then cover it with a sterile gauze bandage and seek medical attention immediately.

CHAIRS

A chair takes more punishment than any other piece of furniture. A simple kitchen chair weighs only a few pounds, but it regularly supports over a hundred pounds. Every day it is dragged across the floor, rocked onto its back legs and twisted as the weight on it shifts.

The joints, the weak points in a chair's structure, are first to succumb to this treatment. A loose or broken joint should be reglued or rebuilt as soon as possible; neglect leads to weakening of other joints. First try to pull a loose joint apart by hand. If it does not separate, look for hidden nails or dowels that lock the joint in place and remove them (page 123). Whenever possible, separate the joint completely, scrape the dried glue from both parts of the joint, then apply new glue and clamp the repair. When the joint cannot be completely separated, pull it apart as far as possible, remove as much of the old glue as you can, work in new glue and clamp the repair. You risk weakening firm joints by forcing a loose one, so inspect other joints before completing the repair.

As you dismantle a chair to clean its joints, note how the pieces are assembled. The pictures at right show two typical chair constructions: platform and frame. The most common joints are dowel and mortise-and-tenon (Tools & Techniques, page 123). Occasionally, a dowel or tenon will have shrunk and should be enlarged before gluing and clamping. One handy trick is to wrap a glue-soaked cloth around the dowel or tenon (page 121). A wood wedge can also be used to build up a shrunken dowel or tenon. Rocking chairs are less susceptible to twisting than regular chairs, but the rockers occasionally split. Glue and reinforce cracks in the rockers (page 22) or have badly worn rockers replaced.

For many chair repairs, the only tools required are a rubber mallet, wood glue and a web clamp (page 123). If you don't own a rubber mallet, use a hammer and block of wood. A tourniquet clamp fashioned from strong cord or rope (page 123) is an effective substitute for the web clamp. Hose clamps, available at hardware or automotive stores, make practical clamps for round pieces. In some cases, heavy books and gravity can do the work of a clamp.

Before clamping a chair, set it upright on a perfectly flat surface. Placing a weight on the seat will often protect the legs from developing the annoying wobble symptomatic of a reglued chair. For best results, clamp a freshly glued chair for 24 hours. On the other hand, if you are repairing all six dining room chairs at once and need the clamp, you can safely release it after three to four hours; but leave the reglued chair undisturbed for the remaining 20 hours.

The stress placed on a chair can split a wood seat or wear an upholstered seat. Cane and rush seats are even more fragile. Prolong the life of a cane seat by regularly moistening its underside with water. Prewoven cane is the easiest to replace. Handweaving individual strands of cane across a seat, or wrapping fiber rush around a chair frame, takes more time and patience, but makes restoration inexpensive and rewarding for the hobbyist. Craft or cane stores stock the necessary supplies.

TROUBLESHOOTING GUIDE

SYMPTOM	POSSIBLE CAUSE	PROCEDURE
Chair wobbly	Foot rail loose	Glue foot rail (p. 14) □○
	Back loose	Separate back and reglue (platform, p. 15; frame, p. 16) ▣●
	Legs uneven	Sand bottoms of legs until even (p. 20) □○
	Glides worn unevenly	Replace glides or insert washers in glides (p. 20) □○
	Legs loose	Separate legs from seat; reglue (platform, p. 15; frame, p. 16) ▣●
Leg, stile or rail broken	Jagged, longitudinal split	Glue split (p. 20) □○
	Clean, complete break	Glue and reinforce with a dowel (p. 21) ▣●
Rocker runner broken	Break along grain	Glue and reinforce with a dowel (p. 22) ▣○
Back splat broken	Wear and tear	Glue splat (p. 20) □○
Bentwood curve split	Stress along bend	Steam the wood, clamp and glue (p. 23) ▣●
Wood seat split	Wood shrinkage	Glue seat (p. 24) □○; or disassemble chair, break seat along split and glue (p. 24) ▣●
Upholstered seat worn	Wear and tear	Replace upholstery fabric (p. 25) ▣●
Cane seat broken	Stress, dry conditions	Replace with prewoven cane (p. 26) ▣●; or reweave cane seat (p. 27) ■●
Rush seat broken	Wear and tear	Reweave rush seat (p. 29) ■●

DEGREE OF DIFFICULTY: □ Easy ▣ Moderate ■ Complex
ESTIMATED TIME: ○ Less than 1 hour ● 1 to 3 hours ● Over 3 hours (Does not include drying time)

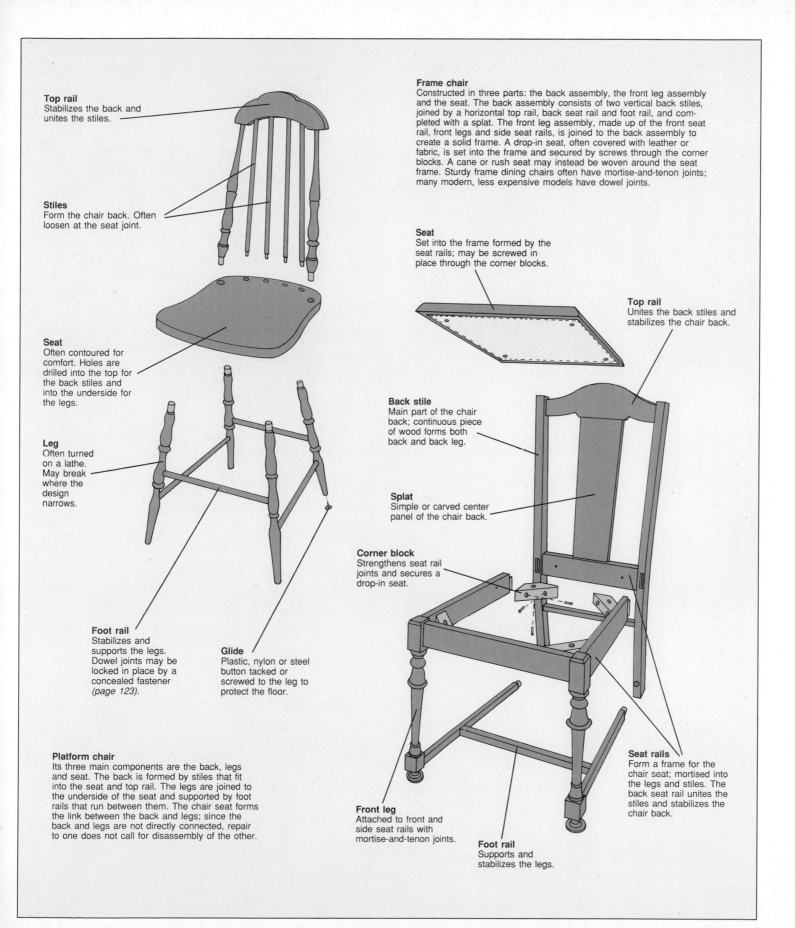

Top rail
Stabilizes the back and unites the stiles.

Stiles
Form the chair back. Often loosen at the seat joint.

Seat
Often contoured for comfort. Holes are drilled into the top for the back stiles and into the underside for the legs.

Leg
Often turned on a lathe. May break where the design narrows.

Foot rail
Stabilizes and supports the legs. Dowel joints may be locked in place by a concealed fastener *(page 123)*.

Glide
Plastic, nylon or steel button tacked or screwed to the leg to protect the floor.

Platform chair
Its three main components are the back, legs and seat. The back is formed by stiles that fit into the seat and top rail. The legs are joined to the underside of the seat and supported by foot rails that run between them. The chair seat forms the link between the back and legs; since the back and legs are not directly connected, repair to one does not call for disassembly of the other.

Frame chair
Constructed in three parts: the back assembly, the front leg assembly and the seat. The back assembly consists of two vertical back stiles, joined by a horizontal top rail, back seat rail and foot rail, and completed with a splat. The front leg assembly, made up of the front seat rail, front legs and side seat rails, is joined to the back assembly to create a solid frame. A drop-in seat, often covered with leather or fabric, is set into the frame and secured by screws through the corner blocks. A cane or rush seat may instead be woven around the seat frame. Sturdy frame dining chairs often have mortise-and-tenon joints; many modern, less expensive models have dowel joints.

Seat
Set into the frame formed by the seat rails; may be screwed in place through the corner blocks.

Top rail
Unites the back stiles and stabilizes the chair back.

Back stile
Main part of the chair back; continuous piece of wood forms both back and back leg.

Splat
Simple or carved center panel of the chair back.

Corner block
Strengthens seat rail joints and secures a drop-in seat.

Seat rails
Form a frame for the chair seat; mortised into the legs and stiles. The back seat rail unites the stiles and stabilizes the chair back.

Front leg
Attached to front and side seat rails with mortise-and-tenon joints.

Foot rail
Supports and stabilizes the legs.

TIGHTENING A LOOSE FOOT RAIL

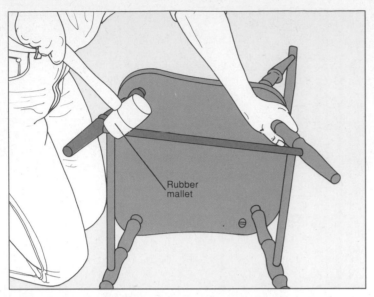

Rubber
mallet

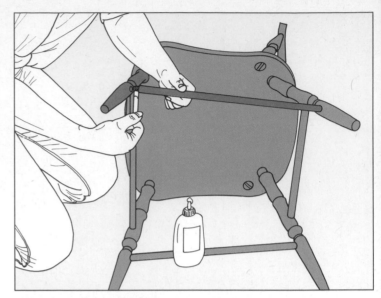

1 **Separating the joint.** Examine the chair leg for signs of a fastener that locks the joint; look for a nail hole, dowel end or patch of wood putty. Remove a fastener *(page 123)* before separating the joint. Set the chair on its side. If there is not much movement in the joint, gently pull it apart as far as it will go, scrape out dried glue with a shop knife, then work in white or yellow glue *(page 121)* and clamp the joint *(step 3)*. If the joint has a lot of movement, separate it completely. To separate a stubborn joint, hold the chair securely and tap the inside of the leg with a rubber mallet *(above)*, then go to step 2.

2 **Cleaning and regluing the joint.** Use a shop knife or coarse sandpaper to scrape away dried glue, taking care not to whittle the wood. A gouge *(page 113)* is especially useful for cleaning a hard-to-reach dowel hole. With a rubber mallet, tap the joint together to see if it is tight, then tap it apart again. Build up a slightly loose joint by wrapping the dowel with a glue-soaked cloth *(page 121)*. Tighten a very loose joint by wedging the dowel *(page 15)*. Spread a thin layer of white or yellow glue on any uncoated gluing surfaces *(above)*, then fit the dowel into the hole, tapping lightly on the outside of the leg with a rubber mallet to seat it completely.

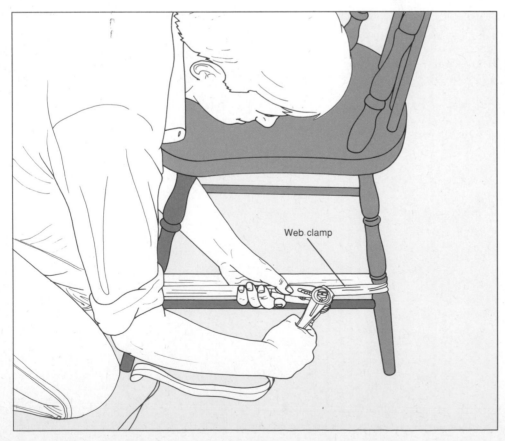

Web clamp

3 **Clamping the joint.** Set the chair upright, with all legs sitting squarely on a flat surface. Wrap a web clamp around the two opposite legs, as shown. Tighten the clamp only enough to close the joint and bring the gluing surfaces in contact. If you don't have a web clamp, use a piece of heavy cord to fashion a tourniquet clamp *(page 123)*. Wipe away excess glue with a clean, damp cloth. Wait 24 hours for the glue to set, then release the clamp.

REGLUING THE BACK OF A PLATFORM CHAIR

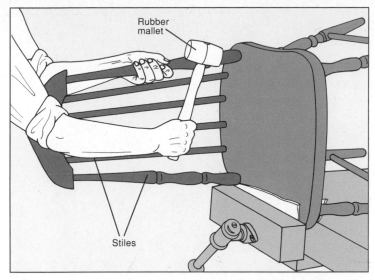

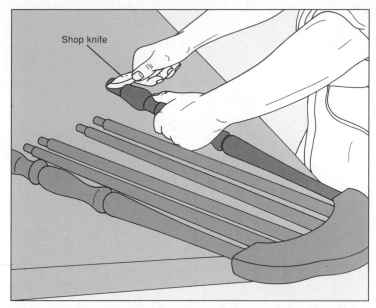

1 **Separating the back from the seat.** For a strong repair to a loose back, separate the back from the seat completely and reglue all the joints. Set the chair on its side and secure the seat in a vise, protecting its finish with cardboard or wood. To loosen a stile, pull it firmly while tapping the seat at the stile joint with a rubber mallet *(above)*. Continue in this manner until all the stiles are separated from the seat.

2 **Cleaning the gluing surfaces.** Scrape dried glue from the dowels and holes with a shop knife *(above)*, taking care not to remove any wood. Use a gouge *(page 113)* to clean out the dowel holes. Fit the joints together to see if they are tight. If the joints fit snugly, separate them again and go to step 4. Build up a slightly loose dowel by wrapping it with a glue-soaked cloth *(page 121)*. Tighten a very loose joint by wedging the dowel *(step 3)*.

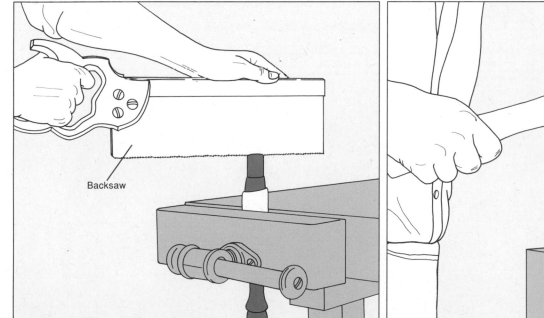

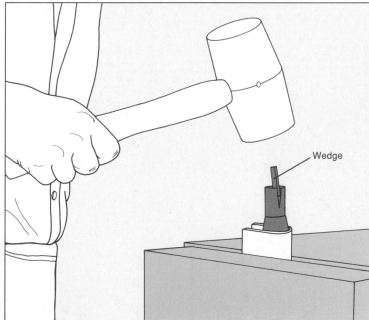

3 **Enlarging a dowel.** Remove the stile from the top rail: While a helper holds the stile, place a block of wood against the top rail next to the stile, and tap the block with a hammer to loosen the stile from the rail. Secure the stile in a vise, protecting its finish with cardboard or cork. With a backsaw, cut a slot down the center of the dowel *(above, left)*, stopping about two thirds of the way into the dowel. Use the backsaw to cut a hardwood wedge slightly longer and wider than the slot. Tap the wedge gently into the slot with a rubber mallet until the dowel widens slightly *(above, right)*. Saw the wedge flush with the dowel, then sand it smooth. Spread a thin layer of white or yellow glue on the dowel that fits into the top rail and in its hole, then tap the stile back into the top rail with the mallet.

REGLUING THE BACK OF A PLATFORM CHAIR (continued)

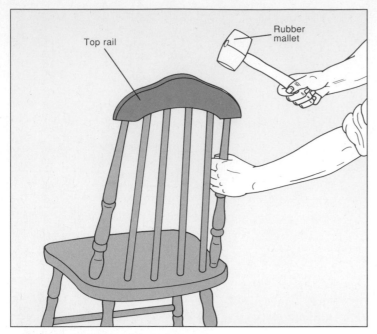

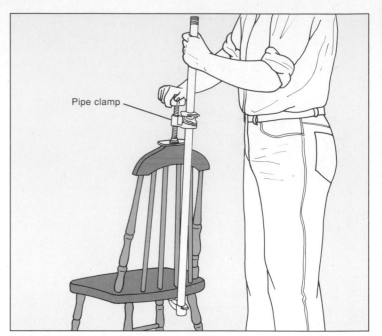

4 **Installing the back.** Spread a layer of white or yellow glue on the dowels and in the holes, then fit each stile into its hole. Tap along the top rail with the mallet to seat the dowels.

5 **Clamping the repair.** Slip a pipe clamp onto the chair, positioning one jaw on the top rail and the other under the seat. Insert pads of wood or cork to protect the finish. Tighten the clamp only enough to close the joints and bring the gluing surfaces together *(above)*. Wipe away excess glue with a clean, damp cloth. Wait 24 hours for the glue to set, then release the clamp.

REGLUING THE BACK OF A FRAME CHAIR

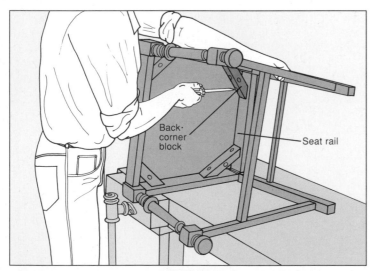

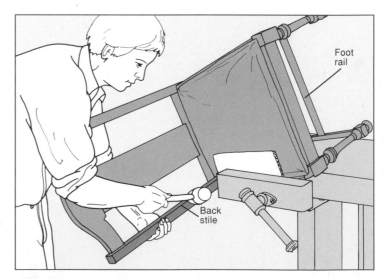

1 **Releasing the back seat rail.** The stress exerted on a frame chair often loosens the joints connecting the seat rails to the back stiles. To make a strong repair, separate the back from the seat and reglue the joints. Set the chair on its side on a work surface. Examine the stiles for fasteners that lock the joints; look for nail holes, dowel ends or patches of wood putty. Remove any fastener *(page 123)* before separating the joints. Remove the screw holding each back corner block to the back seat rail *(above)*. It is not necessary to unscrew the front corner blocks.

2 **Separating the back from the seat.** Secure the seat in a vise padded with cardboard. With a rubber mallet, tap on the lower back stile near the seat joint until the joint separates *(above)*, then tap the foot rail loose from the back stile. Secure the chair on its other side and repeat the procedure to knock apart the other seat joint and foot rail joint. Lift off the back and place it on a work surface. Scrape dried glue out of the joints with a shop knife, then tap the joints together to see if they are tight. If the joints fit snugly, separate them again and go to step 4. Build up a slightly loose joint with a glue-soaked cloth *(page 121)*. Tighten a very loose joint by wedging the tenon *(step 3)*.

REGLUING THE BACK OF A FRAME CHAIR (continued)

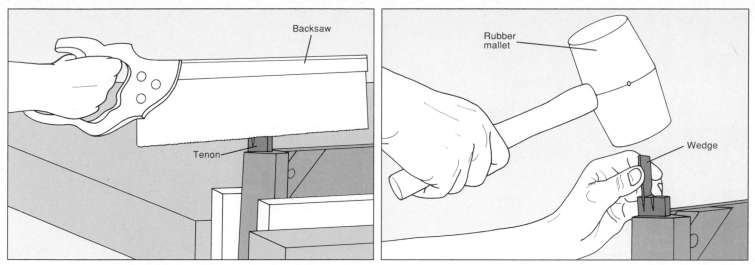

3 **Enlarging a tenon.** One way to rebuild a tenon is by pressing shims of adhesive-backed hardwood veneer on the sides of the tenon, then sanding the shims to make a good fit. To wedge a tenon, use a backsaw to cut two parallel slots across the tenon, stopping about two thirds of the way into the tenon each time *(above, left)*. Use the backsaw to cut two hardwood wedges slightly longer and wider than the slots. Tap each wedge gently into a slot until the tenon widens slightly *(above, right)*, then saw each wedge flush with the tenon and sand it smooth.

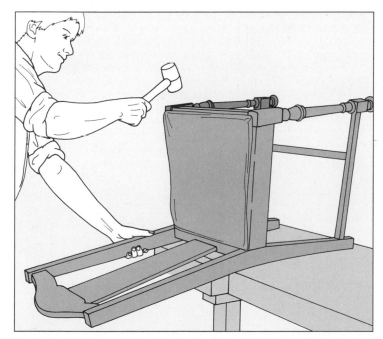

4 **Reassembling the chair.** Spread a thin layer of white or yellow glue on all the gluing surfaces. Set the chair back on the work surface, fit the seat and foot rails into the back stiles and tap the joints together with a rubber mallet, as shown. Screw the corner blocks securely to the seat rail.

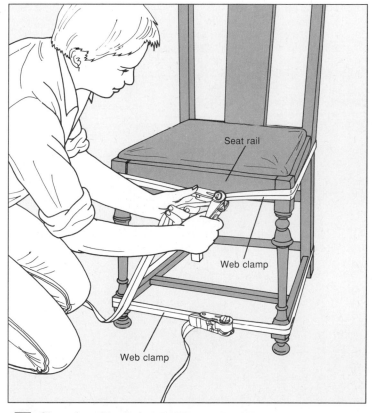

5 **Clamping the chair.** Set the chair upright, with all legs resting squarely on a flat surface. Wrap one web clamp around the seat rails and another around the legs where the foot rails join the back stiles. Tighten the clamps only enough to close the joints and bring together the gluing surfaces. If you do not have web clamps, make tourniquet clamps *(page 123)*. Wipe away excess glue with a clean, damp cloth. Release the clamps after 24 hours.

REGLUING THE LEGS OF A PLATFORM CHAIR

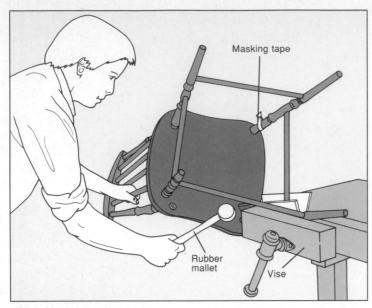

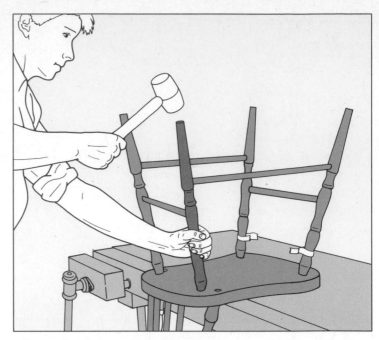

1 **Separating the legs from the seat.** To help you reassemble the chair, mark the front legs with masking tape. Examine the top of the seat for wood wedges that lock the leg dowels in place. Drill out any wedges before separating the legs from the seat. Try to pull the legs free of the seat by hand. If they do not come out of the seat easily, secure a leg in a vise, protecting its finish then use a rubber mallet to knock on the bottom of the seat near the joint to loosen the leg slightly. Loosen all stubborn legs alternately, repositioning the chair in the vise and tapping near the leg *(above)*. Then pull out the legs and foot rails as a unit. If the joints between the foot rails and the legs are loose, mark their positions with tape, then remove and reglue them *(page 14)*, reassembling the foot rails and legs first, then refitting the legs to the seat.

2 **Refitting the legs to the seat.** With a shop knife or coarse sandpaper, scrape dried glue from the gluing surfaces. Place the chair upside down on a work surface and fit the legs into the seat, inserting the marked legs in the front. With a rubber mallet, tap the joints together to see if they are tight *(above)*, then remove them. Build up a slightly loose joint by wrapping the dowel with a glue-soaked cloth *(page 121)*; tighten a very loose joint by wedging the dowel *(page 15)*. Spread a thin layer of white or yellow glue on the dowels and in the holes, then fit each leg into its hole again, tapping on the end of the leg lightly with the mallet to seat the dowel.

3 **Securing the joints.** Remove the masking tape from the front legs. Set the chair upright with all legs sitting squarely on a flat surface. Place heavy books or other weights on the seat to press the chair legs into their holes *(left)*. Wipe away excess glue with a clean, damp cloth. Allow the glue to set for 24 hours.

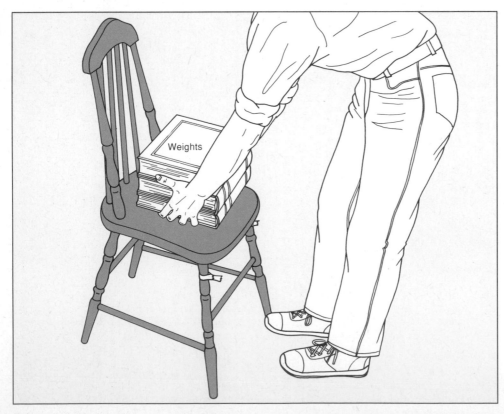

REGLUING LOOSE FRONT LEGS ON A FRAME CHAIR

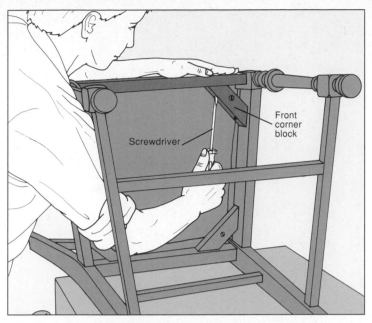

1 **Releasing the corner blocks.** Set the chair on its back on a work surface. Examine the legs for fasteners that lock the joints; look for nail holes, dowel ends or patches of wood putty. Remove any fasteners *(page 123)* before separating the legs from the side seat rails. Use a screwdriver to remove the screws holding each front corner block to the front seat rail *(above)*. It is not necessary to remove the blocks from the side seat rails.

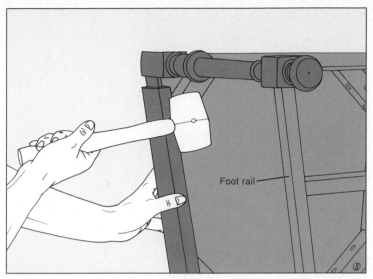

2 **Separating the legs from the chair.** Work slowly and carefully to avoid damaging the chair. Holding the side seat rail securely with one hand, tap on the inside of the leg with a rubber mallet to release the leg from the rail *(above)*. Then hold the foot rail and tap the leg at the foot rail joint until it separates. Repeat the procedure for the other front leg. Lift away the front legs and front seat rail. If the joint between a leg and the front seat rail is also loose, anchor the seat rail with your foot and, with the rubber mallet, tap the joint apart.

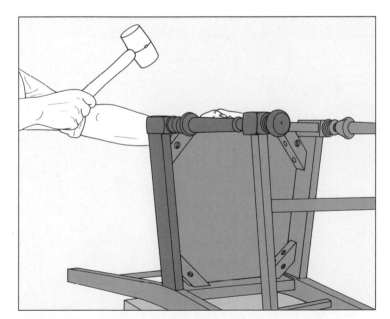

3 **Refitting the legs.** With a shop knife or coarse sandpaper, scrape dried glue from the gluing surfaces, taking care not to remove any wood. Tap the legs onto the seat and foot rails with the rubber mallet to see if the joints are tight *(above)*, then take them apart. Build up a slightly loose joint by wrapping the tenon with a glue-soaked cloth *(page 121)*. Tighten a very loose joint by wedging the tenon *(page 17)*. Spread a thin layer of white or yellow glue on the gluing surfaces. Fit the legs onto the seat and foot rails and tap them in with the mallet. Screw the corner blocks securely to the front seat rail.

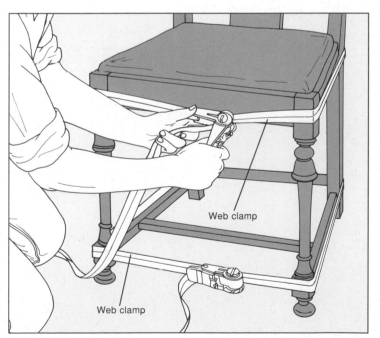

4 **Clamping the joints.** Set the chair upright, with all legs resting squarely on a flat surface. Wrap a web clamp around the seat rails and another around the legs where the foot rails join them. Tighten the clamps only enough to close the joints and bring together the gluing surfaces *(above)*. If you do not have web clamps, make tourniquet clamps *(page 123)*. Wipe away excess glue with a clean, damp cloth. Release the clamps after 24 hours.

LEVELING THE LEGS

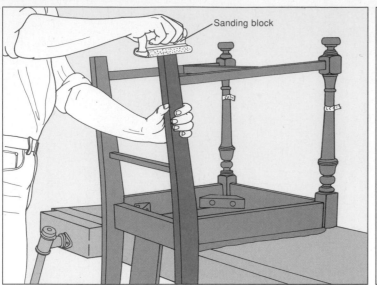

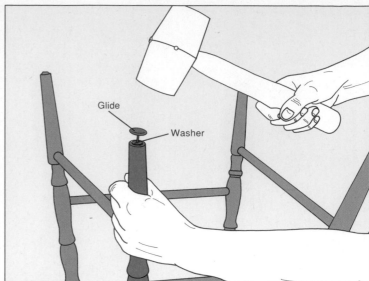

Sanding down or building up. Over the years, the wood in a chair may swell and shrink, or wear unevenly, causing an annoying wobble. A wobble may also result from careless regluing. To identify the uneven legs, set the chair on a flat work surface and rock it. The legs that the chair rests on as it rocks are the long ones; mark them with masking tape. Turn the chair upside down. If there are no glides on the bottoms of the legs, lightly sand down the two marked legs with a sanding block *(above, left)*, setting the chair upright frequently to check the wobble.

If there are glides on the chair legs, check to see that all four are in place. If a glide is missing or worn, pry up the remaining glides with a screwdriver and install a new set. If the entire set is still intact, you can sometimes build up the short legs by prying up the glides on those legs and inserting washers between the glides and the leg bottoms *(above, right)*.

REPAIRING SPLITS

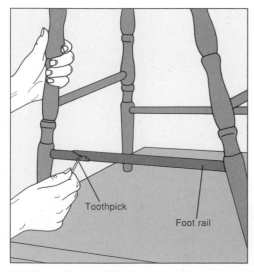

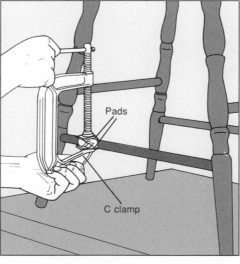

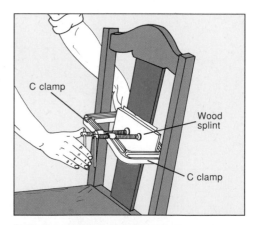

Gluing a long split. To rejoin a long jagged split in a leg, foot rail or back stile, gently separate the split and work white or yellow glue into it with a toothpick *(above, left)*. Press together the split pieces and wipe away excess glue with a clean, damp cloth. Wrap the glued area with waxed paper to keep it from sticking, then tighten a C clamp around the split just enough to draw it together *(above, right)*; insert wood or cork pads to protect the finish. Allow 24 hours for the glue to set, then release the clamp.

Splinting a broken splat. Gently separate the split and apply white or yellow glue with a toothpick. Align the broken sections and press them together by hand. Wipe away excess glue with a clean, damp cloth. To make a splint, place waxed paper and a flat piece of wood across the break on each side, and secure them with a pair of C clamps *(above)*. If the splat is slightly curved, use 1/8-inch hardboard as a splint. Wait 24 hours for the glue to set before removing the splint. To refinish the damaged area, see page 84.

REJOINING A CLEAN FRACTURE

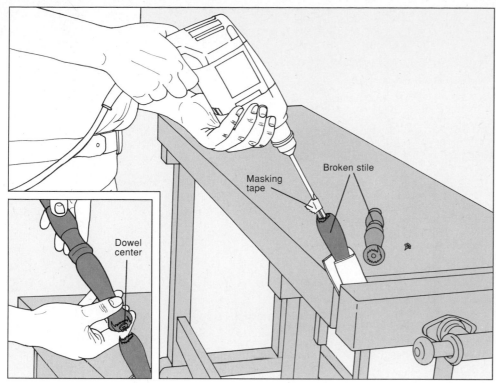

1 Drilling a dowel hole. To repair a clean break across a leg, foot rail or back stile, separate the part from the chair and insert a dowel to rejoin the two pieces. Use a rubber mallet to knock apart the joints holding the broken part, in this case a back stile, to the chair. Secure one piece of the broken stile in a vise, protecting its finish with cardboard or cork. Use an awl to punch a starting point in the center of the stile. Fit a power drill with a bit that matches the size of the dowel you will use (a 1/4-inch dowel for narrow pieces, a 3/8-inch dowel for wide pieces). Wrap masking tape around the drill bit 7/8 inch from the end and bore a dowel hole straight into the center of the stile, stopping when the masking tape touches the wood. Remove the broken piece from the vise and secure the other piece in the vise. To make sure the two pieces will fit together properly, insert a dowel center *(page 124)* into the drilled hole, align the pieces in proper relation to each other *(inset)* and press them together. The dowel center will mark a starting point in the undrilled piece. Using the mark as a guide, drill a matching dowel hole in the second piece *(left)*.

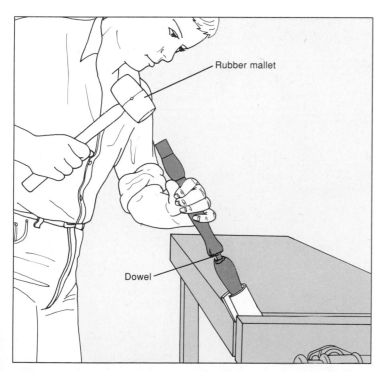

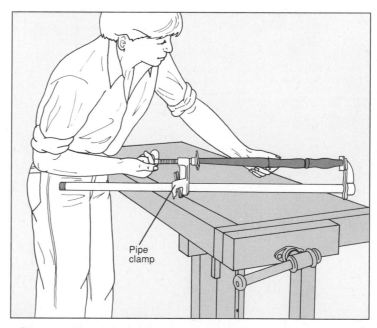

2 Inserting the dowel. Cut a dowel 1 1/2 inch long and bevel both ends slightly with coarse sandpaper. To allow excess glue and air to escape as the dowel is forced into the hole, score the dowel by drawing it through the serrated jaws of pliers. Spread white or yellow glue on the dowel and in the new holes in the stile, then, with the rubber mallet, tap the dowel into the hole in one piece of the stile. Align the other piece of the stile over the dowel, matching the broken edges, and tap the second piece onto the dowel *(above)*.

3 Clamping the repair. Remove the stile from the vise. Place the stile in a pipe clamp padded with wood or cardboard and tighten the clamp just enough to bring the broken ends together *(above)*. Wipe away excess glue with a clean, damp cloth. Let the glue set for 24 hours before releasing the clamp. Reinstall the part as described in this chapter.

MENDING A BROKEN ROCKER

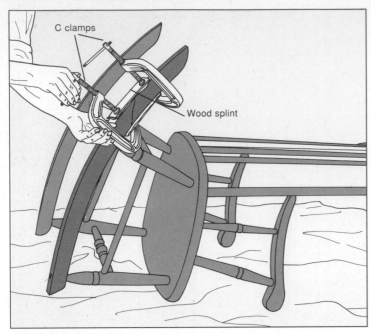

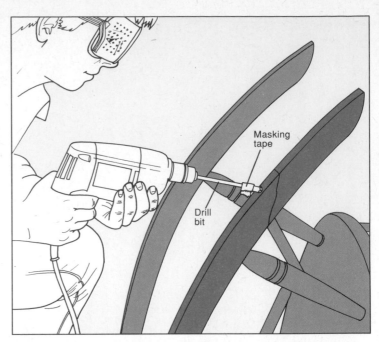

1 **Gluing and clamping the broken rocker.** Wood that is cut in a curve may break along the grain. To repair a broken rocker, lay the rocking chair face down on the floor and gently scrape the break clean with a shop knife. Spread a thin layer of white or yellow glue inside the break, then press the sections together by hand and wipe away excess glue with a clean, damp cloth. To make a splint, place waxed paper and a thin, flat piece of wood along the top and bottom edges of the rocker on each side of the break, and secure them with a pair of C clamps *(above)*. Allow the glue to set for three to four hours, then release the clamps and splint and go to step 2 to reinforce the rocker.

2 **Drilling a dowel hole.** To determine the depth of the dowel hole, measure along the side of the rocker; the dowel will be inserted from the bottom of the rocker, through the break and two thirds of the way into the rocker. Mark the hole position with an awl. Fit a power drill with a bit the same size as the dowel (1/4 to 3/8 inch in diameter) and wrap masking tape around the bit to indicate the depth of the hole. Brace the chair against a wall and drill a hole at the mark *(above)*, stopping when the tape touches the rocker.

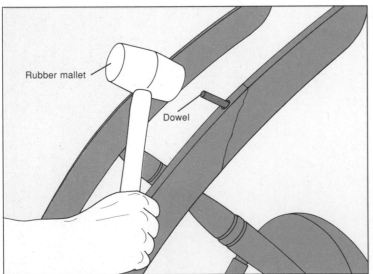

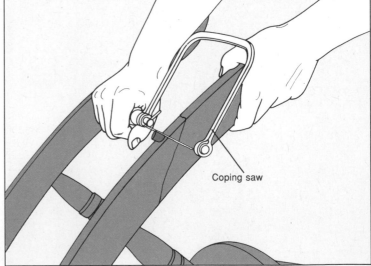

3 **Inserting the dowel.** Cut a dowel 1 inch longer than the depth of the hole and bevel one end slightly with coarse sandpaper. Draw the dowel through the jaws of pliers to score its sides; this will allow excess glue and air to escape as the dowel is forced into the hole. Spread a thin layer of white or yellow glue on the dowel and in the hole. Set the beveled end of the dowel in the hole and tap it in with a rubber mallet *(above, left)*. Wipe away excess glue with a clean, damp cloth. Let the glue set for 24 hours. With a coping saw, cut the dowel flush with the surface of the rocker *(above, right)*. Use medium-grit, then fine sandpaper to sand the dowel smooth.

RESHAPING SPLIT BENTWOOD

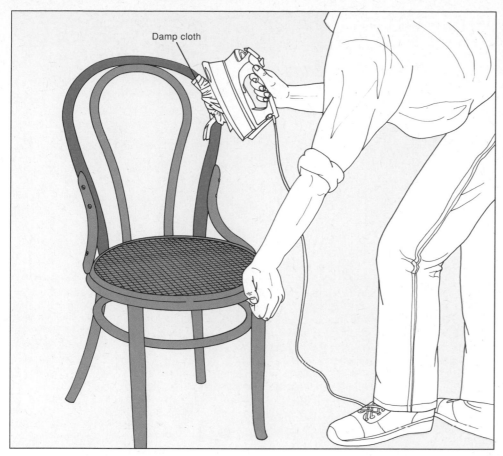

Damp cloth

1 **Softening the wood.** To repair bentwood that has dried and split at the curve, recurve the split area before regluing it. Heat and moisture, used to shape the bentwood piece during construction, can be used to remedy the split. With a shop knife, carefully scrape clean the interior surface of the split, taking care not to cut or break the wood. To make the split wood pliable, wrap a damp cloth around the area, then steam the wood *(left)* by applying a hot steam iron to the cloth on all sides. Steam the split for 15 minutes, wetting the cloth as it dries.

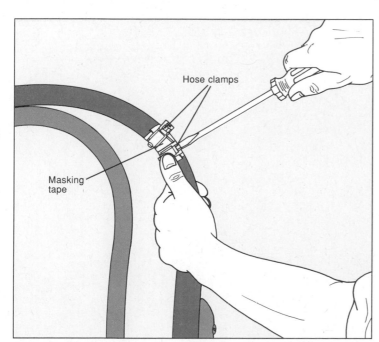

Hose clamps

Masking
tape

2 **Closing the split.** Unwrap the cloth and press the split wood against the curve. To hold the pliable wood in shape, position an automotive hose clamp at each end of the split and tighten the clamps with a screwdriver *(above)*, alternating from one to the other. Do not tighten the clamps so much that their edges cut into the wood. Allow 24 hours for the wood to dry, then release the clamps.

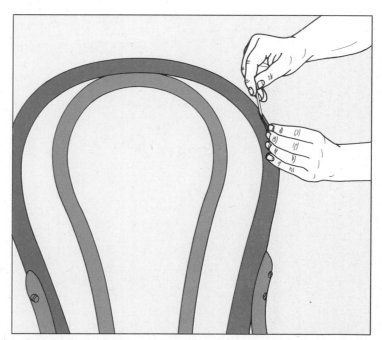

3 **Making it stick.** Ease open the split and, using a toothpick, work in white or yellow glue *(above)*, covering the interior surfaces. Press the split together again and wipe away excess glue with a clean, damp cloth. Wrap the split with waxed paper and reclamp it, as described in step 2. Allow the glue to set for 24 hours, then release the clamps. If necessary, refinish the damaged area *(page 84)*.

REJOINING A SPLIT SEAT

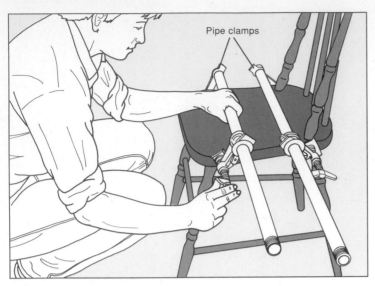

1 **Gluing and clamping the seat.** To repair a small split in the seat, first try to draw the split together with clamps. Place pipe clamps across the seat *(above)*, inserting pads of wood or cork to protect the finish. Tighten the clamps gradually, taking care not to put pressure on another part of the chair. If the clamps do not close the split, release them and go to step 2 to remove and reglue the seat. If the clamps close the split, release them slightly, inject or press in white or yellow glue with a toothpick or glue syringe *(page 121)*, then retighten the clamps. Wipe away excess glue with a clean, damp cloth. Allow 24 hours for the glue to set, then release the clamps.

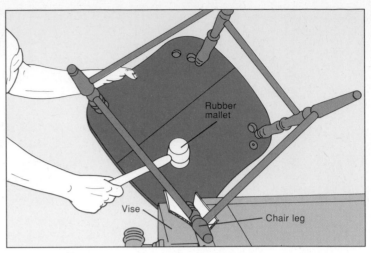

2 **Detaching the seat.** Set the chair on its side and secure the seat in a vise, protecting its finish with cardboard or cork. With a rubber mallet, tap on the seat to loosen the back stiles *(page 15, step 1)*, then lift off the back and set it aside. Next, mark the front legs with masking tape. Examine the top of the seat for a wood wedge that locks each leg in place; drill out any wedges before separating the legs from the seat. Reposition the chair so that one leg is secured in the vise. Knock on the bottom of the seat near the joint to loosen the leg slightly. To keep from twisting the foot-rail frame, loosen all four legs alternately, repositioning the chair in the vise and tapping near each leg so that they loosen together gradually *(above)*. Pull out the legs and foot rails as a unit and set them aside.

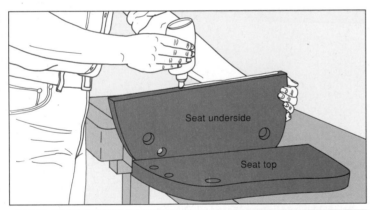

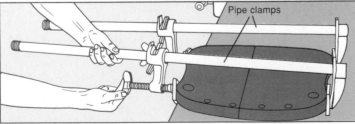

3 **Gluing and clamping the seat.** Remove the seat from the vise and separate it at the split with your hands or tap it apart with the rubber mallet. Spread a thin coat of white or yellow glue along the broken edge of each section *(above, top)*, then press the pieces together. Clamp the joint with two pipe clamps, inserting wood or cork pads to protect the finish. Tighten the clamps only enough to bring together the gluing surfaces *(above, bottom)*. Wipe away excess glue with a clean, damp cloth. Wait 24 hours for the glue to set, then release the clamps.

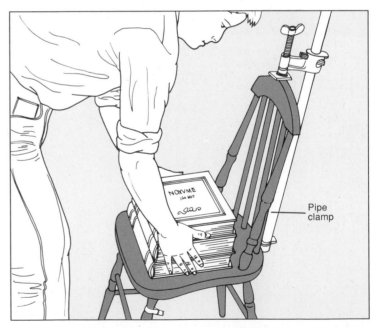

4 **Reassembling the chair.** Use a shop knife to clean the dow-eled ends of the legs and the dowel holes. Take care not to scrape off any wood. Spread a thin layer of glue on the dowels and in the holes, then use the mallet to tap the legs into the seat, placing the marked legs in the sockets at the front of the seat. Remove the masking tape from the legs. Set the chair upright. Apply a coat of glue to the back stiles and holes and tap the back stiles into the seat. Secure the back to the seat with pipe clamps *(page 122)*, inserting pads of wood or cork to protect the finish, and set heavy objects such as books on the seat *(above)*. Wipe away excess glue with a clean, damp cloth. Wait 24 hours, then remove the clamps and weights.

RECOVERING A DROP-IN SEAT

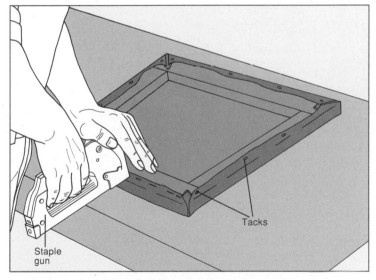

Tacks

1 **Removing the seat from the frame.** Set the chair upside down on a work surface. If there are corner blocks under the seat, release the seat from the frame by removing the center screw from each corner block *(above)*. Set the chair on its side and push on the seat bottom to pop it out of the frame.

Corner block

2 **Taking off the old cover.** If a fabric dust cover is tacked or stapled to the underside of the seat, pry out the fasteners with an old screwdriver and take off the dust cover. Next, pry out any tacks or staples holding the seat cover in place *(above)*, and remove the cover. Buy new seat cover fabric slightly larger than the old cover. Buy replacement fabric for a dust cover if the old one is worn or damaged. If the seat's foam cushion is worn, replace it.

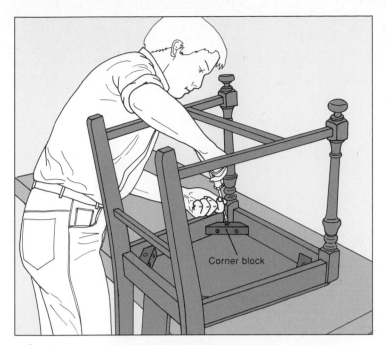

Masking tape

Old seat cover

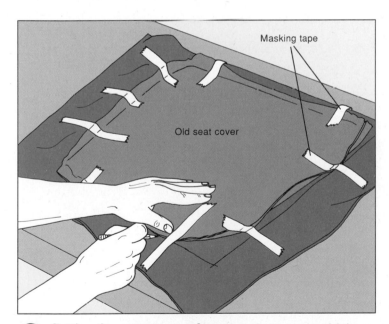

Tacks

Staple gun

3 **Cutting the seat cover to shape.** Lay the new cover fabric face down on a flat work surface. If the old seat cover is very creased, iron it. Lay the old cover face down over the new cover and attach the two pieces with tape if they are vinyl or leather, and with pins if they are cloth. Trace the outline of the old cover on the new cover with a pencil *(above)* or tailor's chalk. Remove the old cover and use strong scissors to cut the new cover along the outline. Use a utility knife to cut heavy vinyl or leather. Cut a new dust cover the same way.

4 **Attaching the new cover.** Set the new fabric face down on a clean work surface, and lay the seat on it, top down. Fold the fabric up around the seat, pulling it tight, and hammer in tacks at each side to hold the fabric temporarily. Pleat the cover at the corners and tack it. Turn over the seat and check for wrinkles in the new cover; if there are any, remove the tack nearest the wrinkle, pull the cover tight and drive the tack back in. Cut away excess material from bulky corner pleats. Drive in all the tacks. With a staple gun, secure the cover to the back of the seat, stapling at 1-inch intervals *(above)*. Fold under the edges of the dust cover 1/2 inch to conceal the raw edge, then staple the dust cover on the back of the seat. Fit the seat into the chair frame and screw it to the corner blocks.

REPLACING A PREWOVEN CANE SEAT

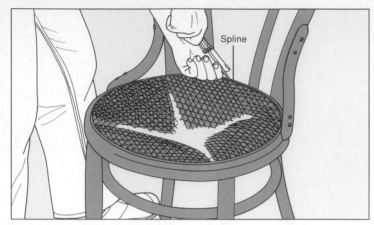

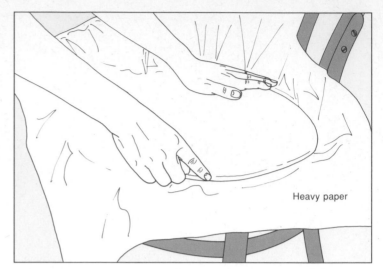

1 **Removing the damaged seat.** To remove a damaged prewoven seat, first cut a large X across the cane with strong scissors. Prewoven cane is held in place by a spline, a cane strip glued into a groove around the perimeter of the seat. Run a utility knife around the outside and inside edges of the spline to loosen it, then locate where the ends of the spline meet, usually at the rear of the seat. Pry out one end with a screwdriver *(above)*. Work along the spline, forcing it out gradually, taking care not to damage the wood. Pull out each section of the seat, then use the screwdriver or a shop knife to scrape dried glue out of the spline groove. Measure the diameter of the seat frame and the circumference of the groove and buy replacement prewoven cane and spline at a craft supply store. Also buy or make five wood wedges about 4 inches long and the same thickness as the spline, for pressing the cane into the groove.

2 **Making a pattern.** Set a piece of heavy paper over the seat frame. Press the paper into the groove in the chair seat with your finger, producing an indentation of the groove in the paper *(above)*. Remove the paper from the chair and draw an outline, adding 2 inches around the indentation. Cut out the pattern along the line. Set the cane on a flat work surface with the lines of the holes running straight from back to front and side to side. Lay the paper pattern over it and tape it down, then, with strong scissors, cut the cane around the pattern. Soak the replacement cane in a bathtub or flat pan of warm water for 15 to 20 minutes or until it is pliable.

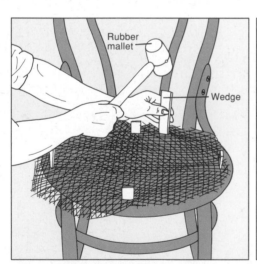

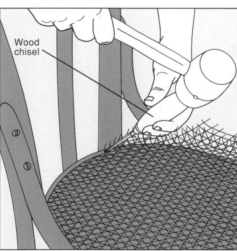

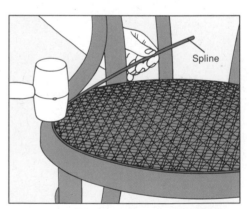

3 **Fitting the new seat.** Lift the cane from the water and shake off the excess. Lay the cane on the seat, with the edges extending equally over the frame and the lines of holes running straight from front to back and side to side. Use a rubber mallet to tap a wood wedge into the groove at the back of the seat, anchoring the cane. Leave the wedge in place. Tap a second wedge into the cane at the front of the seat, drawing the cane across the seat. Repeat the procedure at each side of the seat. If the cane begins to dry, soak the underside with a wet sponge. Once the cane is anchored in four places, use a fifth wedge to force the cane into the groove all around, tapping the wedge with the mallet *(above, left)*. Pull out the wedges, then set the cutting edge of a wood chisel against the cane in the groove and tap the chisel with the mallet to trim off the excess cane *(above, right)*.

4 **Inserting new spline.** Set the strip of spline in the groove to test its fit, then use a utility knife to cut the spline 1 inch longer than the groove. (If the seat is square, cut four pieces of spline and angle the ends so that they butt against each other at the corners.) Soak the spline in water for 15 minutes to make it supple. Squeeze a bead of white glue into the groove, all around. Starting at the rear of the seat, use the rubber mallet to tap the end of the spline into the groove. Continue around the rim *(above)*. Cut the loose spline end to fit against the other end and tap it in. Wipe away excess glue with a clean, damp cloth. Allow the cane and glue to set at least 24 hours.

RECANING A SEAT

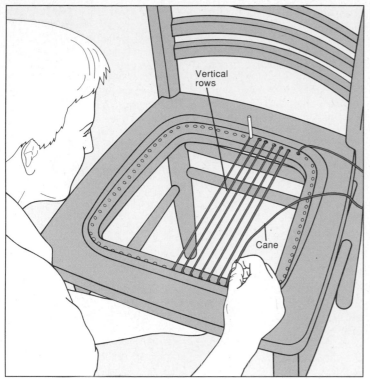

1 **Laying the first set of vertical rows.** With strong scissors, cut the damaged cane from the chair frame. Use a small screwdriver to clean dirt and old cane out of every hole. Measure the diameter of the cane holes and the distance from the center of one hole to the center of the hole beside it. Take these measurements and a piece of old cane to a craft or cane supply store. Buy enough cane to reweave the seat, binder cane to finish the seat and two dozen pegs to hold the strands in place while you work. Golf tees can be used in place of pegs. Pull a strand from the bundle of cane, roll it into a coil and secure it with a clothespin. Soak the coil in warm water for 15 to 20 minutes. Use pegs to mark the center holes at the front and back of the seat. Pull the coil of cane from the water and put in a second coil; put in a new coil every time you take one out. Run the cane through your fingers. In one direction, it will feel smooth, in the other direction, it will feel rough; always pull the cane in the smooth direction. To begin caning, remove the back peg, feed 4 inches of cane through the hole, shiny side up, and anchor it with the peg. Run the cane to the peg at the front of the seat, remove the peg and push all the cane through the hole. Thread the cane up through the hole to the right, then to the corresponding hole at the back of the seat. When you near the end of a strand, anchor it with a peg, then peg a new strand in the same hole. Pull the cane straight but not taut, since it will shrink as it dries. Complete the right half of the seat with parallel strands *(left)*, pegging the cane in the last hole. Return to the back center peg, insert 4 inches of a new strand into the hole to its left and complete the left half of the seat the same way.

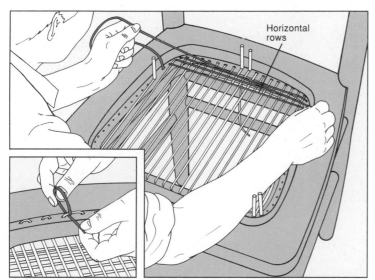

2 **Laying the first set of horizontal rows.** For the side-to-side rows, start at the back of the chair. Insert 4 inches of cane into the side hole beside the right rear corner hole and peg the hole to anchor the cane. Run the cane, shiny side up, across the vertical rows to the corresponding hole on the opposite side without weaving it; leave some slack in the cane. Push the cane down through the hole, then thread it up through the next hole and run it across the seat to the matching hole on the other side. Continue laying side-to-side parallel rows *(above)*, pegging in new strands where needed. Repeat the procedure for the rest of the holes in the sides of the chair and peg the cane at the last hole. Tie off the cane ends that have accumulated under the seat: Turn the chair upside down, moisten the loose ends of cane for pliability, and twist each one twice around the nearest loop of cane that runs between two holes *(inset)*.

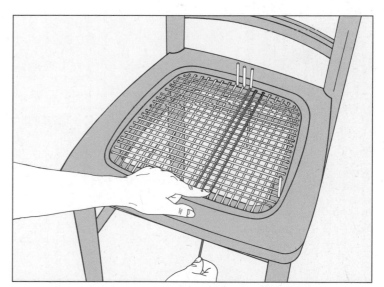

3 **Laying the second set of vertical rows.** Starting at the back center hole once again, remove the peg, insert 4 inches of cane, shiny side up, slightly to the right of the first vertical cane and repeg. Run the second vertical row right next to the first vertical row and over the horizontal rows, without weaving it. Continue running the second vertical rows alongside the first vertical rows *(above)*, starting new strands when necessary. Peg the cane at the last hole. Return to the back center peg, insert 4 inches of a new strand into the hole at its left, and complete the left half of the seat the same way. When several ends of cane have accumulated under the seat, tie them off *(step 2)*.

RECANING A SEAT (continued)

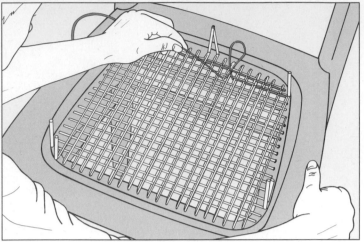

4 **Weaving the second set of horizontal rows.** This is where the weaving begins. Starting at the side hole beside the right rear corner hole (where the first horizontal row was started) insert 4 inches of cane shiny side up, peg it, then weave the strip over the first vertical row and under the second. Continue the over-and-under weave, taking care not to twist the cane. Stop about one third of the way across the seat to pull the strip through *(left)*. Continue weaving until you reach the other side of the chair. Feed the cane down through the opposite hole, then up through the hole beside it. Weave the cane over and under the vertical rows to the other side of the chair. Continue the horizontal weaving, finishing at the front of the chair. Peg in new strands where necessary; when several ends of cane have accumulated under the seat, tie them off. With an awl, gently align the horizontal and vertical pairs of canes into straight, neat rows.

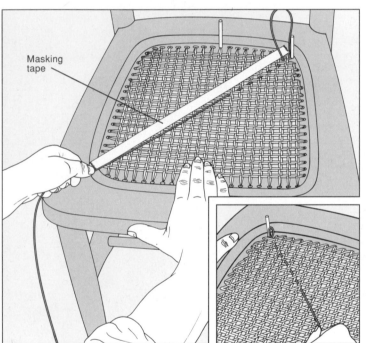

Masking tape

5 **Weaving two sets of diagonal rows.** To create a guideline for the first set of diagonal rows, lay a strip of masking tape across the seat corner to corner. Feed 4 inches of cane into the right rear corner hole and anchor it with a peg, then stretch the cane across the seat to confirm that its intended route leads straight to the opposite corner hole. If it does not, adjust the tape. Weave the diagonal cane over each vertical pair and under each horizontal pair until it reaches the front left corner hole and pull it straight *(left)*. Feed the cane down the hole, then back up the same hole, leaving a loop of cane in the hole, and peg the cane. Remove the masking tape. Continue weaving back and forth, filling in the back half of the chair seat. On an irregularly shaped chair, you may find it necessary to skip or double in some holes to keep the diagonal rows straight and parallel. Weave the front half of the seat, starting next to the right rear and left front corner holes. Tie off the cane ends under the seat.

To weave the second set of diagonal rows, lay masking tape from the left rear corner to the front right corner as you did for the first set of diagonal rows. Peg a strand of cane into the left rear corner hole and weave the second set of diagonal rows the same way as the first set, completing the back half of the seat first. This time, weave the cane under the vertical pairs and over the horizontal pairs *(inset)*. Then starting at the holes beside the corner holes, weave the second set of diagonal rows into the front half of the seat.

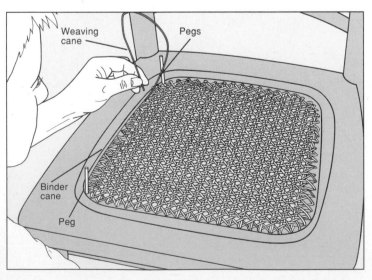

Weaving cane

Pegs

Binder cane

Peg

6 **Laying the binder cane.** Binder cane, wider than weaving cane, covers the holes for a finishing touch. Measure the front, back and sides of the seat along the holes and add 8 inches to each measurement. Cut a strip of binder cane to each of these measurements. Soak the binder cane and four strands of weaving cane for 15 to 20 minutes. Lay a binder cane over the holes along one side of the seat, feed each end into a corner hole and peg it. To lace down the binder cane, tie off a strand of weaving cane under the seat at the back corner hole. Draw the weaving cane up through the first hole covered by the binder cane, loop it over the binder cane, then feed it back down through the same hole. Pull the weaving cane snug, then thread it up through the next hole. Repeat the procedure *(left)* until the binder cane is secured to the seat, then tie the end of the weaving cane under the seat. Continue in the same manner for the remaining three sides. Glue the pegs into the corner holes and use a utility knife to cut them off flush with the seat. Sand the pegs smooth, then cut off the ends of the binder cane under the seat.

REWEAVING A RUSH SEAT

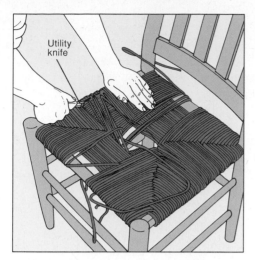

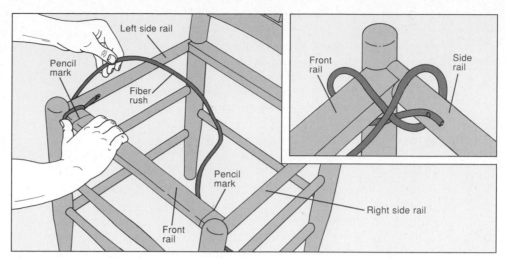

1 Cleaning away the damaged seat. Use a utility knife to cut the damaged rush from the seat frame *(above)*. Remove any tacks on the seat rails with pliers or a nail puller. Examine the chair for loose joints and reglue them if necessary. Buy fiber rush, a durable twisted paper that resembles real rush but is easier to work with, at a craft-supply store. Fiber rush comes in four sizes and several colors. A two- to three-pound coil should be enough to reweave a chair seat.

2 Squaring off the corners. If the front rail of the seat is wider than the back rail, you will have to fill in the front corners with rush to make the seat square before starting to weave. Measure the front and back rails. Subtract the length of the back rail from the length of the front rail, halve the difference and mark the front rail that distance in from each end. If, as in this case, the difference is 2 inches, draw a pencil line on the front rail 1 inch from each corner. Tack one end of a 3- or 4-foot cord of fiber rush to the inside of the left side rail, about 2 inches from the front rail. Feed the rush cord under the front rail, loop it over the front rail, then loop it under and over the left side rail *(above)*. Next, pull the rush across the seat to the right side rail *(inset)*. Pass the cord under the right rail, loop it over the right rail, then loop it under and over the front rail. Tack the cord to the inside of the right rail and cut away the excess. Tack a new cord on the inside of the left rail behind the first cord, then repeat the procedure until you reach the pencil marks.

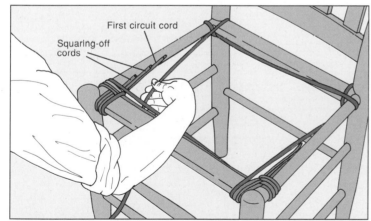

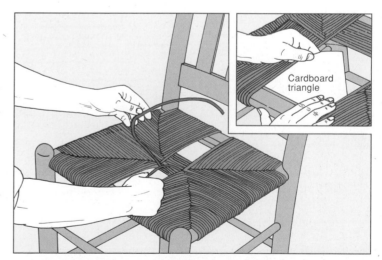

3 Completing a circuit. Cut a 20-foot cord of fiber rush. Roll it into a coil or around a cardboard form. Tack the end of the cord on the left side rail, just behind the last squaring-off cord. Duplicating the pattern produced in the squaring-off procedure, draw the cord under and over the front rail, under and over the left side rail and across the seat to the right side rail. Next, weave it under and over the right side rail and under and over the front rail, then continue to the back rail. Pass the cord under and over the back rail, then under and over the right side rail. Proceed across the seat to the left side rail, then pass the cord under and over the left side rail, then under and over the back rail and return to the front left corner *(above)*. Start a new circuit with the same cord; when the cord runs out, knot a new piece onto the old, positioning the knot in a spot where it will not show.

4 Finishing the seat. Continue weaving circuits, stopping to press the cords together to keep the angles true. When the seat is half woven, reinforce the weave by cutting four triangles from stiff cardboard and fitting them between the upper and lower levels of cord *(inset)* at each seat rail. Cut off the points in the center. Resume weaving until the side rails are completely covered. To fill in the center strip, pull the cord up through the center of the seat and loop it over the back rail. Bring it back up through the center, pull it forward and loop it over the front rail. Pull the cord back up through the center *(above)* and over the back rail again, forming figure eights. To finish, tack the rush to the underside of the back rail or tie it off underneath.

TABLES

A standard, strong wood table consists of three main parts: the top, the apron and the legs. The top is attached to the apron, a horizontal wood understructure, by metal clips or by screws countersunk in pocket holes. In some simple kitchen tables, the apron is glued permanently to the top. Table legs are joined to the apron by a wood joint, either mortise-and-tenon or dowel *(page 123)*, or by a corner brace and hanger bolt *(page 120)*. On small coffee tables or end tables that don't have aprons, the legs are screwed or glued to the top. Two of the tables pictured at right have expandable tops. The drop-leaf table has one or two flaps; each is hinged to the top and supported from underneath. The extension table slides apart, allowing for the addition of one or more center leaves.

A table's surface reveals the use—and abuse—it receives. To repair scratches, nicks and stains, or to fill a minor crack, see Repairing Surfaces *(page 84)*. Fluctuations in humidity cause solid-wood table tops to swell and shrink, resulting in warpage and cracking. Cracks occur along the grain of a board or in a joint between boards. Use wood veneer, available at hardware stores and woodworking supply houses, to fill a wide split in the edge of a table top. When the split is long and deep, first try working in glue and clamping the table top to bring the edges together. If this doesn't close the split, cut the top apart at the split and reglue the two pieces together *(page 39)*. The top should be refinished after the repair.

The stress placed on a table takes its toll at the joints connecting the legs to the apron. Wood joints come unglued and sockets cut into the leg weaken the wood, causing splits at the joint. The corner-brace joint, designed for easy disassembly, wears away the wood where the hanger bolt enters the leg. Before repairing a wobbly table, check that all screws and bolts holding it together are tight. Avoid tampering with a sound joint if possible; separate only the shaky ones, leaving joints that are firm and tight undisturbed.

Most table repairs require the simplest of workshop tools. Use a rubber mallet, which won't mar the wood, to tap pieces apart and together again. White glue or yellow wood glue will bond most joints and fill minute cracks. Pipe clamps *(page 122)* are especially useful for securing the large surface of a table top. Before applying the clamps, set the table upright, the legs resting squarely on a completely flat surface, and place a weight on the table top.

TROUBLESHOOTING GUIDE

SYMPTOM	POSSIBLE CAUSE	PROCEDURE
Table wobbly	Legs uneven	Level legs as for chair legs *(p. 20)* □○
	Mortise-and-tenon or dowel joint loose	Reglue joint *(p. 32)* ◨●
	Mortise-and-tenon or dowel joint broken	Rebuild joint *(dowel, p. 124; mortise-and-tenon, p. 125)* ◨●
	Split in leg at joint	Repair split *(p. 33)* □○
	Hanger bolt loose (corner-brace joint)	Tighten or reseat hanger bolt *(p. 33)* ◨●
	Pedestal leg joint loose	Reglue joint *(p. 34)* □○
	Pedestal leg joint broken	Rebuild dowel joint *(p. 124)* ◨●
Casters do not roll properly	Rollers stiff or dirty	Clean and lubricate rollers *(p. 47)* □○
	Rollers damaged	Replace rollers *(p. 47)* □○
Caster falls out of leg	Pressure against caster socket has enlarged caster hole	Replace caster *(p. 47)* ◨●
Scratches, cracks or gouges in finish	Wear and tear	Spot repair finish *(p. 84)* □○; refinish table *(p. 96)* ■●
Table edge split	Wood shrinkage	Fill split with veneer spline *(p. 38)* ◨●
Long, deep split in table top	Wood shrinkage; loosened glue bond	Work glue into split, then draw it together with clamps as for a chair seat *(p. 24)* □○; split top completely and rejoin *(p. 39)* ◨●
Veneer lifted or damaged	Dryness; aging adhesive	Reglue veneer *(p. 93)* ◨○; glue down blister *(p. 93)* ◨○; patch veneer *(p. 94)* ■●
Extension mechanism sticks	Clogged with dirt and old lubricant	Clean and lubricate *(p. 36)* □○
	Sprocket out of position	Reposition sprocket *(p. 36)* □○
Extension table pin broken	Center leaf not properly aligned	Replace connecting pin *(p. 37)* □○
Drop leaf droops when raised	Pivot arm, gateleg or slider support worn	Add wedge to leaf support *(p. 37)* □○
	Pivot arm damaged	Replace pivot arm *(p. 37)* □●
Drop leaf loose	Hinge screws loose	Tighten screws; reseat screws *(p. 120)* □○
	Hinge damaged	Replace hinge *(p. 38)* □○

DEGREE OF DIFFICULTY: □ Easy ◨ Moderate ■ Complex
ESTIMATED TIME: ○ Less than 1 hour ◔ 1 to 3 hours ● Over 3 hours *(Does not include drying time)*

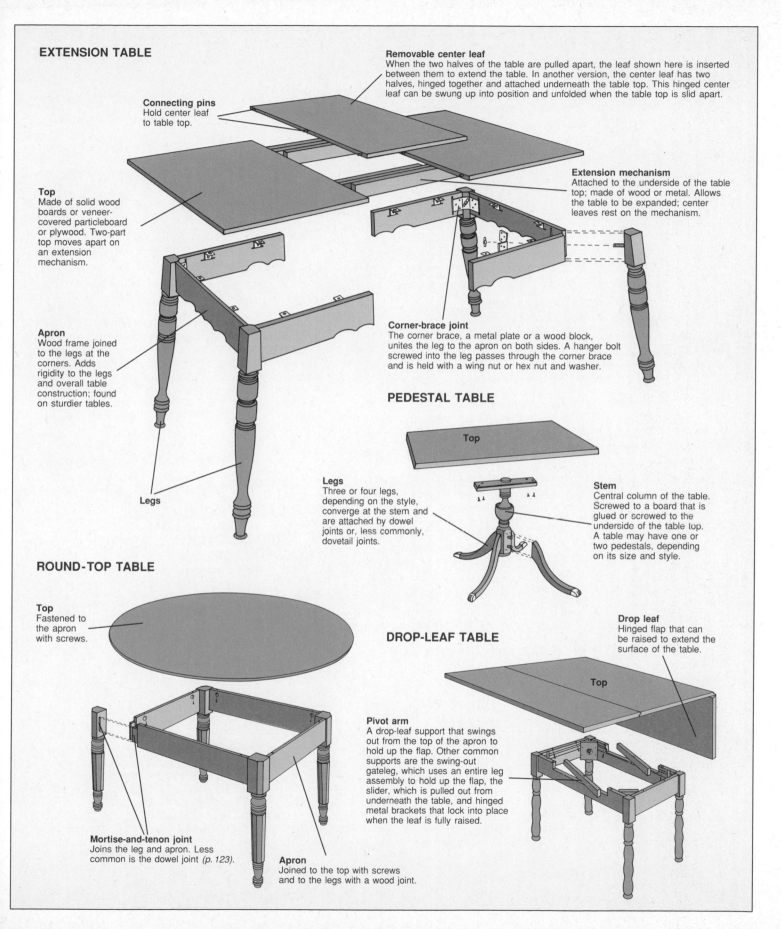

EXTENSION TABLE

Removable center leaf
When the two halves of the table are pulled apart, the leaf shown here is inserted between them to extend the table. In another version, the center leaf has two halves, hinged together and attached underneath the table top. This hinged center leaf can be swung up into position and unfolded when the table top is slid apart.

Connecting pins
Hold center leaf to table top.

Extension mechanism
Attached to the underside of the table top; made of wood or metal. Allows the table to be expanded; center leaves rest on the mechanism.

Top
Made of solid wood boards or veneer-covered particleboard or plywood. Two-part top moves apart on an extension mechanism.

Apron
Wood frame joined to the legs at the corners. Adds rigidity to the legs and overall table construction; found on sturdier tables.

Corner-brace joint
The corner brace, a metal plate or a wood block, unites the leg to the apron on both sides. A hanger bolt screwed into the leg passes through the corner brace and is held with a wing nut or hex nut and washer.

Legs

PEDESTAL TABLE

Top

Legs
Three or four legs, depending on the style, converge at the stem and are attached by dowel joints or, less commonly, dovetail joints.

Stem
Central column of the table. Screwed to a board that is glued or screwed to the underside of the table top. A table may have one or two pedestals, depending on its size and style.

ROUND-TOP TABLE

Top
Fastened to the apron with screws.

DROP-LEAF TABLE

Drop leaf
Hinged flap that can be raised to extend the surface of the table.

Top

Pivot arm
A drop-leaf support that swings out from the top of the apron to hold up the flap. Other common supports are the swing-out gateleg, which uses an entire leg assembly to hold up the flap, the slider, which is pulled out from underneath the table, and hinged metal brackets that lock into place when the leaf is fully raised.

Mortise-and-tenon joint
Joins the leg and apron. Less common is the dowel joint *(p. 123)*.

Apron
Joined to the top with screws and to the legs with a wood joint.

REGLUING A WOOD JOINT

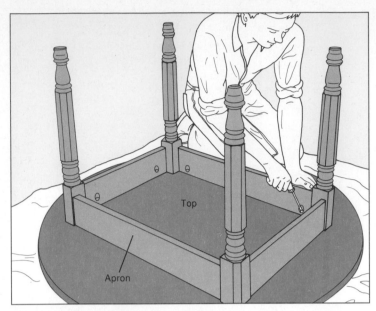

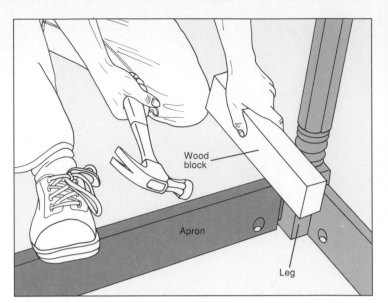

1 Removing the top. To locate the loose leg on a wobbly table, look under the table, inspecting the legs and apron for gaps or splits. If there is a crack around a mortise, you can reglue it without separating the joint *(page 33)*. To repair any wood joint, first remove the top. Cover the floor or work surface with an old blanket, then invert the table on it. Most table tops are fastened to the apron with screws in metal clips or in angled pocket holes, shown here. Unscrew the top *(above)*, then lift off the legs and apron and set them upside down on the floor.

2 Separating the joint. Examine the area around the joint for a concealed fastener that locks the joint in place; look for a dowel or round patch of wood filler at the top of the leg. Remove any fasteners *(page 123)* before separating the joint. Try to pull the joint apart by hand; if it does not come apart easily, anchor the apron with one foot, set a block of wood squarely against the leg and strike the block with a hammer *(above)*. Or give the joint a few sharp taps with a rubber mallet. Take care not to loosen the sound joints.

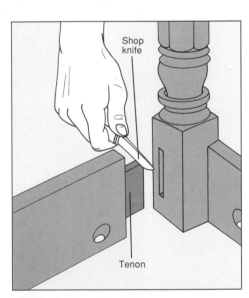

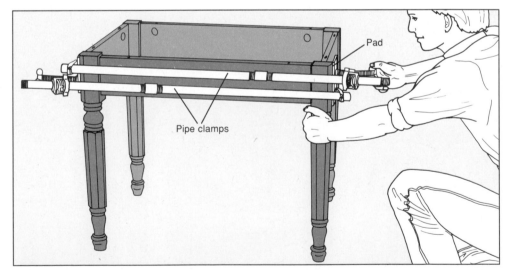

3 Cleaning the joint. Use a shop knife *(above)* or coarse sandpaper to clean the gluing surfaces. Scrape away the dried glue, taking care not to whittle the wood. Wipe the tenon with a dry cloth and vacuum all loose debris from the mortise.

4 Regluing and clamping the joint. With a rubber mallet, tap the joint together to see if it is tight. If not, build up the tenon or dowel by wrapping it with a glue-soaked cloth *(page 121)* or by wedging the tenon *(page 17)* or dowel *(page 15)*. Spread a thin layer of white or yellow glue on the gluing surfaces and push the joint together. Turn the legs and apron upright and set them on a flat surface. Clamp the joint with one or two pipe clamps, inserting pads of wood or cork under the clamps' jaws to protect the finish. If you use two pipe clamps, distribute pressure evenly by facing the clamps in opposite directions *(above)*. Tighten the clamps just enough to close the joint and bring the gluing surfaces in contact. Wipe off excess glue with a clean, damp cloth. Make sure that all four legs rest firmly on the floor. If the table wobbles, loosen the clamps and retighten them gradually, adjusting the fit of the legs and apron until the assembly is square. Let the table stand for 24 hours, then release the clamps. Turn the legs and apron upside down, set them in place over the table top and screw on the top.

REPAIRING A LEG SPLIT AT THE JOINT

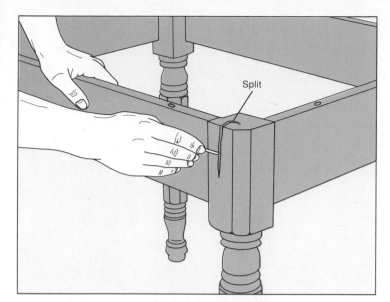

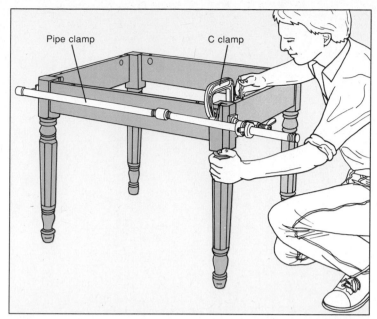

1 **Working glue into the split.** Invert the table on an old blanket and remove the table top as described on page 32. Stand the legs and apron upright. Gently clean debris out of the split with a shop knife. Use a toothpick to work white or yellow glue into the split *(above)*. For a hairline crack, you can use instant glue *(page 121)*, which is thinner in consistency and will flow more readily into the split. Be careful not to get any instant glue on your skin or the wood surface.

2 **Clamping the split.** Place a pipe clamp from one leg to another to close the split, inserting pads of wood or cork in its jaws to protect the finish. Tighten the clamp only enough to bring the gluing surfaces in contact. Next, attach a C clamp across the top of the leg to hold the leg together *(above)*, padding the clamp jaws. Wipe off excess glue with a clean, damp cloth. Let the table stand for 24 hours, then release the clamps. Turn the legs and apron upside down, set them in place over the table top and screw on the top.

TIGHTENING A CORNER-BRACE JOINT

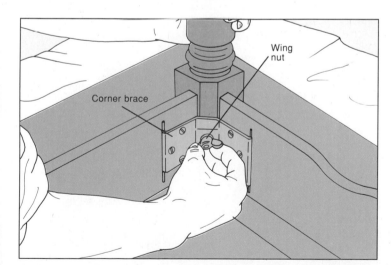

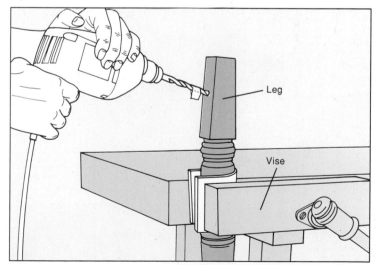

1 **Removing the leg.** The corner-brace joint is secured by a hanger bolt. One end of the hanger bolt has wood-screw threads and is screwed into the leg; the other end has machine-screw threads. This end protrudes through the corner brace and is held tight by a wing nut or hex nut and washer. When a corner-brace joint is loose, first try tightening the nut. Tighten a wing nut by hand *(above)*; tighten a hex nut with locking pliers or a wrench. Wiggle the leg to test the joint. If the bolt is loose in the leg, you will have to reseat it. Cover the floor or work surface with an old blanket and invert the table on this surface. Loosen the nut by hand or with locking pliers or a wrench, and slip the leg and bolt out of the corner brace.

2 **Drilling a hole for a dowel.** Secure the detached leg in a vise, protecting its finish with cardboard or cork. Grip the un-threaded center strip of the bolt with locking pliers and unscrew the bolt. At a hardware or building supply store, buy hardwood dowel stock with a diameter slightly larger than that of the bolt. Measure the depth of the bolt hole. Choose a drill bit of the same diameter as the dowel and use masking tape to mark the bit to the depth of the bolt hole. Drill the dowel hole *(above)*, carefully following the angle of the original hole. Stop when the tape touches the leg. Tap wood particles out of the hole.

TIGHTENING A CORNER-BRACE JOINT (continued)

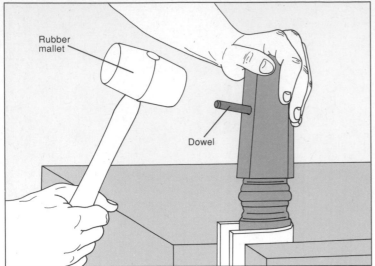

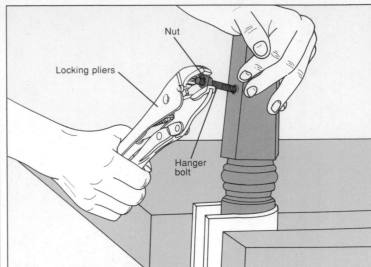

3 **Seating the bolt.** Cut the dowel 1 inch longer than the depth of the hole. Use coarse sandpaper to bevel one end of the dowel slightly, and score the dowel by drawing it through the serrated jaws of pliers. The striated surface will allow excess glue and air to escape as the dowel is forced into the hole. Coat the gluing surfaces with a thin layer of white or yellow glue. Insert the beveled end of the dowel into the hole and knock in the dowel with a rubber mallet *(above, left)*. Use a coping saw to trim off the protruding end of the dowel, and sand it flush with the leg. Wait three to four hours for the glue to set, then, with an awl, punch a starting hole for the drill bit in the center of the dowel. Choose a drill bit 1/8 inch smaller than the diameter of the

bolt. Measure the wood-screw end of the bolt and use masking tape to mark the drill bit 1/4 inch less than this depth. Bore into the center of the dowel, stopping when the tape touches the leg. With locking pliers, grasp the bolt at its unthreaded middle and screw it in the hole. If the serrated jaws of the pliers threaten to damage the bolt's threads, screw a hex nut onto the bolt until it reaches the base of the threads, fasten the pliers onto the nut and screw the bolt into the hole *(above, right)*. Remove the nut. Release the leg from the vise and position it against the apron, passing the hanger bolt through the corner brace. Put the washer on the bolt, then tighten the wing nut or hex nut.

REJOINING A WOBBLY PEDESTAL LEG

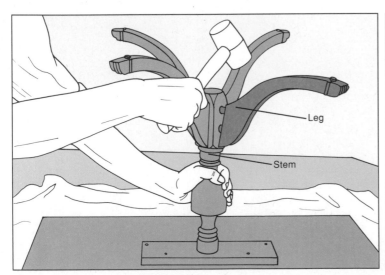

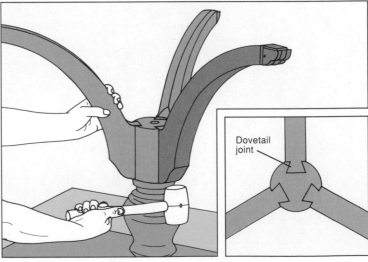

1 **Removing a loose leg.** Cover the floor or work surface with an old blanket, then invert the table on this surface. On most smaller tables, the legs are connected to the column or stem with dowels; less common is the dovetail joint. Try to determine what type of joint holds the legs to the stem before knocking the leg free. Examine the underside of the pedestal; the dovetail joint can usually be identified by its shape *(inset)*. Work slowly to separate the leg. Using a rubber mallet, strike a doweled leg from above and below, as close to the stem as possible, so that it comes straight out without damaging the dowels *(above, left)*; strike a dovetailed leg at the top of the leg so that it slides up out of its groove in the stem *(above, right)*.

REJOINING A WOBBLY PEDESTAL LEG (continued)

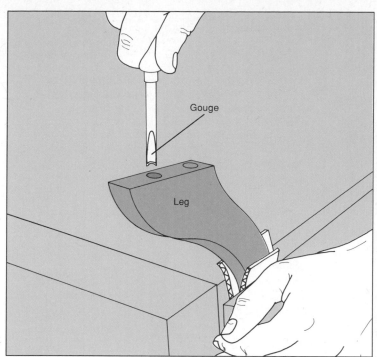

Gouge

Leg

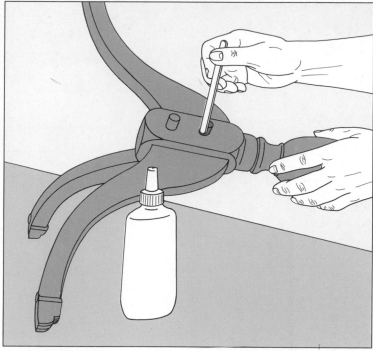

2 **Regluing the joint.** Use a shop knife or coarse sandpaper to clean the gluing surfaces. Scrape away dried glue, taking care not to whittle the wood. A gouge *(above, left)* is especially useful for cleaning hard-to-reach areas such as the dowel holes shown here. With the rubber mallet, tap the joint together to see if it is tight. If not, build up a dowel by wrapping it with a glue-soaked cloth *(page 121)* or by wedging it *(page 15)*. Spread a thin layer of white or yellow glue on the gluing surfaces of the joint *(above, right)*, then set the leg back in place on the stem. Tap the leg with the mallet to seat the dowels or dovetail.

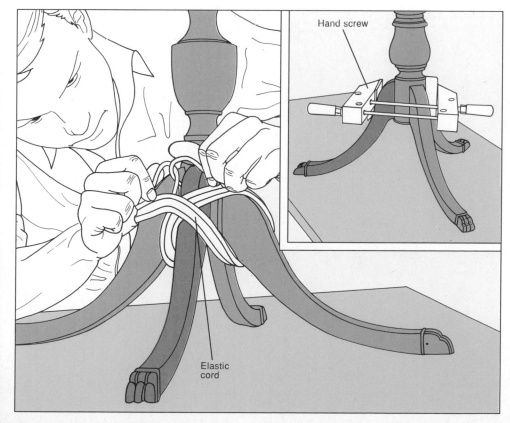

Hand screw

Elastic cord

3 **Clamping the leg.** Turn the table upright and make sure all legs are sitting firmly on a completely flat surface. On a small table, you can use a bungee cord—an elastic cord with a hook at each end—to secure a newly glued pedestal joint. Wrap the cord around the legs, crisscrossing it over the repaired leg *(left)* and hook the ends together. For a larger pedestal, on a dining-room table for example, use a hand screw and a block of wood to secure the joint *(inset)*. Wipe off excess glue with a clean, damp cloth and let the table stand for 24 hours before releasing the cord or clamp.

SERVICING A WOOD EXTENSION MECHANISM

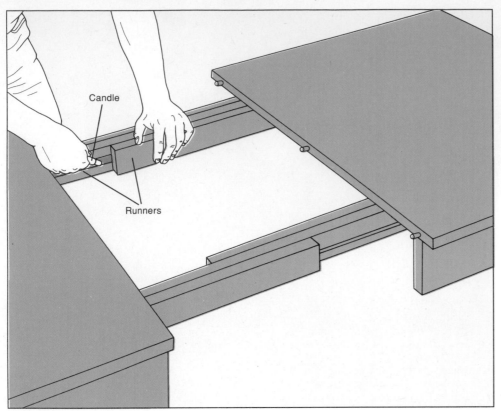

Lubricating wood runners. Extend the table top as wide as possible to allow you to reach the entire length of the wood runners. With a shop knife or old wood chisel, scrape dirt and gummed-up lubricant from the runners. Scrub wax or grease buildup with a cloth soaked in turpentine or mineral spirits, then wipe the runners clean with a dry cloth. Rub a candle or block of paraffin in the runners, leaving a thin coat of wax *(left)*. Open and close the table several times to distribute the lubricant evenly.

SERVICING A SPROCKET EXTENSION MECHANISM

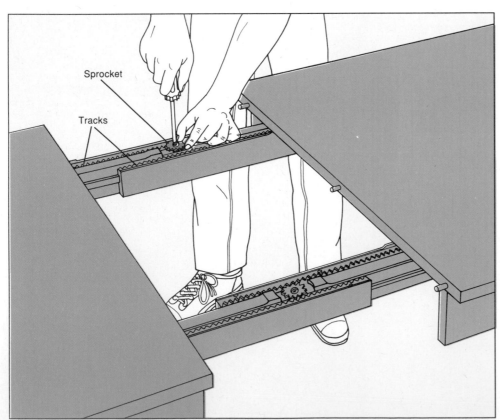

Repairing a sticking sprocket. Extend the table top as far as possible. If the sprocket is loose, use a screwdriver to tighten the screw at its center *(left)*. If the screw hole has become enlarged so that the screw no longer tightens, remove the screw and sprocket, fill the hole in the wood runner with toothpicks and glue to provide a tighter fit *(page 120)* and reinsert the screw. If the sprocket is clogged with dirt, remove the screw and lift out the sprocket. Spray silicone lubricant on the sprocket and scrub it with an old toothbrush. Screw the sprocket back in position, making sure that the sprocket teeth mesh with the teeth on the tracks, and spray the tracks with silicone lubricant.

REPLACING A CONNECTING PIN IN AN EXTENSION TABLE

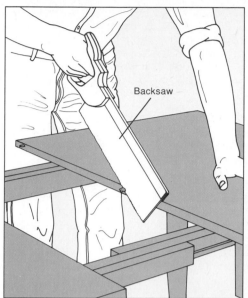

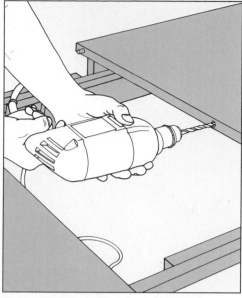

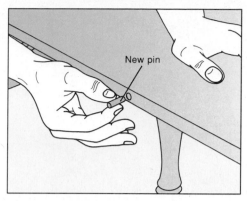

2 **Installing the new pin.** Buy a replacement pin of the same diameter and material as the old one at a hardware or woodworking supply store. If you prefer, cut one from a dowel, scoring it with the serrated jaws of pliers to allow air and excess glue to escape. Coat the replacement with a thin layer of white or yellow glue and insert it into the hole, as shown. Wipe off excess glue with a damp cloth. If you glued in a dowel, round off the protruding end with fine sandpaper. Wait three to four hours for the glue to set before closing the table.

1 **Removing the broken pin.** Connecting pins, tapered wood or plastic dowels that hold a center leaf in place, can split or break if the leaf is not properly aligned before the table top is pushed together. To remove a damaged connecting pin, open the table to its full extension. If you can, pull the pin out by hand or with pliers, and scrape dried glue out of the hole with a shop knife or gouge. If the broken pin does not come out, use a backsaw to cut off the end flush with the edge of the table top *(above, left)*. Using a drill bit the same diameter as the pin (usually 3/8 inch), bore out the remaining piece of pin *(above, right)*.

SHORING UP A DROP LEAF

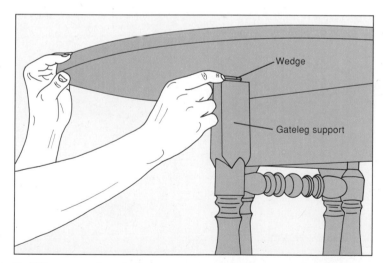

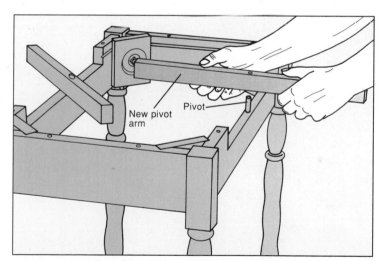

Building up a drop-leaf support. To raise a slanting drop leaf so that it sits level with the table top, use a backsaw to cut a softwood wedge 2 to 3 inches long, the same width as the leaf support—in this case a gateleg—and thick enough to hold the leaf straight. Coat the bottom of the wedge with a thin layer of white or yellow glue and insert it, glue side down, between the support and the raised drop leaf *(above)*. The weight of the leaf will hold the wedge in place until the glue dries. To avoid gluing the wedge to the underside of the leaf, slip a piece of waxed paper between them. Wipe off excess glue with a damp cloth. Let stand 24 hours, then pull out the waxed paper.

Replacing a damaged pivot arm. Cover the floor or work surface with an old blanket, then invert the table on it and remove the top as described on page 32. Turn the leg-apron assembly upright and unscrew or lift off the damaged pivot arm. With a backsaw, cut a hardwood replacement arm of the same dimensions as the old one. Secure the replacement in a vise. Punch a position mark with an awl at the point where the pivot will be inserted. Using a drill bit the same diameter as the pivot, drill a hole straight into the replacement pivot arm at the mark. Set the new arm on the pivot *(above)* and replace the screw if it had one. Turn the legs and apron upside down, set them on the inverted table top and screw on the top.

REPLACING A DROP-LEAF HINGE

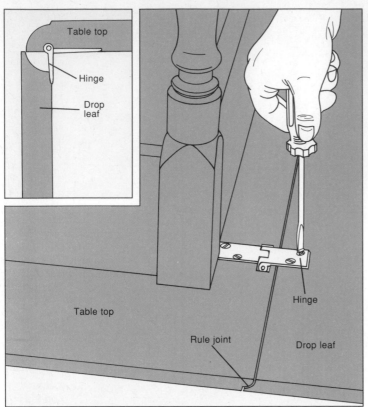

Curing a loose drop leaf. Cover the floor or work surface with an old blanket and invert the table on this surface. Extend the loose drop leaf to expose the loose or damaged hinge. With an awl or pencil, trace the outlines of all hinges on that leaf and on the table top, then remove the hinges *(left)*. To determine the type of replacement hinge to buy, examine the hinge and the way the table-top and drop-leaf edges meet. Tables like the one shown, with a rounded rule joint, use hinges with leaves of unequal length *(inset)*. These hinges are available at a woodworking supply store. Simple kitchen tables, whose drop leaf and table top have straight mating edges, use regular butt hinges, available at hardware stores. Along with the replacement hinge, buy hinge screws short enough not to pierce the top surface of the table.

Pack the screw holes with toothpicks or dowels *(page 120)*. Align the drop leaf snugly against the table top. Open the new hinge and set it on the outline of the old hinge, fitting the hinge knuckle into the notch in the table top. Use an awl to punch position marks for the screws. Fit a power drill with a bit slightly smaller in diameter than the screws and wrap it with masking tape to indicate the screw-hole depth. Drill the screw holes, stopping when the tape touches the wood. Set the hinge in position and tighten the screws. Install the other hinges the same way.

CLOSING A SPLIT EDGE

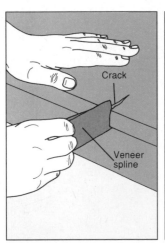
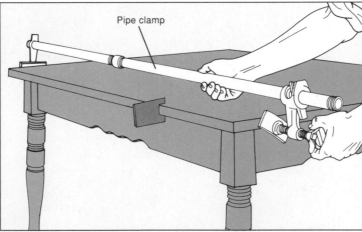
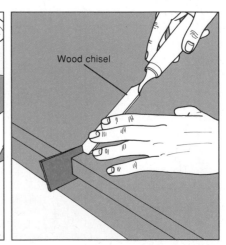

Adding a veneer spline. Use wood veneer to fill a split that goes through the edge of a table top. At a woodworking or hardware store, buy a strip of veneer that matches the table top and has no backing. Cut the veneer slightly longer and wider than the crack and sand it thin enough to fit snugly into the split. Coat both sides of the veneer with a thin layer of white or yellow glue, then wedge it into the split edge *(above, left)*. Close the split with a pipe clamp *(above, center)*, inserting pads of wood or cork to protect the finish and tightening the clamp only enough to bring the gluing surfaces in contact. Wipe away excess glue with a damp cloth. Let the table stand for 24 hours, then release the clamp. Use a wood chisel carefully to trim the veneer flush with the table top *(above, right)*. If the edge of the veneer is rough, smooth it with fine sandpaper. Refinish the patch to match the table *(page 92)*.

REJOINING A SPLIT TABLE TOP

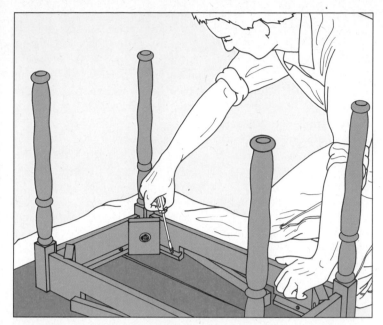

1 **Removing the top.** Many cracks in table tops can be filled with a shellac stick or wood putty *(pages 89 and 90)*, or glued and drawn together with pipe clamps *(page 24)*. But to repair a deep split that extends from one end of the table nearly to the other, and is narrower than the kerf of a circular saw blade (1/8 inch), you will have to remove the table top, saw it in two along the split and rejoin the top. Cover the floor or work surface with an old blanket, and invert the table on this surface. Use a screwdriver to remove the screws from the metal clips or pocket holes *(above)*, then lift off the legs and apron and set them aside. Unscrew any drop leaves and set them aside.

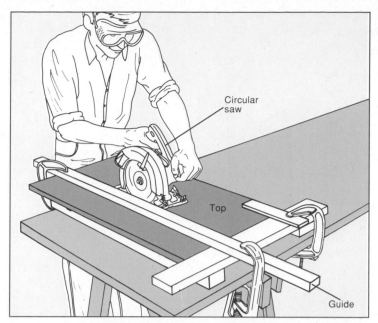

2 **Completing the split.** Draw a line along the crack, extending it to the opposite end of the table. Before beginning to cut the top, familiarize yourself with the proper use of a circular saw *(page 119)*. Make a saw guide from two C clamps and a straight-edged board. To avoid splintering the wood, set the table top face down on 2-by-4 wood blocks and butt a block against the top on the far side of the cut. Set a new carbide-tipped saw blade to a depth of one tooth-length below the table top. Wearing goggles to protect your eyes, cut along the split carefully and slowly with the circular saw, keeping the base of the saw flush against the guide.

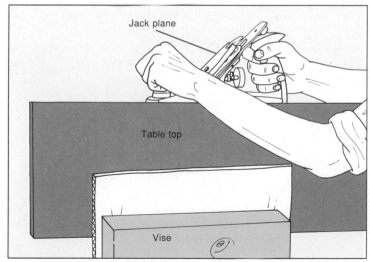

3 **Preparing the gluing surface.** Once the top is split completely, set the pieces together and examine their fit. If the joint has any gaps, smooth the edges slightly with a sanding block. Or secure one piece in a vise, protecting its finish with wood or cardboard, and very carefully and sparingly level the edge with a jack plane *(page 116)*, taking care not to splinter the wood. Smooth the edge of the other piece the same way until the parts fit together snugly.

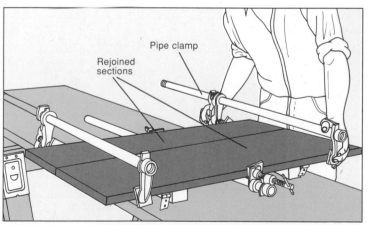

4 **Gluing and clamping the table top.** Set the pieces side by side on scraps of 2-by-4 lumber. Spread a thin coat of white or yellow glue along the edges of both pieces and join them. Clamp the joint with three pipe clamps, inserting wood or cork pads to protect the finish. Run the middle clamp underneath the table top, as shown, to distribute the force evenly. Tighten the clamps only enough to bring the gluing surfaces together, then wipe off the excess glue with a clean moist cloth. Let stand for 24 hours, then release the clamps. Sand the joint lightly. To reassemble the table, place the top on an old blanket, screw on any drop leaves, then position the legs and apron on the top and reattach them. Refinish the top *(page 96)*.

BEDS

We adorn a bed with fine linens and perhaps turn the mattress from time to time, but otherwise take for granted that the bed will give us unlimited service. Most beds do have a strong and flexible design, but their wood frames are vulnerable to wear and stress.

Beds such as the ones pictured at right are built to be taken apart; without knock-down joints, they would be very cumbersome to move and repair. Usually, the bedposts are joined to the headboard and footboard with glued mortise-and-tenon joints. The long, narrow side rails are the removable parts, attached to the bedposts with metal hooks, concealed bolts, or wedged wood tenons to form a frame for mattress slats. Knock-down fasteners with hooks provide a strong temporary joint; even after years of being locked in place, a side rail can be unlatched with a sharp upward tug or a few taps from below with a rubber mallet.

If a headboard wobbles or the frame creaks with movement, something is loose or cracked. Don't wait for the bed to break in the middle of the night; lift off the mattress and box spring and inspect the joints, then tighten any loose hardware. Bedrail fasteners are made of heavy metal and last nearly forever; it is the wood they are mounted on that weakens with age. Weight and movement wear away the wood around screws, or split a side rail along the grain. Constant stress can bow out the sides of a frame, or crack one of the ledges that support the mattress and box spring.

The burden carried by the side rails and ledges is shared by the slats that span the rails. A broken slat can easily be replaced with a board you cut yourself. Position slats squarely and fully on the ledges. Cut them neither so long that they push out the side rails nor so short that they work free and fall through the rails. To make your mattress firmer if you have no box spring, replace old slats with a posture board of plywood or particleboard. Since these panels are very heavy, check the condition of the side rail ledges and reinforce them *(page 44)* if necessary. A posture board made in two pieces will be easier to disassemble and move.

A good mattress and box spring set will last from 10 to 25 years with minimal maintenance. For uniform wear, rotate the mattress from end to end and from one side to the other every few months. Periodically remove the mattress and flip the box spring on its edge to vacuum dust from the bottom. A metal box spring has a riveted, heavy steel frame. It is sturdy and lasts virtually forever, but is susceptible to rust. Remove rust with steel wool, then paint the frame with rust-resistant paint.

The platform bed has a rigid plywood or particleboard base inside a rectangular wood frame that is joined at the four corners by angle irons or knock-down fasteners. If the screws come loose at these joints, reposition the fasteners or reseat the screws *(page 120)*.

Most bed repairs require no tool more sophisticated than those found in a home tool box; a power drill, assorted screwdrivers, pipe clamps *(page 122)* and No. 8 round-head wood screws will usually do the job. Supplies may include casters or replacement knock-down fasteners, available at a hardware or home improvement store. When buying bedrail fasteners, choose a sturdy design with more than one hook to hold the headboard and footboard stable.

TROUBLESHOOTING GUIDE

SYMPTOM	POSSIBLE CAUSE	PROCEDURE
Bed creaks or wobbles	Fasteners loose	Tighten fasteners
	Side rail cracked	Glue crack and install new fastener *(p. 42)* ▪◐ Replace side rail *(p. 43)* ▪◐
	Wood joint loose between bedpost and headboard or footboard	Reglue joint *(p. 46)* ▪◐
Mattress sags or tilts to one side	Mattress worn	Replace mattress
	Side rail ledge loose	Tighten or reposition screws
	Side rail ledge sagging or broken	Replace ledge *(p. 44)* ▪◐
	Slat broken or warped	Replace slat *(p. 45)* ☐○ Install posture board *(p. 45)* ▪◐
Frame bows outward	Side rail warped	Pull in side rail and secure it to slats *(p. 46)* ▪○ Replace side rail *(p. 44)* ▪◐
Casters do not roll properly	Rollers stiff or dirty	Clean and lubricate rollers *(p. 47)* ☐○
	Roller damaged	Replace roller *(p. 47)* ☐○
Caster falls out of leg	Weight on caster has enlarged socket hole	Replace caster *(p. 47)* ▪◐
Scratches, cracks or gouges in finish	Wear and tear	Spot repair finish *(p. 84)* ☐○ Refinish bed *(p. 96)* ☐○

DEGREE OF DIFFICULTY: ☐ Easy ▪ Moderate ■ Complex
ESTIMATED TIME: ○ Less than 1 hour ◐ 1 to 3 hours ● Over 3 hours *(Does not include drying time)*

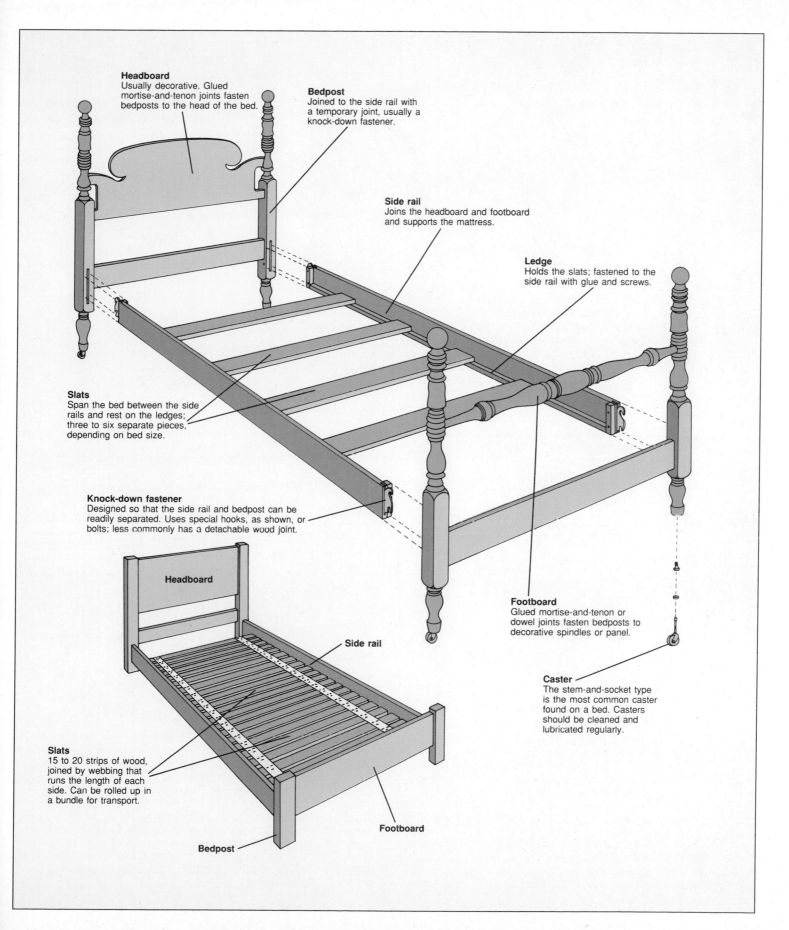

Headboard
Usually decorative. Glued mortise-and-tenon joints fasten bedposts to the head of the bed.

Bedpost
Joined to the side rail with a temporary joint, usually a knock-down fastener.

Side rail
Joins the headboard and footboard and supports the mattress.

Ledge
Holds the slats; fastened to the side rail with glue and screws.

Slats
Span the bed between the side rails and rest on the ledges; three to six separate pieces, depending on bed size.

Knock-down fastener
Designed so that the side rail and bedpost can be readily separated. Uses special hooks, as shown, or bolts; less commonly has a detachable wood joint.

Headboard

Footboard
Glued mortise-and-tenon or dowel joints fasten bedposts to decorative spindles or panel.

Caster
The stem-and-socket type is the most common caster found on a bed. Casters should be cleaned and lubricated regularly.

Side rail

Slats
15 to 20 strips of wood, joined by webbing that runs the length of each side. Can be rolled up in a bundle for transport.

Footboard

Bedpost

BEDRAIL FASTENERS

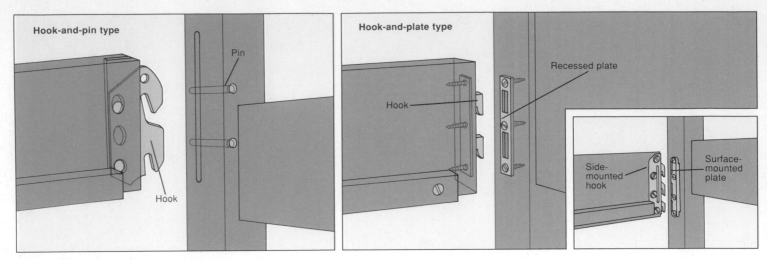

Knock-down joinery. Because beds are such large pieces of furniture, they would be difficult to move or store without knock-down fasteners that allow you to disengage the side rails from the bedposts. Shown here are three types of gravity-lock hook fasteners. The hooked metal part of the hook-and-pin fastener *(above, left)* is screwed into a slot in the end of the side rail. The hooks fit into a slot in the bedpost, where they engage hidden metal pins.

The hook-and-plate fastener has two variations. In the recessed type *(above, right)*, the base of the hook part is mortised into the end of the side rail and its mating part, the plate, is mortised into the bedpost. The surface-mounted hook-and-plate fastener *(inset)* makes ideal replacement hardware, since it requires no slots or mortise.

CLOSING A CRACK IN A SIDE RAIL

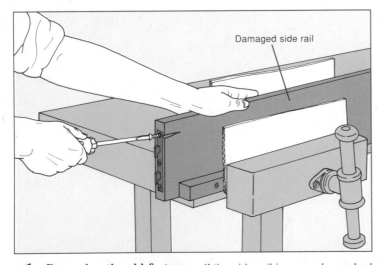

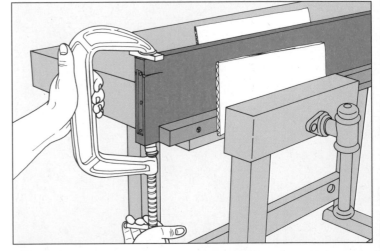

1 Removing the old fasteners. If the side rail is severely cracked or damaged, make a new side rail *(page 43)*. If the side rail has been cracked by a loosened fastener, close the crack, then install a surface-mounted fastener. Lift out the mattress, box spring and slats. To help you position the side rail correctly when reinstalling it, trace the outline of the damaged end of the side rail on the bedpost. Disengage the side rail from the bedposts by lifting it at one end, then the other, or by tapping the rail up with a rubber mallet. Secure the damaged end of the side rail in a vise, protecting its finish with cardboard or wood. Unscrew the old fastener from the side rail *(above)* and from the corresponding bedpost. Buy a surface-mounted hook-and-plate fastener at a hardware or home improvement store.

2 Clamping the crack. Use a toothpick to work white or yellow glue into the crack. Place a C clamp on the top and bottom edges of the side rail, inserting pads of wood or cork to protect the finish, then tighten the clamp just enough to bring the crack together *(above)*; do not overtighten. Wipe away excess glue with a clean, damp cloth. To strengthen the end of the rail, use a backsaw to cut a hardwood patch to fit into the mortise left by the old fastener. Glue the patch in place. Allow the glue to set for three to four hours, then release the clamp and sand the patch flush with the side rail. Remove the side rail from the vise. Install the surface-mounted fastener on the side rail and the bedpost, following the instructions on page 43.

MAKING A NEW SIDE RAIL

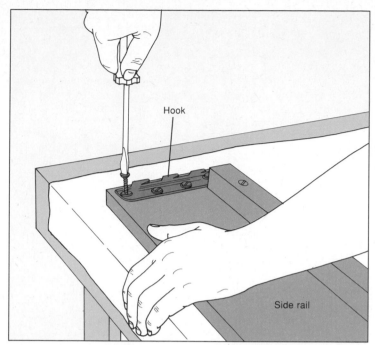

Hook

Side rail

1 **Making a side rail and installing new hooks.** If you are simply replacing a fastener on the old side rail, go to the next paragraph. To make a new side rail, trace the outline of the ends of the damaged side rail on both bedposts, then lift it off or tap on the bottom with a rubber mallet to separate it from the bedposts. Take the side rail to a hardwood lumber store. Buy a board of the same wood as the side rail and have it cut to size and planed at the store. Also buy a replacement for the old ledge, usually 1-by-1-inch hardwood, and a set of two surface-mounted hook-and-plate fasteners. Install the ledge on the new side rail *(page 44, step 2)*, and stain and finish the side rail to match the bed *(page 96)*.

Place the side rail on a work surface padded with an old blanket. Position the hook part of the fastener on one end of the side rail, with the ends of the hooks lined up flush with the end of the wood. Use an awl to punch position marks for the mounting screws. Fit a power drill with a drill bit slightly smaller in diameter than the screws and mark the screw length on the bit with masking tape. Drill screw holes at the marks, stopping when the tape touches the wood. Screw the hook part to the side rail *(left)*. Attach a hook at the other end of a new side rail the same way.

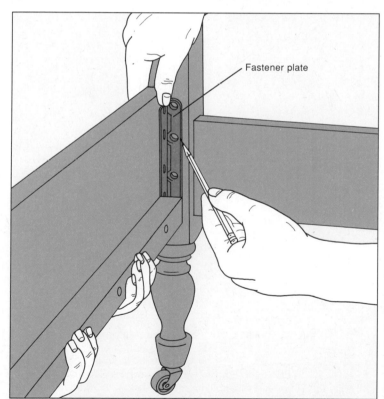

Fastener plate

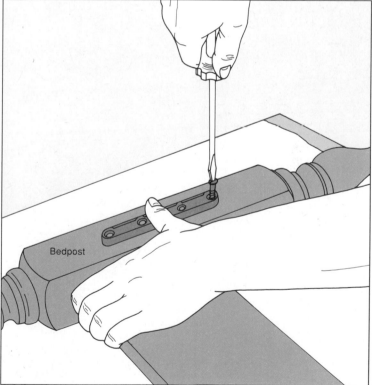

Bedpost

2 **Installing new fastener plates.** Mate the fastener plate to the hook at the end of the side rail. Have a helper hold the side rail in position, lining up the end of the side rail with the outline on the bedpost. With the side rail correctly positioned, use a pencil to trace the outline of the new fastener plate on the bedpost *(above, left)*, then use an an awl to punch position marks for the mounting screws. If installing new fasteners at both ends of the side rail, mark the other bedpost the same way. Detach the headboard or footboard and set it on a work surface, padded with an old blanket. Prepare a drill bit as in step 1, drill screw holes in the bedpost, then screw on the fastener plate *(above, right)*. Repeat the procedure for the opposite bedpost, if necessary. Reassemble the bed frame and reinstall the slats, box spring and mattress.

REPLACING A LEDGE

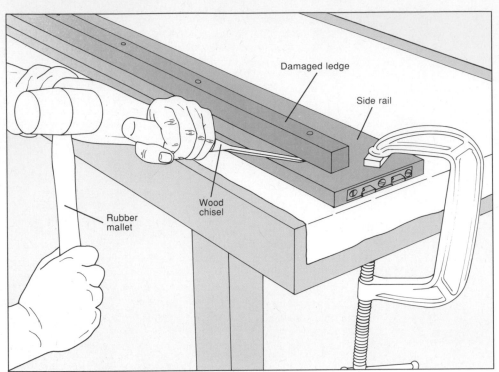

1 **Removing the ledge.** If the ledge on a side rail is sagging or broken, remove the old ledge and install a new one. Lift off the mattress, box spring, and slats. Detach the side rail by pulling it up, or by tapping it from below with a rubber mallet. Place the side rail on a work surface, padded with an old blanket, and secure it to the work surface with C clamps. To guide you when installing the new ledge, use a pencil to trace an outline of the old ledge on the rail. Remove the screws that secure the ledge to the side rail. The ledge is probably glued as well; pry it off using an old wood chisel and a rubber mallet *(left)*. With a shop knife, scrape dried glue from the side rail. Release the C clamps.

Damaged ledge

Side rail

Wood chisel

Rubber mallet

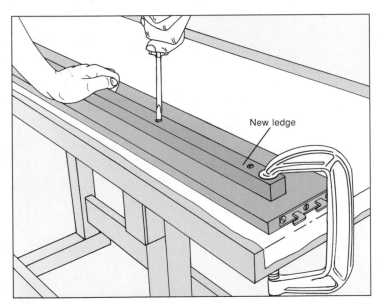

New ledge

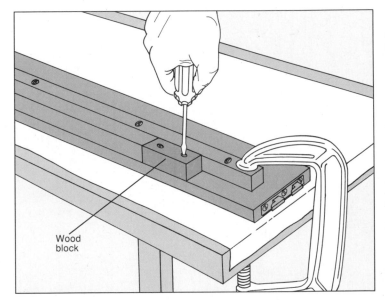

Wood block

2 **Installing the ledge.** Buy a replacement for the old ledge, usually 1-by-1-inch hardwood. If there is space for ledge supports between the ledge and the bottom of the side rail, buy an extra 2 feet of the same wood to make support blocks *(step 3)*. Spread a thin layer of white or yellow glue on the ledge and side rail, then press the ledge onto the rail, aligning it within the traced outline. Secure the ledge with a C clamp at each end and in the middle. Use an awl to punch position marks for screws at 12-inch intervals along the ledge. To avoid piercing the finished side of the rail when you drill, choose No. 8 wood screws 1/4 inch shorter than the combined thickness of the ledge and side rail, and mark the screw length on a 3/32-inch drill bit with masking tape. Bore a screw hole through the ledge into the side rail at each mark, stopping when the tape touches the wood. Install a countersink bit *(page 114)* on the drill and bore countersink holes for the screw heads. Drive the screws into the holes *(above)*.

3 **Adding support to the ledge.** If the ledge does not run along the bottom edge of the side rail, you can bolster the ledge by adding wood support blocks beneath it. Use a backsaw to cut six or seven wood blocks approximately 3 inches long. Spread a thin coat of white or yellow glue on the blocks and the side rail, and press on the blocks, spacing them about 10 inches apart. With an awl, pierce two screw-position marks in each block. Drill screw holes through the blocks into the side rail below, as you did for the ledge in step 2. Drive No. 8 wood screws into the holes. Reinstall the side rail, then put back the slats, box spring and mattress.

REPLACING DAMAGED SLATS

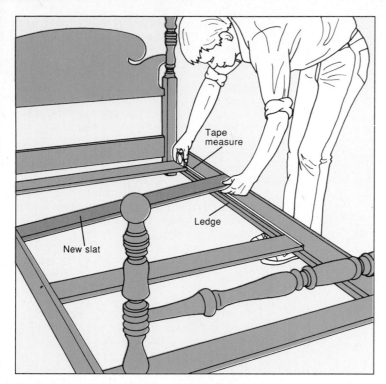

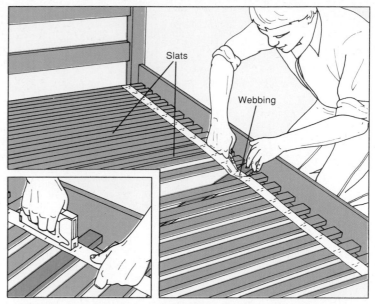

Replacing a single slat. Lift out the mattress, box spring and damaged slat. Buy a replacement hardwood slat of the same dimensions as the damaged one. Have it cut to length at the lumber yard or cut it yourself with a backsaw. Set in the new slat (above), spacing the slats equally within the bed frame. Replace the box spring and mattress.

Repairing bundled slats. Lift off the mattress and box spring. Trace the position of the damaged slat onto the webbing at both sides. With long-nose pliers (above) or a screwdriver, pull out the staples or tacks that hold the damaged slat to the webbing. Lift out the slat. Buy a replacement hardwood slat of the same dimensions as the old one. Have it cut to length at the lumber yard or cut it yourself with a backsaw. Slip the new slat between the webbing and the side rail ledge and use a staple gun to fasten the webbing to the slat (inset). Replace the box spring and mattress.

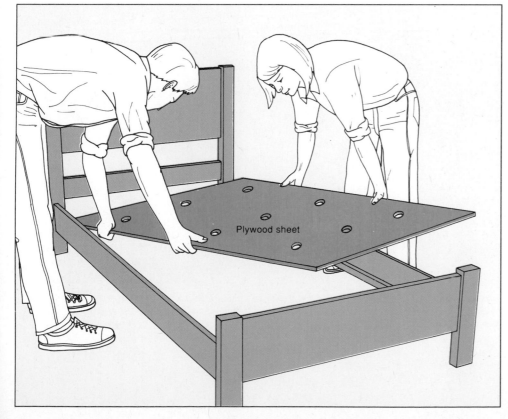

Dropping in a posture board. A posture board can be installed in place of slats to make a mattress firmer. To replace slats with a 3/4-inch plywood or particleboard sheet, have the panel cut to the inside dimensions of the bed frame, allowing for a 1/8-inch gap on all edges of the panel. Lift out or roll up the slats. Tighten any loose screws securing each ledge to its side rail and, if possible, reinforce them following the instructions on page 44. To ventilate the mattress, use a 1-inch drill bit to bore holes through the posture board, spacing them 9 to 12 inches apart. With a helper, carefully lower the board onto the ledge, smooth side up.

STRAIGHTENING A BULGING SIDE RAIL

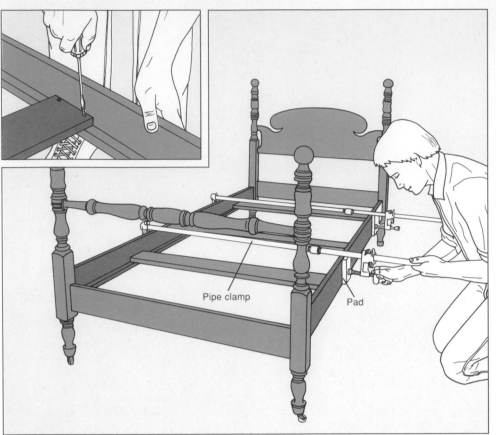

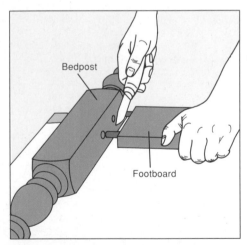

Pipe clamp

Pad

Correcting the warp. If you have separate bed slats, you can use them to anchor a bulging side rail. If your slats are 3 inches wide or less, either have three 1-by-4 hardwood slats cut to the same length as the old slats, or replace the warped side rail *(page 43)*. Lift out the mattress, box spring and slats. If necessary, tighten or reposition the screws that hold each ledge to its side rail. Remove all but three slats and space them evenly between the headboard and footboard. Place two pipe clamps across the side rails, inserting wood or cork pads to protect the finish. Tighten the clamps, as shown, until the side rails straighten and each of the three slats is 1/8 inch from the inside surfaces of both side rails; this ensures that the side rail is pulled in squarely. Mark the edges of each slat on the ledges with a pencil, then remove the two outer slats. With an awl, punch two screw-position marks in each end of the slat. Drill 3/32-inch holes at the marks and into the ledge below. If the side rail interferes with the drill, use a drill-bit extension long enough to raise the drill above the top of the side rail. Countersink each hole with a countersink bit and drive in No. 8 wood screws *(inset)*. Install the other two slats the same way. Release the clamps and put back the remaining slats, then set in the box spring and mattress.

REGLUING A WOOD JOINT

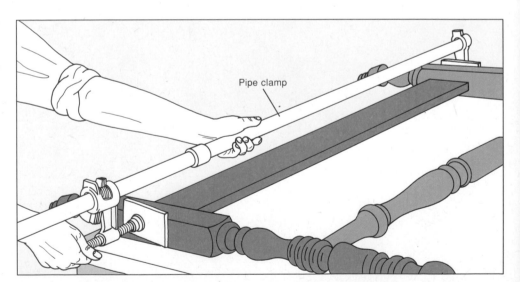

Bedpost

Footboard

Pipe clamp

1 **Cleaning the joint.** To repair a loose joint at the headboard or footboard, lift out the mattress, box spring and slats. Detach the headboard or footboard from the side rails and set it on a padded work surface. For a strong repair, separate the joint completely. Try to pull the joint apart by hand, or tap it apart with a rubber mallet. Use a shop knife *(above)* to scrape dried glue from the gluing surfaces, taking care not to carve away any wood.

2 **Gluing and clamping.** Spread a thin coat of white or yellow glue on the dowels and in the dowel holes, then tap the joint together with the mallet. Clamp the freshly glued joint with a pipe clamp *(above)*, inserting pads of wood or cork to protect the finish. Tighten the clamp only enough to close the joint; do not overtighten. Wipe away any excess glue with a clean, damp cloth. Wait 24 hours for the glue to set, then release the clamp. Reassemble the bed and set in the slats, box spring and mattress.

REPLACING A DAMAGED CASTER ROLLER

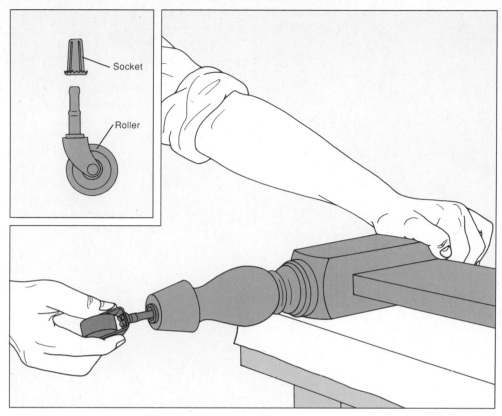

Socket

Roller

Inspecting and servicing a caster. The most common type of caster found on the narrow legs of a bed (or a table or chair) is the stem-type caster *(inset)*. A metal sleeve or socket is fitted into a hole drilled in the bottom of the leg; the teeth on the socket collar hold it firmly in place. The metal stem of the roller snaps into the socket, attaching the caster to the leg and allowing it to swivel. If a caster does not roll properly, lift out the mattress, box spring and slats, then detach the headboard or footboard from the frame and set it on a work surface padded with an old blanket. Remove any rug fibers and debris that clog the roller; then spray the roller and stem with silicone lubricant. If the roller appears badly worn or damaged, pull it out of the socket *(left)*. At a hardware store, buy a replacement caster with a stem and roller that match the dimensions of the old caster and rated to support the same load. If possible, buy a caster with a nylon roller, which will not rust. Lubricate the stem of the new roller with paraffin wax, then push it firmly into the empty socket until it snaps into place. Reassemble the bed frame, then set in the slats, box spring and mattress.

REPAIRING A LOOSE CASTER SOCKET

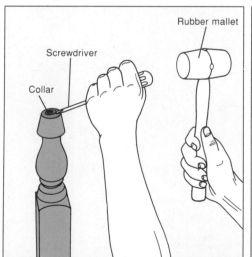

Rubber mallet

Screwdriver

Collar

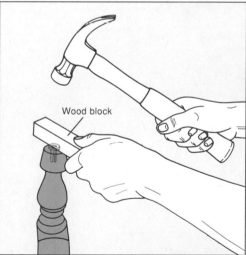

Wood block

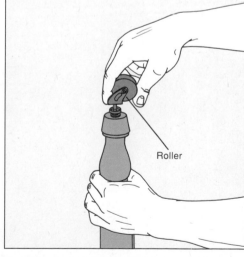

Roller

Installing a new socket. Stress on a caster can loosen the socket, making it rub against the wood and enlarge the socket hole. The result is a wobbly caster or one that falls out when the bed is lifted. Lift off the mattress, box spring and slats, then disassemble the bed. Secure the leg with the loose caster in a vise, protecting the finish with cardboard or cork. Pull the roller out of the socket. To remove the socket, drive an old screwdriver under the socket collar *(above, left)*. Pry the socket straight up out of its hole at a 90-degree angle to avoid fracturing the leg. Fill the socket hole by plugging it with a wood dowel *(page 120)*. If the old caster is damaged, buy a replacement caster with a stem and roller that match the dimensions of the old one. Select a drill bit the same diameter as the new socket and use masking tape to mark the bit to the depth of the socket. Bore into the center of the dowel glued in the leg, stopping when the tape touches the wood. Insert the new socket into the hole, then place a wood block over the the collar and hammer in the socket until the teeth are seated in the leg *(above, center)*. Rub paraffin wax on the roller stem to lubricate it, then push the stem into the socket *(above, right)* until it snaps into place. If you are replacing the entire set, repeat the procedure for the other legs. Reassemble the bed.

DRAWERS, DOORS AND SHELVES

Cabinet drawers and doors suffer constant swinging, sliding and pulling. In time, they can develop annoying ailments: Drawers slide crookedly, doors fit imperfectly, and shelves develop a wobble or an unbecoming sag.

A drawer slides in and out of the cabinet on a system of runners and guides. The drawer sides may be grooved, forming guides that slide along wood runners in the sides of the cabinet, as in the cabinet below. In other styles, the bottom edges of the drawer sides may serve as runners, as in the chest of drawers below. Wide drawers sometimes have a middle runner on the bottom to help distribute the weight.

If a drawer refuses to slide freely, check for a loose item lodged in the sliding apparatus. Severely worn bottom runners require what cabinetmakers refer to as reshoeing, a method of replacing the worn part of the runner with a new hardwood strip, then reshaping the runner to its original dimensions *(page 52)*. Drawers in some modern cabinets slide on metal tracks screwed to the sides or bottom of the drawer and cabinet. To keep the tracks operating smoothly, spray them occasionally with silicone lubricant, extending the drawer as far as possible. If the tracks are clogged with dirt, first scrub them with a old toothbrush.

Every time a drawer is pulled out, the joints take stress. Often you can reglue one loose joint without taking the drawer apart. If the drawer is loose and rickety, however, carefully knock apart the joints and rebuild the drawer *(page 56)*.

The doors in the cabinet below show two variations: one fits flush within the cabinet frame and the other is lipped to butt

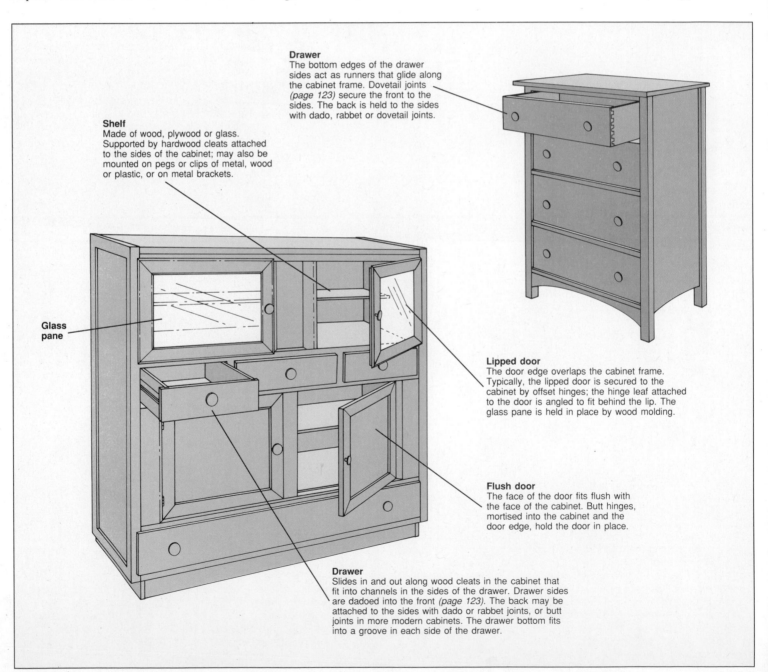

Drawer
The bottom edges of the drawer sides act as runners that glide along the cabinet frame. Dovetail joints *(page 123)* secure the front to the sides. The back is held to the sides with dado, rabbet or dovetail joints.

Shelf
Made of wood, plywood or glass. Supported by hardwood cleats attached to the sides of the cabinet; may also be mounted on pegs or clips of metal, wood or plastic, or on metal brackets.

Glass pane

Lipped door
The door edge overlaps the cabinet frame. Typically, the lipped door is secured to the cabinet by offset hinges; the hinge leaf attached to the door is angled to fit behind the lip. The glass pane is held in place by wood molding.

Flush door
The face of the door fits flush with the face of the cabinet. Butt hinges, mortised into the cabinet and the door edge, hold the door in place.

Drawer
Slides in and out along wood cleats in the cabinet that fit into channels in the sides of the drawer. Drawer sides are dadoed into the front *(page 123)*. The back may be attached to the sides with dado or rabbet joints, or butt joints in more modern cabinets. The drawer bottom fits into a groove in each side of the drawer.

against the frame edges. Hinges attach each door to the cabinet. These common door types are described further on page 57. When a cabinet door sags or sticks, the problem could be caused by loose or improperly aligned hinges. Before sanding or planing an ill-fitting door, first try tightening the hinge screws, then, on a flush door, try resetting the hinge. Use the diagnostic diagram on page 58 to help you decide when to build up the mortise or shave it down. If the door is warped or the cabinet is twisted out of square, it may be necessary to reshape the door *(page 60)*. Proceed slowly, test-fitting often to prevent taking off too much wood and destroying the door's appearance.

The greatest problem with shelves is sagging, as the shelf bows under the weight of the articles it stores or displays. The solution can be as simple as flipping the shelf. Badly warped or cracked shelves should be replaced. Refer to the load-bearing chart on page 63 before choosing a new shelf.

When a shelf wobbles or tips, a weakened support is usually to blame. If the mounting holes of adjustable peg supports are worn, the pegs can simply be repositioned to unworn holes. If space requirements make this impossible, reseat the pegs *(page 62)*. The metal clip-and-track system found in many modern bookcases seldom requires repair. Bent or lost clips are easily fixed or replaced.

Common repairs to doors, drawers and shelves do not require advanced carpentry skills. Most of the repairs in this chapter can be accomplished with a plane, a chisel, wood glue and pipe clamps *(page 113)*.

TROUBLESHOOTING GUIDE

SYMPTOM	POSSIBLE CAUSE	PROCEDURE
DRAWERS		
Drawer sticks	Cabinet warped or floor uneven	Insert wood shim under cabinet to make it sit squarely; inspect cabinet for structural flaws and have it rebuilt professionally
	Sliding surfaces need lubrication	Rub soap or wax on runners and guides *(bottom runners, p. 50; side runners, p. 53)* □○
	Nail head catching on sliding area	Countersink or remove nail *(p. 53)* □○
	Bottom runners worn unevenly	Add tacks or glides to runners or guides *(p. 50)* □○; sand or plane runners *(bottom runners, p. 50; side runners, p. 53)* □○
	Bottom runners worn or rutted	Build up runners *(p. 51)* ◨◗; replace runners *(p. 52)* ■◗
	Drawer bottom sagging or damaged	Flip or replace drawer bottom *(p. 54)* □○
	Drawer joint loose	Reglue joint *(p. 55)* □○; rebuild drawer *(p. 56)* ◨◗
Drawer fits loosely in cabinet	Bottom runners worn unevenly	Add tacks or glides to runners or guides *(p. 50)* □○; sand or plane runners *(bottom runners, p. 50; side runners, p. 53)* □○
	Bottom runners worn or rutted	Build up runners *(p. 51)* ◨◗; replace runners *(p. 52)* ■◗
Drawer handle loose	Screw holes enlarged	Pack screw holes and reseat screws *(p. 120)* □○
DOORS		
Cabinet door sticks or gaps	Hinge loose or improperly mounted	Tighten screws or replace screws with longer ones; pack screw holes and reseat screws *(p. 120)* □○; read gaps to locate sticking areas *(p. 58)*, then build up hinge with shim *(p. 58)* ◨○ or deepen hinge mortise *(p. 59)* ◨○
	Door warped or cabinet frame twisted	Read gaps to locate sticking areas *(p. 58)*, then build up hinge with shim *(p. 58)* ◨○, deepen hinge mortise *(p. 59)* ◨○, or sand or plane door *(p. 60)* □○; inspect cabinet for structural faults and have it rebuilt professionally
Door does not stay closed	Door latch broken or missing	Install latch to hold door closed *(p. 57)* □○
	Hinge too deeply mortised	Build up mortised hinge with shim *(p. 58)* ◨○
Glass pane in door broken	Accidental damage; door warped	Replace pane *(p. 61)* ◨◗
SHELVES		
Shelf sags	Warpage caused by excess weight	Turn shelf over; replace shelf *(p. 63)* ◨◗
Shelf wobbly	Shelf supports loose or misaligned	Reposition or anchor shelf supports *(p. 62)* □○

DEGREE OF DIFFICULTY: □ Easy   ◨ Moderate   ■ Complex
ESTIMATED TIME: ○ Less than 1 hour   ◗ 1 to 3 hours   ● Over 3 hours *(Does not include drying time)*

UNSTICKING A DRAWER WITH BOTTOM RUNNERS

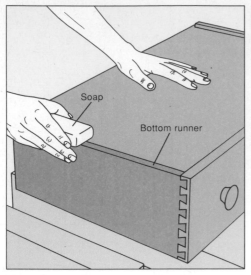

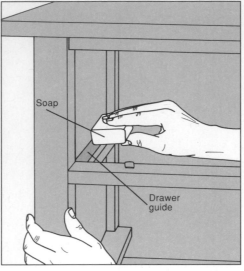

Waxing sliding surfaces. Pull the sticking drawer out of the cabinet and place it upside down on a work surface. Runners that feel rough or dry require waxing. Rub soap or paraffin wax along the entire length of the drawer runner *(far left)*. Drawer guides on the inside of the cabinet may also need lubrication. If necessary, remove an adjoining drawer to gain access to the drawer guides. Use a hammer and nail set to countersink any protruding nail heads *(page 120)*, then coat the sliding surfaces with soap or paraffin wax *(near left)*. If there is a center runner on the drawer bottom, lubricate it and the mating guide inside the cabinet frame.

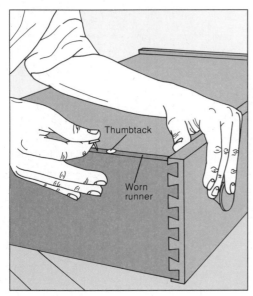

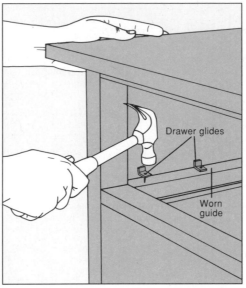

Raising a worn edge. The runners of heavily used drawers tend to wear at the front. If the drawer does not slide in and out evenly, or it fits loosely in the cabinet, pull the drawer out of the cabinet and set it on a work surface. Inspect the bottom runners on the drawer for signs of wear. Fill in a curve in the drawer runner by firmly pressing in a row of thumbtacks *(far left)*. If the entire runner is badly worn or rutted, build it up with veneer *(page 51)* or nylon tape, or replace the runner *(page 52)*. If the runner does not show signs of wear, inspect the guides inside the cabinet. To raise a worn guide, tap thumbtacks or purchased drawer glides into the worn area *(near left)*.

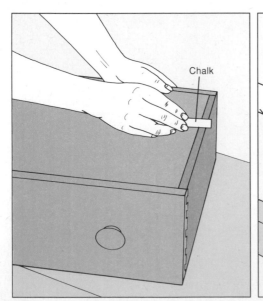

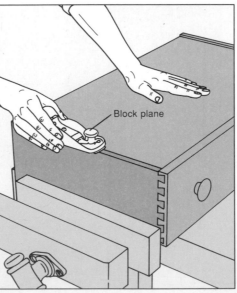

Leveling an uneven edge. Pull the drawer out of the cabinet and invert it on a work surface. To locate the sticking spot, rub chalk along the edges of both drawer runners *(far left)*, then return the drawer to the cabinet and slide it in and out several times. Pull out the drawer, flip it over and inspect the chalked edges; the chalk will rub off any high areas on the runners that are causing the drawer to stick. Use a sanding block with medium-grit sandpaper to smooth the protrusions, then test the drawer. If it still sticks, secure it in a vise to shave down high spots sparingly with a properly adjusted block plane or jack plane *(page 113)*. Keeping even pressure on the plane, shear the wood along the grain *(near left)*.

BUILDING UP A WORN BOTTOM RUNNER

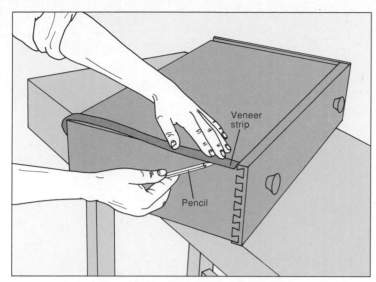

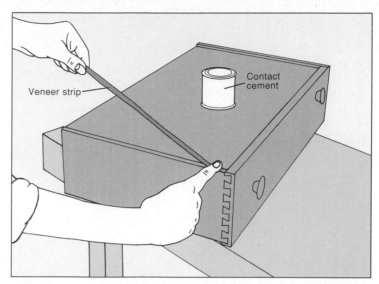

1 Measuring and cutting the veneer strip. Set the drawer upside down on a work surface. Use sandpaper to smooth the bottom runners, then measure their length. Buy a hardwood veneer strip wide enough to cover the runner and twice as long; double that measurement if both runners are worn. Extend the veneer strip along the runner and mark the width and length of the runner on it *(above)*. Place the strip on a work surface and use a utility knife and metal straightedge to trim the veneer to size. Cut a strip for the other runner the same way.

2 Gluing on the veneer strip. Lay the trimmed veneer along the worn runner to make sure it fits. Use a small brush to spread a thin, even layer of contact cement on both surfaces to be joined. (Veneer edging also comes with a pre-glued backing that must be ironed on.) Allow about 5 minutes for the contact cement to dry, then, aligning the veneer strip exactly, press it onto the runner *(above)*. Apply pressure along the entire length of the veneer strip to ensure that the edges are bonded. Repeat the procedure to install the strip on the second runner.

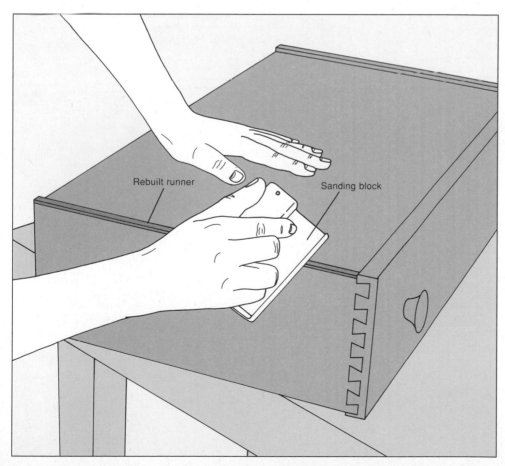

3 Sanding to fit. Use a sanding block with medium-grit sandpaper to smooth the veneer strip lightly along its edges *(left)*. Return the drawer to the cabinet and slide it in and out several times to test the fit. If the runners are too high, sand them down. If the runners require more rebuilding, add a second layer of veneer, following the same procedure. Lubricate the rebuilt runners with paraffin wax *(page 50)*.

REPLACING BOTTOM RUNNERS

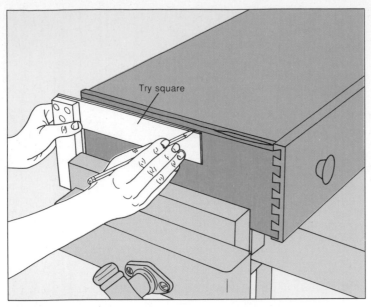

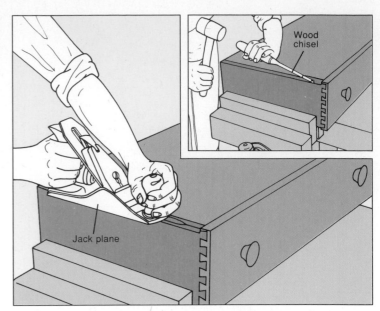

1 Drawing planing lines. Place the drawer upside down on a work surface and secure it in a vise. To guide you when trimming the damaged runners, use a try square or steel square to draw a line on each drawer side just below the area of most wear *(above)*. The line cannot extend past the drawer bottom. At each drawer side, measure for a hardwood strip to replace the runner: Measure the length of the drawer side, its thickness and, at the back of the drawer side, where the wear is least, measure the depth of the piece to the planing line. Note these measurements for later use.

2 Trimming away the worn runners. Use a jack plane *(page 116)* to pare down a runner to the line drawn in step 1. Plane along the grain of the wood *(above)*, maintaining even pressure. The blade of the jack plane will not reach into the front corner of the drawer; to shave this section, use a wood chisel slightly wider than the runner. Hold the chisel at an angle, beveled side facing down, and lightly tap the handle end with a mallet *(inset)*. Chisel the wood in very thin layers, taking care not to remove any wood below the guideline. Trim away the second runner in the same manner.

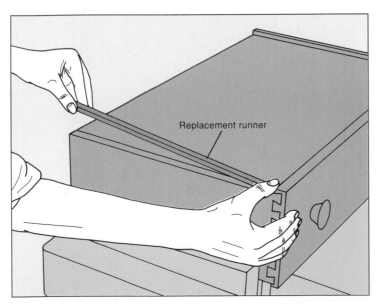

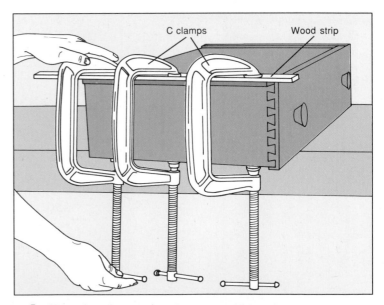

3 Installing new runners. At a lumber yard, have two pieces of hardwood cut to the dimensions noted in step 1. Maple or birch make the best runners; make sure there are no knots on the sliding surfaces. Spread a thin layer of white or yellow glue on the surfaces to be joined. Align the first piece on the corresponding drawer side and press it into place *(above)*. Glue the second piece to the other side the same way.

4 Clamping the repair. Clamp the replacement runner to the drawer side with C clamps. Insert a wood strip between the clamp jaws and the replacement runner to distribute the clamping pressure; a sheet of waxed paper between the wood strip and the runner will prevent oozing glue from sticking. Tighten the clamps just enough to bring the two gluing surfaces evenly together *(above)*; do not over-tighten. Wipe away excess glue with a clean, damp cloth. Clamp the runner on the other side the same way. Wait 24 hours for the glue to set, then release the clamps. Test the drawer in the cabinet. Sand the new runners to fit and lubricate them with paraffin wax.

UNSTICKING A DRAWER WITH SIDE RUNNERS

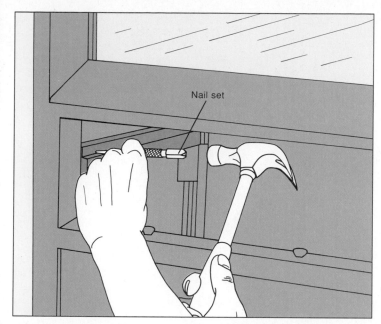

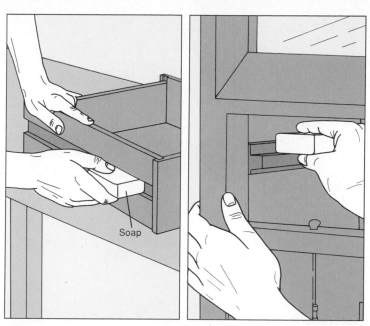

1 Setting a nail. Sliding assemblies are sometimes mounted with finishing nails. With wear, the nails may loosen and protrude. Slide the binding drawer out of the cabinet and inspect the guides on the drawer and the runners inside the cabinet. If you find a protruding nail head, use a hammer and nail set *(page 120)* to set the nail head *(above)*. If a nail is loose or bent, remove it with a nail puller or pliers and drive a new nail close to the old hole. Set the new nail.

2 Waxing the sliding surfaces. With a shop knife or an old wood chisel, scrape old wax from the runners and guides. Rub soap or paraffin wax on the sliding surfaces of the drawer *(above, left)*, then coat the mating sliding surfaces inside the cabinet frame *(above, right)*. Return the drawer to the cabinet and slide it in and out several times. If the drawer still binds, pull it out again and go to step 3.

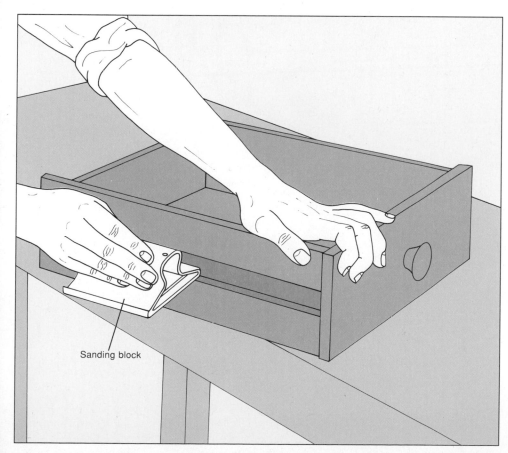

3 Sanding runners and guides. To locate raised surfaces that might be binding, run chalk along the edges of the drawer guides, then return the drawer to the cabinet and slide it in and out several times. Pull out the drawer and inspect the chalked edges; the chalk will rub off any binding areas. Use a sanding block with medium-grit sandpaper to smooth these areas *(left)*. Do not over-sand and do not round off sharp edges. Test-fit the drawer several times during the sanding procedure to avoid removing too much wood. If necessary, apply chalk to the cabinet runners and sand them as well. When the drawer slides freely in and out of the cabinet, lubricate the sliding surfaces with paraffin wax or silicone.

REPAIRING A DRAWER BOTTOM

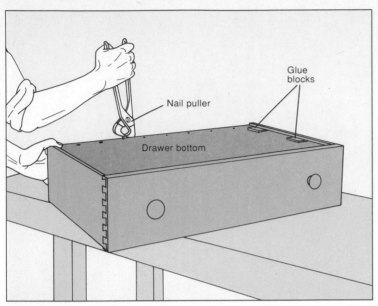

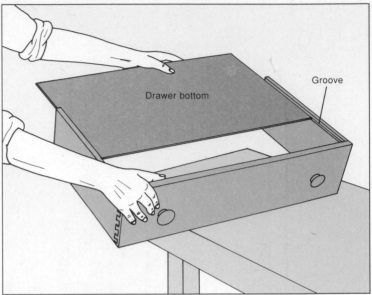

1 **Removing the drawer bottom.** Pull the drawer out of the cabinet and place it upside down on a work surface. Use a nail puller to take out any nails fastening the drawer bottom to the back *(above, left)*. If the nails are set, turn over the drawer and use a wood block and hammer to hit inside the drawer bottom near the back, popping the nail heads. Turn the drawer upside down again and extract the nails. Use an old wood chisel to pry off any glue blocks holding the bottom to the drawer sides. Slide the bottom out of its grooves *(above, right)*. If the bottom sags, but is otherwise in good condition, flip it. A badly worn or cracked drawer bottom should be replaced. Measure the old drawer bottom and buy a piece of hardboard or plywood of the same thickness (normally 1/4 inch, but may range from 1/8 inch to 1/2 inch). Have the bottom cut to fit, or cut it yourself. Smooth all cut edges with medium-grit sandpaper.

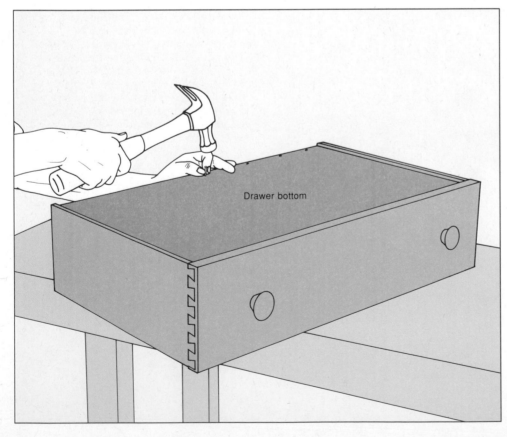

2 **Installing the drawer bottom.** Slide the drawer bottom into the grooves in the drawer sides. To secure the bottom, drive box nails through it into the back of the drawer, spacing them about 2 inches apart *(left)*. If the drawer has glue blocks, use a shop knife to scrape off any dried glue, then spread a thin layer of white or yellow glue on the gluing surfaces and install the blocks on the drawer bottom in their original positions against the sides. Wait three to four hours for the glue to set before returning the drawer to the cabinet.

REGLUING A LOOSE JOINT

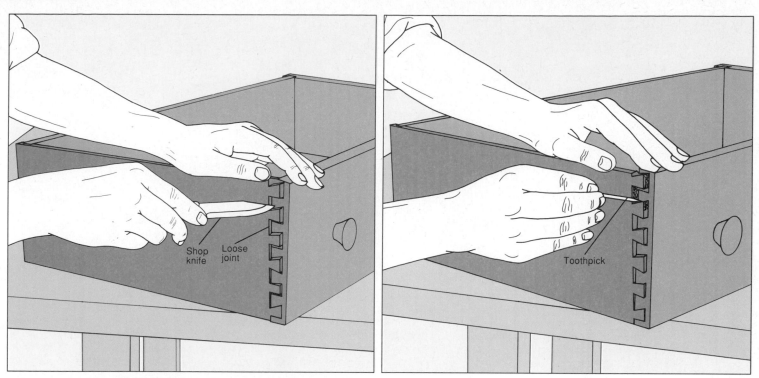

1 **Working glue into the joint.** Slide the drawer out of its cabinet and set it on a work surface. Examine all joints for soundness. In the drawer shown, the loose joint is a dovetail joint, but a dado, rabbet or butt joint is repaired the same way. If one joint is shaky, separate the joint by hand, taking care not to loosen the firm joints. Use a shop knife to scrape out as much dried glue as possible without cutting into the wood *(above, left)*. With a toothpick *(above, right)* or a glue syringe *(page 121)*, inject glue into the crevices of the joint. Push the joint back together by hand or tap it gently with a rubber mallet.

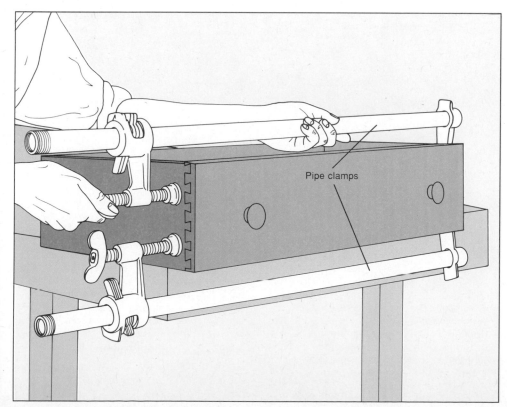

2 **Clamping the drawer joint.** Attach pipe clamps to the drawer at the reglued joint *(left)*. Tighten the clamps only enough to bring the gluing surfaces in contact. To make sure that the drawer is clamped squarely, measure diagonally from the front right corner to the back left corner, and from the front left corner to the back right corner. Adjust the fit of the clamps until the two measurements are equal. Use a clean, damp cloth to wipe away any glue that beads out of the joint. Release the clamps after 24 hours and return the drawer to the cabinet.

REBUILDING A RICKETY DRAWER

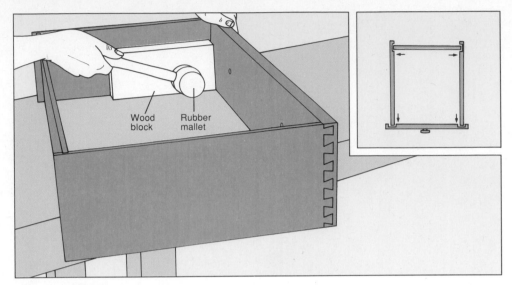

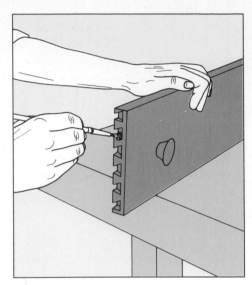

1 Knocking the drawer apart. Pull the drawer out of the cabinet and set it on a work surface. Remove the drawer bottom *(page 54)*. Use a nail puller to extract any nails fastening
the joints. Examine the way the drawer front and back are attached to the sides before
you begin to knock the drawer apart. If the drawer front is dovetailed to the sides and the back
is dadoed into the sides, as in this drawer, tap on the sides inside each corner. Place a hardwood block against the side of the drawer at the front corner, and strike the block sharply with a
mallet *(above)* or a hammer. Repeat the procedure at the back corner, then on the opposite
side, tapping the corners alternately so that all four joints loosen together gradually. If the sides
are dadoed into the drawer front and the drawer back is dadoed into the sides *(inset)*, tap on the
drawer front at the corners, then tap the sides at the back corners. Separate the back and front
from the sides.

2 Gluing the joints. Use a shop knife
to scrape dried glue out of the drawer
joints, taking care not to break the
fingers of a dovetail. Spread a thin layer of
white or yellow glue on the gluing surfaces;
use a small brush *(above)* or a toothpick to
spread the glue. Reassemble the drawer
immediately *(step 3)*.

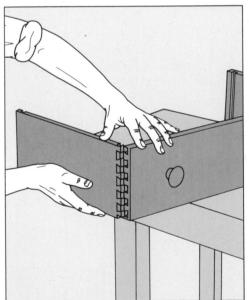

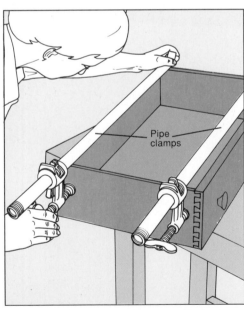

3 Reassembling the drawer. First fit together the joints at the front *(above, left)* then
attach the back. Push the joints together with your hands or tap them into place with the
rubber mallet. Slide the drawer bottom into the grooves in the sides. Attach pipe clamps
on the drawer at the reglued joints *(above, right)*. Pad the clamp jaws if they contact the drawer
front. Tighten the clamps only enough to bring the gluing surfaces in contact. To make sure that
the drawer is clamped squarely, measure diagonally from the front right corner to the back left
corner, then from the front left corner to the back right corner. If these two measurements are
not equal, adjust the fit of the clamps. With a clean, damp cloth, wipe away any glue that
beads out of the joints. Release the clamps after 24 hours.

4 Reinforcing the repair. If the drawer
is used to store heavy items, you can
reinforce it with glue blocks. Use a backsaw to cut four small, rectangular blocks of softwood, slightly less than the interior depth of
the drawer. Apply a thin layer of glue to two
sides of a block and an inside corner of the
drawer. Press the block into the corner *(above)*,
rubbing it up and down several times to exclude
any air bubbles. Glue the other blocks the same
way. Wait three to four hours for the glue to
set before returning the drawer to the cabinet.

TWO KINDS OF DOORS AND HINGES

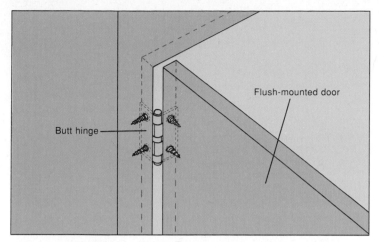

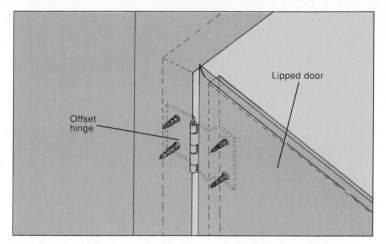

Doors that fit flush within the frame. A flush door is cut to the size of the cabinet opening, so that when closed, it sits flush inside the opening. Typically, standard butt hinges, which have two equal leaves joined in a knuckle, attach a flush door to the cabinet *(above)*. One leaf of the hinge is mounted in a mortise on the cabinet, while the other is surface-mounted or mortised into the door edge. Some butt hinges have loose pins that can be pulled out of the knuckle, making it easy to remove the door. Because of the precise fit of flush doors, slight warpage of the door, settling of the cabinet frame or sags in the hinges can make the door stick or can cause noticeable gaps between the door edges and the cabinet opening.

Doors that overlap the frame. A lipped, or inset, door is partially recessed into the cabinet opening and fitted with a lip that overlaps the framework of the cabinet. Lipped doors are hung with offset hinges, which have one leaf shaped at a 90-degree angle to fit against the back of the lip *(above)*. Precise fit is far less important in the lipped door; the lip hides gaps between the door edge and the cabinet opening, and allows for much more play between them. It is seldom necessary to adjust the hinges on a lipped door.

INSTALLING A DOOR LATCH

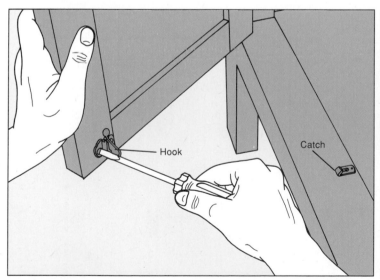

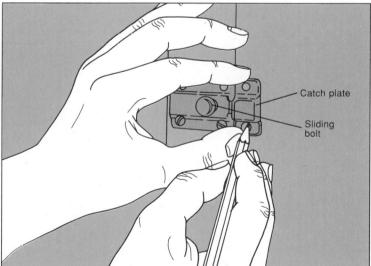

Holding a door closed. Install a new latch if the old latch is broken, or if the door has no latch and does not stay closed. If the cabinet has double doors, you can install a finger latch inside the cabinet. This latch has two parts: an L-shaped catch and a spring-loaded hook. The catch sits inside the cabinet and the hook fits on the back of the door; when the door is closed, the two pieces latch together. To open the door, you must open the adjacent door and press back the hook. To install the latch, hook the two parts together and position the catch on the floor of the cabinet and the hook on the back of the door. Use an awl to punch position marks for the mounting screws. Remove the latch and drill pilot holes at the marks. Screw the catch to the cabinet and the hook to the door *(above, left)*. Test the fit of the finger-latch

assembly and adjust it by loosening the screw on the catch and sliding the catch forward or backward along its oblong screw hole. Latches with roller, friction and magnetic catches are installed in a similar manner.

A bar latch can be installed on the outside of the door. Bar latches are available in a variety of sizes, styles and finishes. Choose a bar latch with a straight bolt for a flush door or one with a bent bolt for a lipped door. Position the sliding-bolt assembly on the door and mark its screw-hole positions with a pencil or an awl. Drill pilot holes at the marks and screw the sliding-bolt assembly in place. Next, position the catch plate on the cabinet frame, or on the divider between double doors, and fit the bolt into the catch plate to align it. Mark the screw-hole positions *(above, right)*, drill pilot holes and screw the catch plate to the door.

DIAGNOSING DOOR PROBLEMS

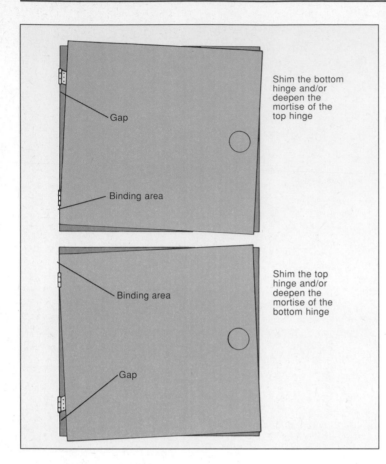

Gap

Binding area

Shim the bottom hinge and/or deepen the mortise of the top hinge

Binding area

Gap

Shim the top hinge and/or deepen the mortise of the bottom hinge

Reading gaps and locating binding areas. When a door sticks or jams against its opening in the frame, the problem could be as simple as a loose hinge screw or as complex as a twisted door or cabinet frame. First try to solve the problem by tightening all hinge screws on the door and on the cabinet frame. If the screw holes are worn, install longer screws or rebuild the holes *(page 120)* and remount the hinges.

Close the door and check whether it sags; note any uneven gaps between the door edges and the cabinet frame. Use the diagrams at left to read the gaps and binding to help determine solutions to your fitting problem.

Rub marks or burnished wood along the edges of a door or the cabinet frame can provide clues to where a door is sticking. If the tight spots are hard to see, rub chalk along the door edges, then open and close the door several times. The chalk will rub off at the points where the door is sticking. Alternatively, insert a sheet of paper between the edge of a flush door and the cabinet; the paper should move freely around the door except at the sticking points. To eliminate very slight rubbing, lightly sand the raised areas with medium-grit sandpaper. Otherwise, adjust the hinges.

Rubbing may occur in a flush door if one hinge leaf is mortised too deeply or not deeply enough in the wood, or if the wood of the door or cabinet has swollen or shrunk. Examine the hinge leaves for one that does not sit flush with the surface; to shim, or build up, a hinge leaf that is too deep, follow the steps below; to deepen the mortise of a raised hinge leaf, go to page 59. If hinge adjustments do not solve the problem, you may have to reshape the door to fit the cabinet *(page 60)*.

SHIMMING A HINGE

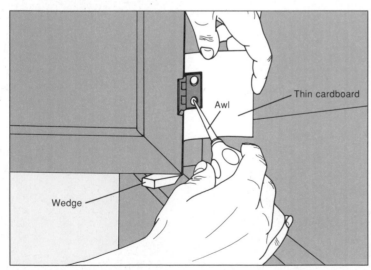

Thin cardboard

Awl

Wedge

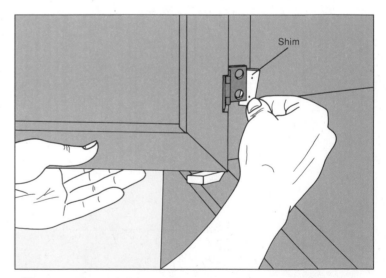

Shim

1 **Fitting the shim.** Open the door and wedge a piece of wood or cardboard under the bottom corner to prevent the door from sagging. Remove the screws that mount the hinge leaf to the cabinet frame. Slip a thin piece of cardboard behind the detached hinge leaf. Use an awl to trace the outline of the hinge leaf on the cardboard and punch holes at the screw-hole positions *(above)*. Take out the cardboard and use a utility knife or scissors to cut the shim about 1/16 inch smaller than the traced outline.

2 **Installing the shim.** Slide the shim behind the detached hinge leaf into the mortise, aligning the punched holes with the screw holes *(above)*. Screw the hinge to the cabinet. Pull out the wedge and open and close the door to test it. If it sticks, the hinge may still be too deep. Shim it again until the hinge leaf sits flush with the wood surface, or deepen the mortise of the other hinge *(page 59)*.

DEEPENING A HINGE MORTISE

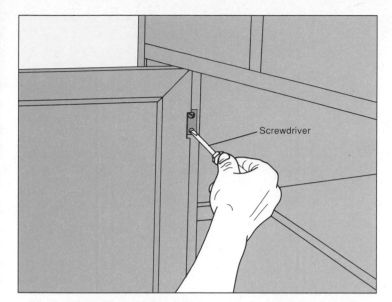

1 **Dismounting the door.** Open the door and wedge a piece of wood or cardboard under the bottom corner to prevent the door from sagging. Unscrew the hinge leaves from the cabinet frame *(above)*, starting with the lower hinge. Do not unscrew the hinge leaves attached to the door. Remove the door from the cabinet.

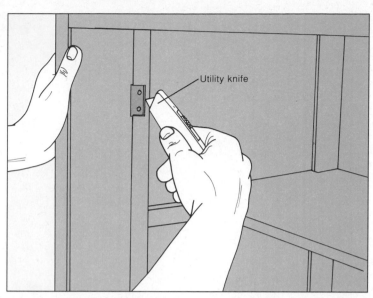

2 **Deepening the edges of the mortise.** To prevent the chisel from enlarging the outline of the mortise, use a sharp utility knife to score the mortise perimeter to a depth of 1/16 inch *(above)*.

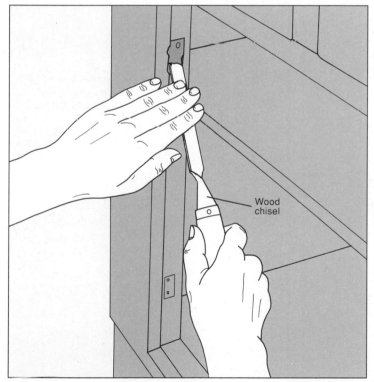

3 **Chiseling the mortise.** Using a wood chisel with the beveled edge facing down, shave a thin, even layer of wood out of the mortise *(above)*. Use hand pressure only; do not push hard on the chisel. Fit the door back into place with the hinge leaf positioned in the deepened mortise. If the leaf does not sit evenly, the mortise is not flat; use the wood chisel to even out the surface.

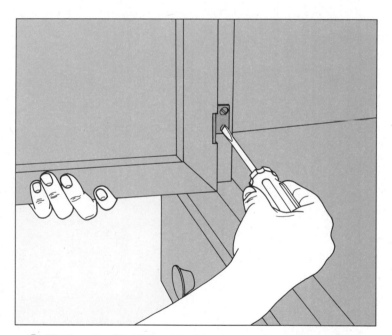

4 **Testing the fit.** Fit the door into place again and remount the hinges *(above)*, replacing screws that are worn or damaged; choose slightly longer screws for a better grip. Close the door to test the fit. If the binding persists, unscrew the hinge leaves from the cabinet, lift off the door and deepen the mortise a little more *(step 3)*. As a final resort, reshape the door *(page 60)*.

LEVELING A STICKING DOOR

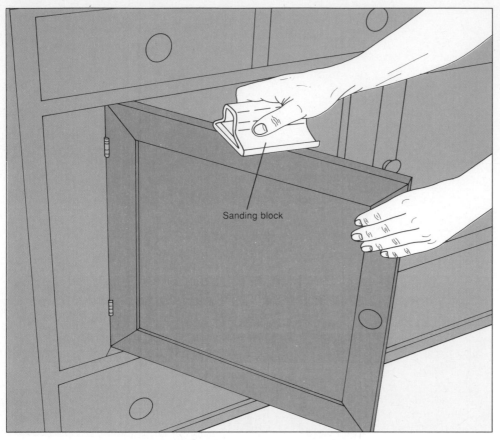

Sanding block

1 **Sanding down a high area.** To locate the areas to be leveled, rub chalk along the door edges, open and close the door several times and look for the points where the chalk has rubbed off. Use a sanding block with medium-grit sandpaper to smooth down the tight spots *(left)*. Do not over-sand; test-fit the door several times during the sanding procedure to ensure that you are not removing too much wood. If the binding area is at the bottom, or close to the hinged side of the door where the sanding block does not reach, or if you must remove more than 1/16 inch of wood, dismount the door *(page 59)* and plane it *(step 2)*.

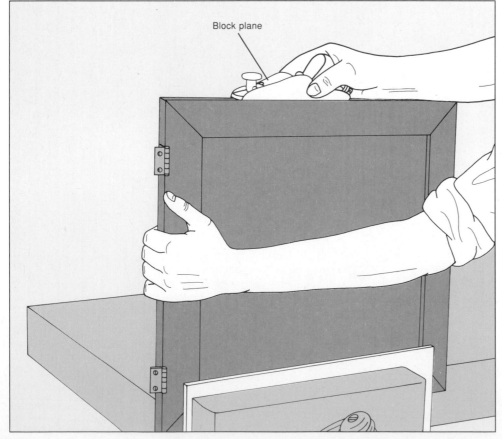

Block plane

2 **Planing the binding edge.** Place the door in a vise, protecting its finish with wood or cardboard. Use a properly adjusted block plane or jack plane *(page 113)* to level the edge, shaving along the grain *(left)*. Keep even pressure on the plane and use long shearing strokes, working from the corners toward the center to ensure that the ends of the side rails don't splinter. Remove the wood sparingly, remounting the door often to test its fit.

REPLACING A BROKEN PANE OF GLASS

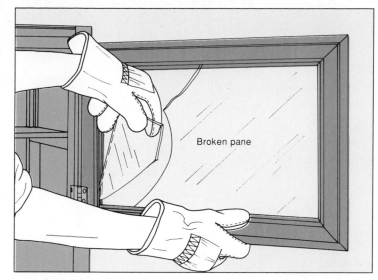

Broken pane

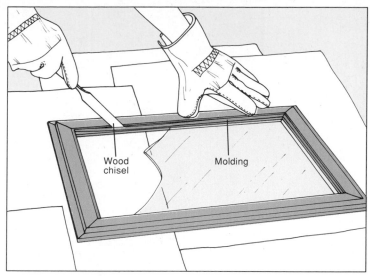

Wood chisel

Molding

1 **Picking out loose shards.** Before replacing a broken pane in a cabinet door, spread several layers of newspaper on the floor around the cabinet. Wearing heavy work gloves to protect your hands and safety goggles to protect your eyes, pull loose shards of glass out of the door frame *(above)*. Gently wiggle the fragments free, but leave stubborn pieces of glass in the door. Wrap the fragments in thick layers of newspaper and discard them.

2 **Removing the stubborn pieces.** Open the door and wedge wood or cardboard under the bottom corner to stabilize it. Unscrew the hinge leaves from the door and lift the door free of the cabinet. Set the door on a work surface covered with newspaper. The molding that secures a pane of glass is normally fastened to the door frame with small finishing nails. To remove the molding, insert the tip of an old wood chisel between the molding and the frame, close to each nail head, and gently pry away the molding. Use a nail puller to extract any nails that remain in the door. If the molding is in good condition, set it aside to reuse it. If it is damaged during removal, replace it *(step 3)*. Wearing work gloves, lift the broken glass out of the door frame, wrap it in several layers of newspaper and throw it away. Clean debris out of the glass groove.

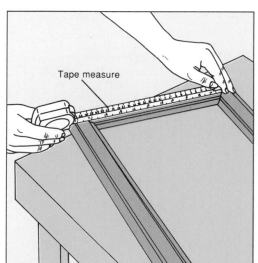

Tape measure

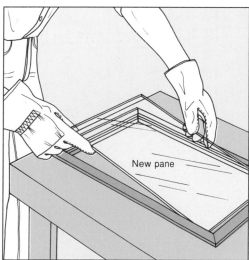

New pane

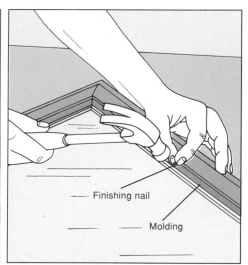

Finishing nail

Molding

3 **Installing a new pane.** To determine the size of the replacement pane, measure the length and width of the recess for the pane *(above, left)*, then subtract 1/8 inch from each dimension to allow for clearance. At a glass supplier or home improvement store, have a replacement pane cut to these dimensions from 1/8-inch glass. If the molding was damaged during removal, buy replacement molding of the same wood and dimensions. Have the new moldings cut to size, or cut them yourself with a backsaw and miter box *(page 115)*, matching the miters of the original pieces. Wearing work gloves to protect your hands, set the pane into its recess in the door *(above, center)*. Position the molding pieces over the edges of the pane and press the corners into place. Use a hammer to tap finishing nails every 5 or 6 inches through the molding into the door *(above, right)*, angling the nails to avoid hitting the glass. Remount the door on the cabinet.

ANCHORING SHELF SUPPORTS

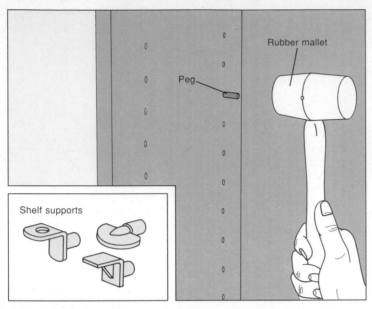

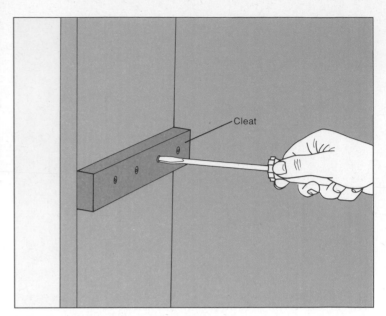

Remounting loose pegs. Plastic, wood and metal peg-style shelf supports fit into a series of holes drilled into the sides of a shelving unit. They come in a variety of shapes and are found in cabinets and bookcases with adjustable shelving. Metal spade pins and angled brackets *(inset)* have a flat surface, offering greater stability than the round dowel shown above. If the peg holes are worn, causing the shelf to wobble, lift out the shelf and relocate the pegs either up or down from the worn holes. To keep the shelf at the same height, pack the holes *(page 120)* and drill new holes. (Manufactured pegs generally fit into 1/4-inch holes, but measure the peg diameter to be sure.) Use a rubber mallet to tap the peg into its hole *(above)*, if necessary.

Securing a loose cleat. Large shelves that bear heavy loads often rest on wood ledges called cleats, screwed to the sides of the cabinet. With wear, the screws may loosen. Lift out the shelf; if the shelf is nailed to the cleats, tap it up from below with a rubber mallet. Tighten any loose screws holding the cleats *(above)*. If the screw holes are enlarged, unscrew the cleat and pack the screw holes *(page 120)*, then reinstall the cleat. To give the shelf extra strength, cut a 1-by-2 cleat to run the length of its back edge. If the back panel of the cabinet is less than 3/4 inch thick, attach the cleat to it with white or yellow glue; otherwise, drill pilot holes through the cleat into the back panel and screw the cleat in place as for the side cleats.

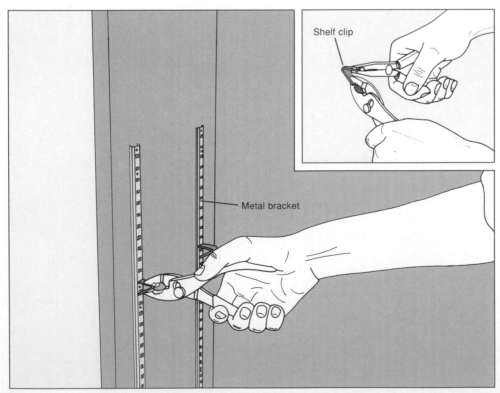

Repairing movable clips. Metal clips and the vertical metal tracks that they snap into are a highly adjustable shelf support system often found in bookshelves and modern wall units. A wobbly shelf may be caused by a bent or damaged clip, or a clip placed in the wrong slot. To remove a metal clip of the type shown here from its track, lift out the shelf, then squeeze the clip between the jaws of pliers and pull it up from its slots *(left)*. Use two sets of pliers gently to straighten a slightly bent clip *(inset)* or buy replacement clips to match the damaged clips. Squeeze the clip with pliers to remount it in the track.

REPLACING A DAMAGED SHELF

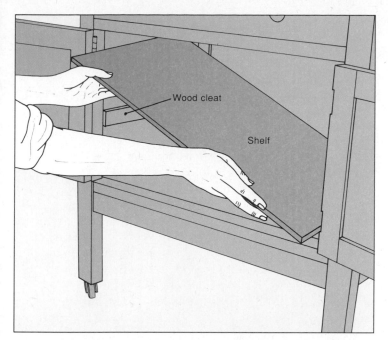

SHELF REPLACEMENT MATERIALS

Material	Characteristics	Thickness and maximum span
Plywood	Available with a wide variety of hard-wood veneers. Buy panel veneered on both sides; add veneer edging.	3/4" ......36"
Particleboard	Surfaced with a variety of veneers or plastic laminates, or with a smooth surface ready for painting. Add veneer edging; paint or finish both sides.	3/4" ......36"
Solid wood	A variety of softwoods and hardwoods, available in several grades. Buy kiln-dried boards that match cabinet. Apply a clear finish to both sides and edges.	3/4" ......36" 1 1/2" ......48"
Glass	Clear or smoked, with beveled or polished edges.	1/4" ......24" 1/2" ......36"
Acrylic	Available in translucent, transparent and tinted sheets. Sand edges smooth with medium-grit, then fine, sandpaper.	1/2" ......24" 3/4" ......36"

1 Lifting out the shelf. If the shelf is attached to a wood cleat with screws or nails, remove them as described on page 63. Lift the shelf, angle it to provide clearance and ease it out of the cabinet *(above)*. If the shelf sags, but is otherwise in good condition, turn it over and reinstall it, refinishing the bottom first *(page 96)*, if necessary. If the shelf is badly damaged, replace it.

2 Choosing a replacement shelf. Measure the old shelf to determine the dimensions of the replacement. Consider the weight that the shelf will bear and the length it will span between supports, and refer to the chart above to determine the appropriate replacement material. Have the new shelf cut to the length and width of the old one at a lumber yard, home improvement store or glass supplier. If the back corners of the old shelf are notched to accommodate the cabinet frame, have notches cut in the replacement at the same time, or cut them yourself with a backsaw. To add veneer edging to a plywood or particleboard shelf, go to step 3.

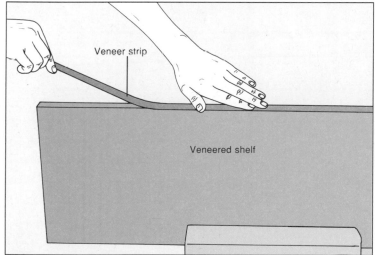

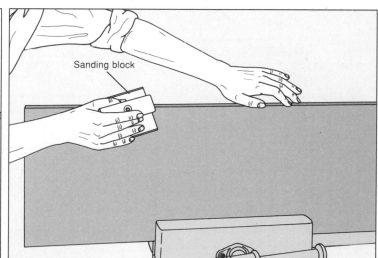

3 Veneeering the edge of the shelf. Use veneer in strip form, sold at hardwood lumber stores, to match the front cut edge of a plywood or particleboard shelf to its veneered surface. Veneer strips are available unglued, or with a self-adhesive backing, or backed with heat-activated glue that is ironed on. Buy a veneer strip of the proper width for the shelf's thickness, and a bit longer than the shelf. To apply unglued veneer, brush a thin layer of contact cement on the back of the veneer and the edge of the shelf. Wait five minutes for the cement to become tacky. Align the veneer strip precisely with the shelf edge and, starting at one end, press it in place along the edge *(above, left)*. Work carefully; once glued, the strip cannot be repositioned. Allow the contact cement to set for two hours, then trim off excess edges with a razor blade or very sharp wood chisel, taking care not to cut into the edge of the shelf. Use a sanding block with medium-grit sandpaper to smooth the veneer edges *(above, right)*. Refinish the new shelf *(page 96)* to match the cabinet, and install the shelf.

UPHOLSTERED FURNITURE

It might surprise you to discover that the comfortable wing chair you relax in to read the newspaper is a multi-layered system built of padding, fabric and springs supported by a wood frame. The seat is a prime example of the system. A stuffed cushion is often the first layer. Below it, fabric covers layers of stuffing, then burlap separates the stuffing from the springs. Strips of webbing may support the springs from beneath. Finally, a dust cover tacked to the very bottom of the seat catches any stuffing that falls out of the chair.

The three upholstered chairs at right show three types of springs commonly used to support seats. Hourglass-shaped coil springs are individually attached to the burlap at the seat bottom and require webbing to hold them in position. Conical, or drop-in, springs are manufactured in a set held together by sturdy wires or metal bars that run across their coils. The ends of the bars or wires are anchored to the seat frame. The zigzag, or serpentine, spring is a piece of tough steel wire shaped in a series of U bends. These springs run parallel from front to back beneath the seat stuffing. They are found extensively in furniture built after 1950.

This chapter includes instructions for bolstering sagging seats, refastening loose trim and buttons and lifting stains from upholstery fabric. All these repairs can be accomplished without removing the covering or disturbing the stuffing; repairs that make it necessary to reupholster are not included. Even the spring repairs, done from the underside of the chair, call only for the removal of the dust cover. Although the repairs shown here are carried out on upholstered chairs, they may be done on love seats and sofas as well.

Everyday wear and tear subject upholstery fabric to soiling and staining, but you can prevent much of the damage. Position upholstered furniture away from heat or direct sunlight. Vacuum the fabric with an upholstery brush every week or two and turn the cushions regularly. When spills occur, work fast to mop them up (page 10). Follow the manufacturer's instructions and the directions on page 66 to clean the fabric and remove stains. Spray a clean chair or sofa with a soil protectant (page 66) to help the fabric resist dirt and stains.

If a once-shapely seat develops an unsightly dip in the center, the problem may be a seat cushion that has lost its volume. Replace dried-out foam stuffing with a new piece of polyurethane or latex foam, sold in several densities ranging from soft to firm. A saggy seat may also point to misaligned springs or overstretched webbing. Tighten old webbing and add a new layer of webbing to reinforce it; replace rotted webbing altogether. The Troubleshooting Guide below directs you to these repairs and more.

Upholstered furniture is filled with dust and stuffing bits, so work in a well-ventilated, non-carpeted area. When setting up for repairs to the underside of a chair or sofa, place it upside down on the floor with its bottom level, and prop it up with sturdy supports. To avoid back injury, have someone help you when moving heavy furniture. Protect the fabric by covering the floor and supports with padding such as an old blanket. Repairs to upholstered furniture are not expensive; all you need are a handful of tools and supplies of the upholstery trade, described on page 67, and a few tools from the basic tool kit (page 113).

TROUBLESHOOTING GUIDE

SYMPTOM	POSSIBLE CAUSE	PROCEDURE
Upholstery fabric stained	Spills not cleaned immediately; fabric has no protective finish	Remove stain (p. 66) ◨○; apply protective finish (p. 66) □○
Upholstery fabric dirty	Grime, pollution, hair and body oils	Vacuum and shampoo fabric (p. 66) □◕
Leather or vinyl upholstery dull	Grime, pollution, hair and body oils	Clean leather or vinyl (p. 66) □○
Decorative trim loose	Glue that holds trim has lost adhesion	Reglue trim (p. 67) □○
Decorative tacks missing		Replace decorative tacks (p. 67) □○
Button on seat back loose	Button twine loose or broken	Resew button to back (p. 68) ◨◕
Seat sagging or lumpy	Stuffing in seat cushion deteriorated	Restuff cushion (p. 69) ◨◕
	Webbing holding coil springs stretched	Tighten webbing and add second layer (p. 70) ◨◕
	Webbing holding coil springs torn	Replace webbing (p. 73) ◨◕
	Twine connecting coil springs broken	Retie springs and replace webbing (p. 73) ◨◕
	Twine connecting conical springs broken	Retie springs (p. 74) ◨◕
	Zigzag spring loosened from frame	Reconnect spring (p. 75) ◨◕
Chair or sofa wobbly	Loose joints in wood frame	Have frame repaired and chair or sofa reupholstered

DEGREE OF DIFFICULTY: □ Easy ◨ Moderate ■ Complex
ESTIMATED TIME: ○ Less than 1 hour ◕ 1 to 3 hours ● Over 3 hours

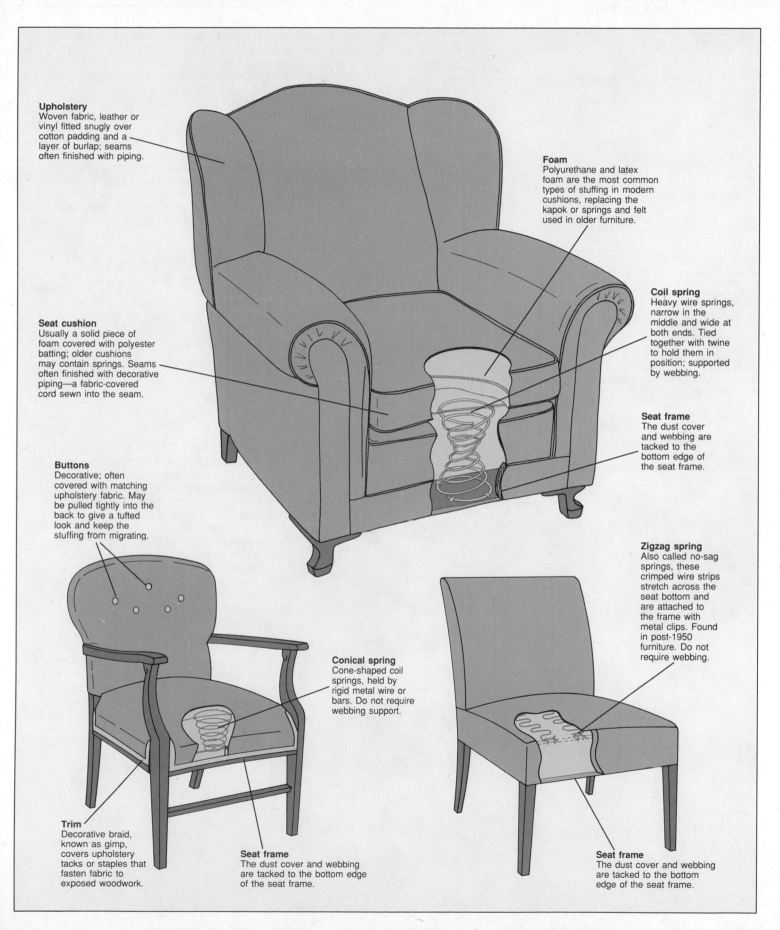

Upholstery
Woven fabric, leather or vinyl fitted snugly over cotton padding and a layer of burlap; seams often finished with piping.

Foam
Polyurethane and latex foam are the most common types of stuffing in modern cushions, replacing the kapok or springs and felt used in older furniture.

Coil spring
Heavy wire springs, narrow in the middle and wide at both ends. Tied together with twine to hold them in position; supported by webbing.

Seat cushion
Usually a solid piece of foam covered with polyester batting; older cushions may contain springs. Seams often finished with decorative piping—a fabric-covered cord sewn into the seam.

Seat frame
The dust cover and webbing are tacked to the bottom edge of the seat frame.

Buttons
Decorative; often covered with matching upholstery fabric. May be pulled tightly into the back to give a tufted look and keep the stuffing from migrating.

Zigzag spring
Also called no-sag springs, these crimped wire strips stretch across the seat bottom and are attached to the frame with metal clips. Found in post-1950 furniture. Do not require webbing.

Conical spring
Cone-shaped coil springs, held by rigid metal wire or bars. Do not require webbing support.

Trim
Decorative braid, known as gimp, covers upholstery tacks or staples that fasten fabric to exposed woodwork.

Seat frame
The dust cover and webbing are tacked to the bottom edge of the seat frame.

Seat frame
The dust cover and webbing are tacked to the bottom edge of the seat frame.

CARING FOR UPHOLSTERY FABRICS

STAIN-LIFTING PROCEDURES

Stain	Solution Sequence
Alcoholic beverages	2, 4
Blood	2, 3
Candle wax, crayon	1, 2
Chocolate, fruit juices, soft drinks	2, 3, 4
Coffee, tea	2, 4, 1
Grease, oil, unknown stains , water	1, 2, 3, 4
Cosmetics, furniture polish, ink, shoe polish	1, 2, 3
Ice cream, milk	2, 3, 4, 1
Wine	2, 4, 3

Cleaning Solutions

1	Dry-cleaning fluid, available at grocery and hardware stores
2	1 teaspoon mild colorless dish detergent mixed with 1 cup water
3	1 teaspoon ammonia mixed with 1/2 cup water
4	1/3 cup white vinegar mixed with 2/3 cup water

Removing and preventing fabric stains. The longer a stain remains in the fabric of upholstered furniture, the more difficult it is to remove. When you discover a stain, look for a tag on the chair or sofa listing the manufacturer's cleaning recommendations. If there is no tag, use the chart at left to determine the cleaning solutions to use on a stain and the order in which to apply them. Before applying each cleaning solution to the stain, test its effect on the fabric: Dab several drops of the solution in an inconspicuous area and blot it with a clean cloth. If the fabric changes color or the dye bleeds, have the furniture professionally cleaned. If the fabric color does not react, apply the solution to the stain with a clean cloth, working from the outside edge of the stain toward the center. Do not overwet the fabric. Blot the area by placing a clean, dry, absorbent cloth on the stain and patting it gently. Allow the fabric to dry. If after several applications the stain does not fade, repeat the procedure with the next recommended solution on the chart. Dry-cleaning fluid and ammonia can burn skin and eyes; when using them, wear rubber gloves and work in a well-ventilated area. Dry-cleaning fluid is flammable; do not use it near an open flame or while smoking.

A protective chemical coating can prevent fabric stains. Buy a spray-on soil protectant at a furniture store or home-improvement center, or have the furniture sprayed professionally. Follow the protectant manufacturer's instructions.

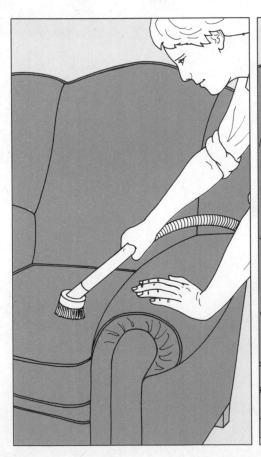

Cleaning woven fabric and leather. Before shampooing the fabric of an upholstered chair or sofa, remove dust and surface dirt with a vacuum cleaner brush attachment *(far left)*. Use a commercial upholstery shampoo. Pre-test the shampoo on an inconspicuous area of the fabric *(above)*; if the color runs, do not use it. Spray the foam on an area, then with a soft, clean cloth, scrub it into the fabric with parallel strokes, overlapping each stroke to avoid streaks. To remove dirty suds, wipe the area with a clean, slightly damp towel. Let the fabric dry, then rub it briskly with a clean towel or vacuum it again to raise the nap.

When old leather upholstery begins to lose its original sheen, dust it with a soft cloth, then use a damp cloth to work in saddle soap, rubbing it to a lather *(near left)*. Wipe off excess saddle soap with a second damp cloth, then polish the leather with a soft, dry cloth. To restore dry leather, pour lanolin or castor oil into a glass jar and warm it in a pan of warm water. Wipe on the oil with a clean, soft cloth and allow it to soak in for 24 hours. Buff the leather with a second cloth. To clean new leather or vinyl, wash the surface with a solution of mild soap and warm water, rinse and dry. Remove stubborn stains with a solution of water and baking soda, rubbing gently with a soft cloth. Do not apply ammonia or abrasives.

UPHOLSTERY TOOLS AND SUPPLIES

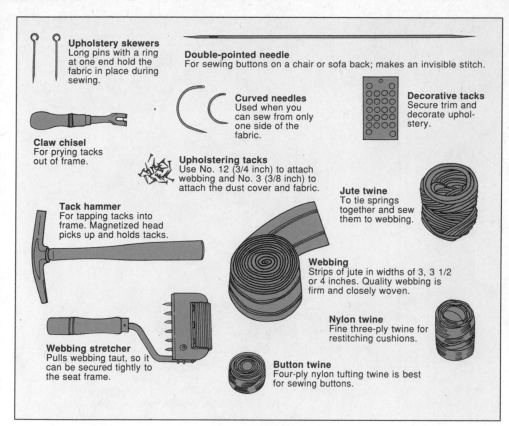

Upholstery skewers
Long pins with a ring at one end hold the fabric in place during sewing.

Double-pointed needle
For sewing buttons on a chair or sofa back; makes an invisible stitch.

Curved needles
Used when you can sew from only one side of the fabric.

Decorative tacks
Secure trim and decorate upholstery.

Claw chisel
For prying tacks out of frame.

Upholstering tacks
Use No. 12 (3/4 inch) to attach webbing and No. 3 (3/8 inch) to attach the dust cover and fabric.

Jute twine
To tie springs together and sew them to webbing.

Tack hammer
For tapping tacks into frame. Magnetized head picks up and holds tacks.

Webbing
Strips of jute in widths of 3, 3 1/2 or 4 inches. Quality webbing is firm and closely woven.

Nylon twine
Fine three-ply twine for restitching cushions.

Webbing stretcher
Pulls webbing taut, so it can be secured tightly to the seat frame.

Button twine
Four-ply nylon tufting twine is best for sewing buttons.

Basic upholstery repair kit. The venerable art of upholstering has developed its own unique set of tools. Pictured at left are some simple tools and supplies useful for the repairs to upholstered furniture shown in this chapter. The metal teeth of a webbing stretcher puncture the webbing, allowing the strip to be pulled tightly. The rubber-covered head rests snugly against the frame without slipping or marring the fabric. The long, narrow head of a tack hammer allows you to tap tacks into tight corners of the frame; the magnetic end is for picking up and placing a tack and the opposite end is for driving it in. To simplify picking up tacks, spread them out on a flat surface. Many tools from a regular woodworking kit also come in handy, including a flexible steel measuring tape to measure the frame and all-purpose white glue for regluing loose trim. Also useful are strong, sharp sewing scissors and a thimble to protect your thumb. Needles, skewers and other tools of the trade can be obtained at an upholstery supply store. Decorative tacks and twine are available at hardware and home improvement stores. Buy foam for restuffing cushions at an upholstery or foam supply store; polyester batting can be found at fabric stores.

RENEWING DECORATIVE EDGING

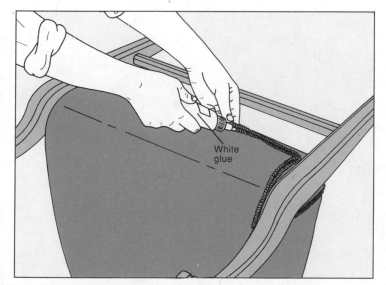

White glue

Regluing loose decorative trim. If the ornamental braid, or gimp, that finishes the joint between the upholstery and frame comes unglued, pull it back from the chair and apply a thin line of white glue down the center of the trim *(above)*. Press the trim evenly into position. To secure the trim to the frame while the glue dries, tap 1/2-inch gimp tacks partway into the trim, carefully inserting their points into the weave of the trim. Wait 24 hours, then use a claw chisel gently to pull out the tacks.

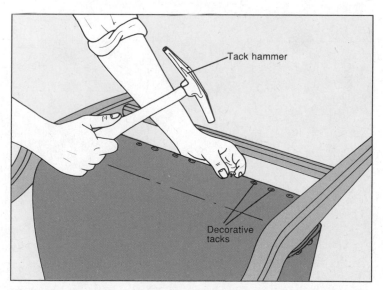

Tack hammer

Decorative tacks

Replacing decorative tacks. To replace missing decorative tacks that join the upholstery to the frame, use a claw chisel to pry a sample tack from the chair or sofa. At a hardware or upholstery store, buy matching tacks. If matching tacks are not available, buy enough tacks to replace the entire set. Using a tack hammer, tap the decorative tacks into the edge of the fabric in a straight line *(above)*, spacing them evenly. If you are replacing the original tacks, pry up each old tack and replace it, one at a time.

SEWING ON A BUTTON

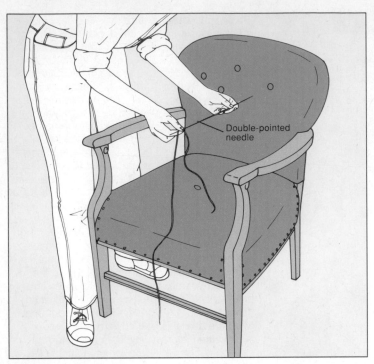

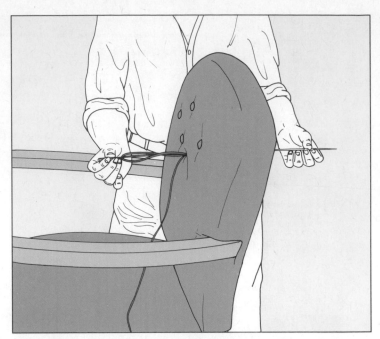

1 **Inserting the needle.** A double-pointed upholstery needle can be used to resew a button on a chair or sofa back upholstered with a sturdy, large-weave fabric. For a very delicate fabric, consult a professional. Use scissors to clip away the twine holding the loose button to the chair or sofa and pull out any loose pieces of twine. Thread 4 feet of button twine through one eye of the needle. Insert the unthreaded tip of the needle into the fabric at the button's original position *(above)*, taking care not to break threads in the fabric. Push the needle through the stuffing and out the back of the chair or sofa, stopping just short of pulling the threaded end through the fabric.

2 **Making an unseen stitch.** Keeping the threaded end of the needle inside the back, angle the threaded tip to one side by 1/2 inch and push it toward the front of the chair or sofa, doubling the thread back toward the front of the chair. Guide the threaded tip through the fabric at the front, right next to its entry point *(above)* and pull through the free end of the twine. Remove the needle and pull on the ends of twine until they are of even lengths.

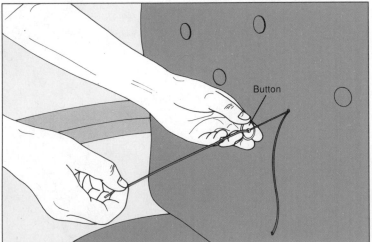

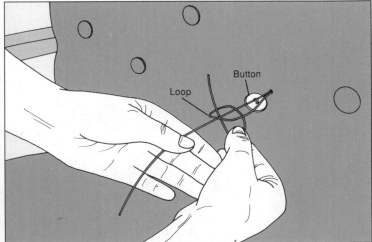

3 **Tying on the button.** Thread the button onto one end of the twine and push it up against the fabric *(above, left)*. Tie an upholsterer's slip knot with the twine ends: Make a loop with one twine end, and lay the loop over the other end of twine. Feed the twine end with the loop up through the loop *(above, right)*, then pull it all the way through. Push the knot against the fabric until the button rests against the fabric as tightly as the other buttons on the chair or sofa. Wrap the loose ends of twine several times around the back of the button, then tie a knot and clip the loose ends of twine close to the button.

GIVING NEW SHAPE TO A SAGGING CUSHION

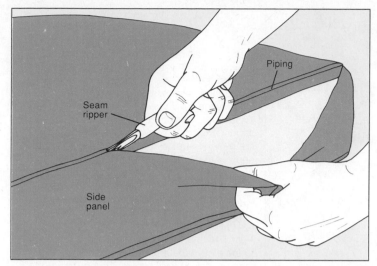

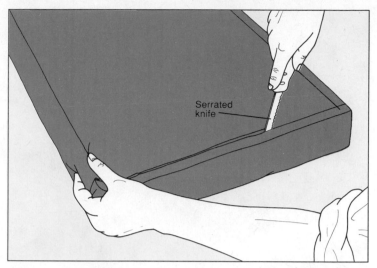

1 **Removing the old stuffing.** Measure the cushion's dimensions. Buy a piece of polyurethane or latex foam; if possible, have the foam cut to the required dimensions *(step 2)* at the store. Also buy a piece of polyester batting large enough to wrap around the foam. If the cushion cover is zippered, open the zipper, remove the old stuffing and go to step 2. If the cushion cover is stitched, examine all four sides for a hand-stitched seam; this seam will be easier to open than a machine-stitched seam. To open the seam between the piping and the side panel, cut the thread at one corner and pull the thread to unravel the seam from corner to corner. Or run a seam ripper slowly along the seam just below the piping *(above)*.

2 **Cutting the foam to fit.** Set the foam on a work table. Lay the cushion cover on the foam and trace the outline of its top panel with a fine-point felt marker. Add 1/2 inch all around if the foam is soft, and 1/4 inch if the foam is firm. Wet the blade of a broad, serrated knife to ensure that it slides smoothly through the foam. To cut the foam, hold the knife upright and cut only on the upward stroke *(above)*; a sawing motion tends to give a jagged edge. An electric carving knife can also be used to cut foam.

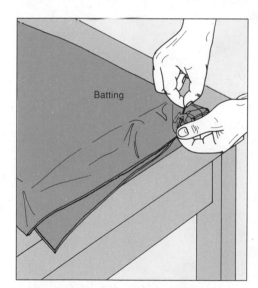

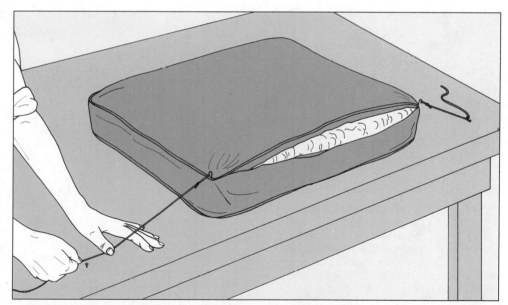

3 **Wrapping the foam in batting.** A layer of polyester batting will protect the foam from disintegration and minimize lumpiness. Place the foam on the batting, wrap the batting up and around the foam and hand-stitch the ends together *(above)*. Restuffing the cushion takes time and patience; hold the cushion cover open and push in the new stuffing with seams facing the rear of the cushion, filling one corner at a time. Rezip a zippered cushion cover. To restitch a seam, go to step 4.

4 **Making a seam stretcher.** A homemade seam stretcher holds the unstitched edge of the cushion cover taut so that you can resew it evenly. Place the cushion on a wood work surface or a plywood sheet that you don't mind marking with tacks. Push an upholstery skewer straight down deeply into the corner of the cushion at one end of the open seam. Tie 15 to 20 inches of nylon twine to the skewer ring. Tap a tack halfway into the work surface 8 to 10 inches from the skewered corner. Loop the twine tightly around the tack, then drive in the tack to secure the twine. Partially tap in a second tack beside the first one, loop the twine around it in the opposite direction, making a figure eight, then drive in the tack fully. Repeat this procedure at the opposite corner *(above)*, drawing the seam edges taut.

GIVING NEW SHAPE TO A SAGGING CUSHION (continued)

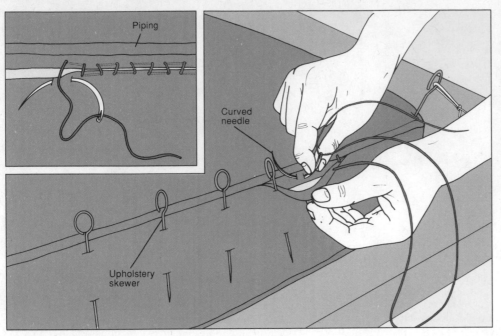

5 **Stitching the seam.** To hold the seam in position, pinch together the seam allowance of the piping and the seam allowance of the side panel. Insert a skewer through them and push it back out through the side panel. Insert skewers every 2 or 3 inches to close the seam. Thread nylon twine on a curved needle and knot the twine at the long end. Begin stitching at a corner. From the ouside of the cushion, insert the needle into the top edge of the side panel and curve it back out the top edge, forming a 1/4-inch stitch. Next, cross to the piping and insert the needle in the fabric just beneath the piping cord, across from where the thread emerges from the side panel. Curve the needle back out, forming a 1/4-inch stitch *(left)*. Pull the thread through and cross back to the side panel. Continue stitching in this manner *(inset)* until you reach the end of the seam. Remove the skewers as you go. Tie a knot to secure the thread, and cut off the thread next to the fabric.

FIRMING AND REINFORCING OLD WEBBING

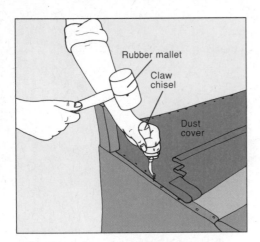

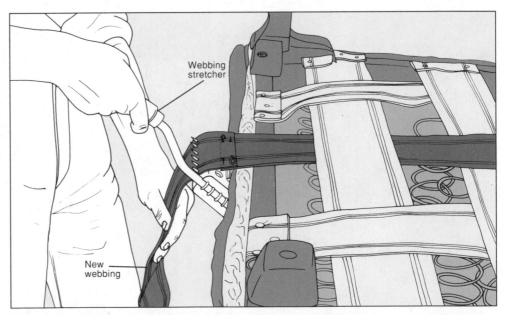

1 **Exposing the webbing.** Cover the floor of the work area with an old blanket to protect the upholstery. Working with a helper if the piece is heavy, bend your knees to support your back and turn the chair or sofa upside down. Prop it on padded supports so that the bottom is level. Use a rubber mallet and claw chisel to pry up the tacks holding the dust cover to the frame *(above)*. Set aside the dust cover, then pry up the tacks holding the upholstery fabric to the frame, and gently fold it back.

2 **Tightening up old webbing.** To prepare a solid foundation for a second, reinforcing layer of webbing, tighten the old webbing strips one by one. Tighten the vertical strips first. Use the claw chisel and rubber mallet to pry up one end of the center vertical strip. To temporarily lengthen the old webbing, cut a 12-inch strip of new webbing, overlap its end with the old webbing by 2 inches, then fasten the strips together with two upholstery skewers, as shown. Set the head of a webbing stretcher against the edge of the frame and wrap the webbing over the teeth of the stretcher, so the teeth puncture the jute. Push down on the stretcher handle to tighten the webbing *(above)* and tap three tacks through it into the frame. Release the stretcher and pull out the skewers to detach the extension piece. Fold the end of the webbing over the tacks and hammer in three more tacks through the double layer of webbing. Tighten the remaining vertical strips the same way, then repeat the procedure to tighten the horizontal strips. If the webbing tears as you tighten it, remove and replace it *(page 73)*. Once the old webbing is tight, go to step 3 to stretch a second layer of webbing over the springs.

FIRMING AND REINFORCING OLD WEBBING (continued)

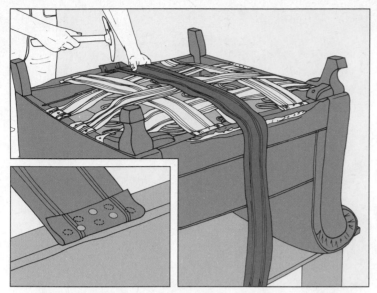

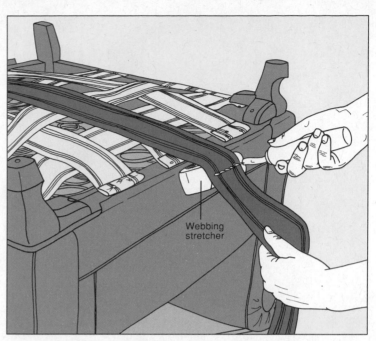

3 **Tacking down vertical webbing.** To add a second layer of webbing, buy a roll of 10-ounce jute webbing from an upholstery supply dealer; 6 yards will reweb a typical chair. Attach the vertical strips of webbing to the frame first, then weave in the horizontal strips. To begin, position the new webbing over the center strip so that its end overhangs the frame back by 1 inch. With a tack hammer, tack the webbing to the frame back *(above)*, placing five tacks in a staggered pattern to create a W shape. Next, fold the inch of overlap over the tacks and hammer three more tacks through the double layer of webbing *(inset)*, then press the fold flat. Go to steps 4 and 5 to stretch and secure the webbing to the front of the frame. Do not cut the strip from the roll until it has been secured to the front of the frame.

4 **Stretching the webbing.** To pull the webbing taut across the springs, set the rubber head of the stretcher against the outer edge of the chair and wrap the webbing over the teeth of the stretcher, so the teeth puncture the jute *(above)*. Press down on the stretcher handle until the webbing is stretched tightly.

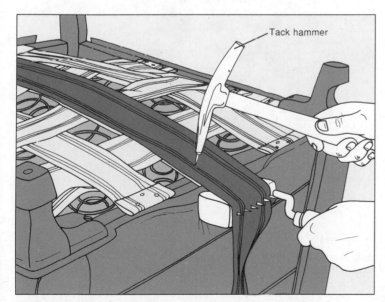

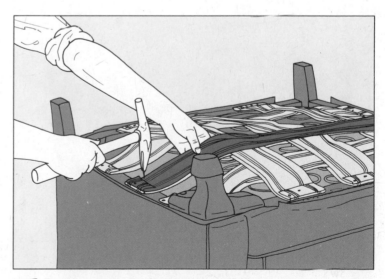

5 **Securing the webbing.** Holding the webbing tight with the webbing stretcher, use the magnetic end of the hammer to pick up five tacks one at a time, and tap them through the webbing into the frame in a W pattern *(above)*. Release the webbing from the stretcher, then with scissors cut off the webbing from the coil 1 inch beyond the frame's outer edge. Fold the inch of overlap over the tacks and hammer in three more tacks through the double layer of webbing as in step 3, then press the fold flat. Repeat steps 3, 4 and 5 to tack, stretch and secure the remaining vertical strips.

6 **Tacking down the horizontal webbing.** Tack, weave, stretch and secure the horizontal strips one at a time. Begin by laying the new webbing over the center horizontal strip with its end overhanging one side of the frame by 1 inch. Tack the webbing to the frame as in step 3. Fold the inch of overlap over the tacks and tap in three more tacks *(above)*, then press the fold flat.

FIRMING AND REINFORCING OLD WEBBING (continued)

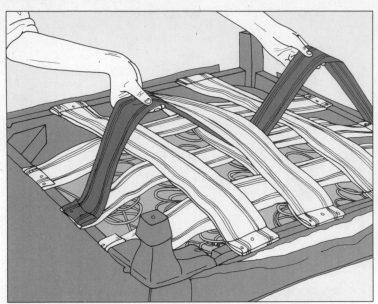

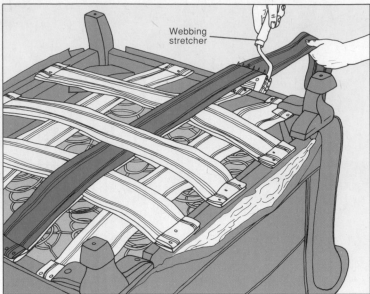

7 **Weaving the horizontal webbing.** Cut the unattached end of the webbing, allowing 10 inches of overhang at the other side of the frame. Weave the webbing across the vertical strips, passing it over one strip, under the next and over the next *(above, left)*. Once the strip reaches the other end of the frame, wrap the end over the webbing stretcher and pull the strip taut *(above, right)*. Tack down the webbing as in step 3. Weave in the remaining horizontal strips following the instructions in steps 6 and 7. To fit webbing around legs, go to step 8.

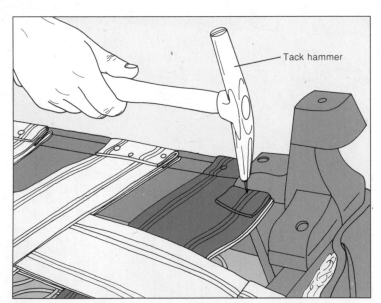

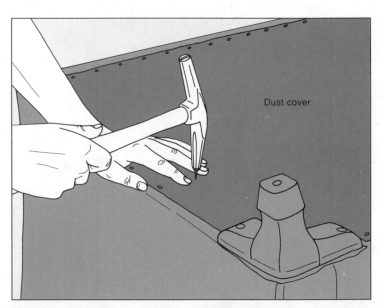

8 **Fitting webbing around a leg.** If a row of springs is placed close to the frame, lay a strip of webbing over the springs and cut one end of the webbing to fit around a leg. Slit the end of the webbing and drive two tacks to secure it to the frame around the leg. Fold the end over the tacks and tap in two more tacks through the double thickness. At the opposite side of the frame, cut the webbing to allow 10 inches of overhang, then weave it over and under the vertical strips. Pull the strip taut with the webbing stretcher, then tap in a tack to secure the webbing to the frame. Cut the webbing 1 inch beyond the frame's edge, then slit it to fit around the leg. Tack the remaining part around the leg, then fold back the end and drive tacks through the double thicknesses *(above)*. Press the folds flat.

9 **Covering the webbing.** Pull the upholstery fabric up around the frame and tack it in place. If the original dust cover is too worn to be reused, buy replacement fabric of the same dimensions as the old cover. Fold the new fabric on all four sides to make a finished edge and iron the folds. Tack the dust cover onto the frame: Start at the middle of one side of the frame and work toward the leg, placing the tacks 2 inches apart. Stop 2 inches before reaching the leg, start again at the middle and work toward the other leg. For a tight fit, stretch the cover as you tack it. Repeat the procedure at each side of the frame *(above)*. To fit the dust cover around a leg, cut into the corner of the fabric, then fold it in and tack it down next to the leg.

RETYING COIL SPRINGS AND REPLACING WEBBING

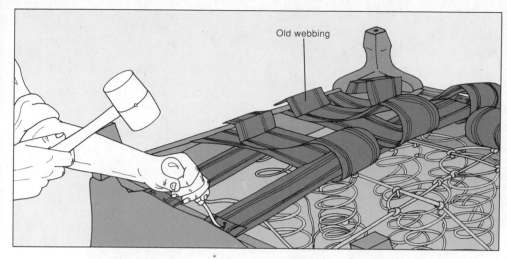

Old webbing

1 **Removing the old webbing.** Set the chair or sofa upside down on padded supports so that the bottom is level, and remove the dust cover and upholstery fabric *(page 70, step 1)*. Use scissors to clip away the twine holding the webbing to the springs. Do not cut the twine linking spring to spring. With the claw chisel and rubber mallet, pry up the tacks holding the webbing to the frame *(left)*. Turn the chair or sofa upright to shake out loose dust and stuffing. If the twine that links a row of springs and anchors it to the frame is broken, retie the springs *(step 2)*. If the twine is intact, go to step 3 to replace the webbing.

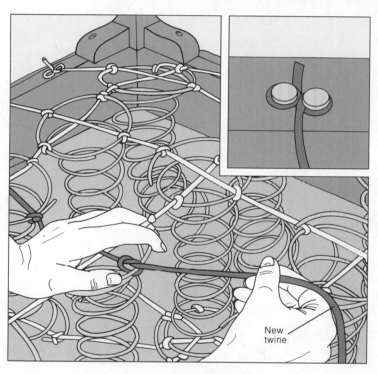

New twine

2 **Anchoring the springs.** Cut the broken twine and pry up the tacks holding it to the frame. Cut a new piece of twine 1 1/2 times longer than the width of the frame. To secure the new twine to the frame, tap a tack halfway into the frame at the point where you removed the old twine. Loop one end of twine around the tack, then drive in the tack. Tap in a second tack beside the first tack and loop the twine around it in the opposite direction, forming a figure eight *(inset)*. Drive in the second tack. Pull the twine firmly to the first spring in the row. Tie it around the closest part of the top coil, pull it across the coil and tie it again. Use one hand to push down on the spring, keeping it as vertical as possible, and pull the knot tight with the other hand. Pull the twine across to the next spring in the row and continue tying the twine the same way *(left)*. Once you have tied the final spring in the row, anchor the twine to the frame, making a figure eight around two tacks, as before. Repeat the procedure to replace other rows of broken twine, both horizontal and vertical.

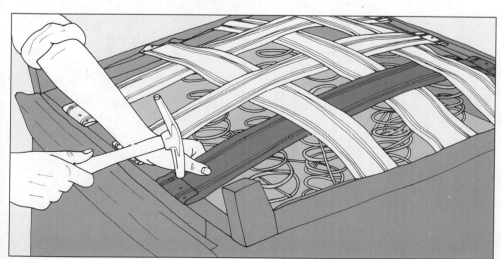

3 **Laying down new webbing.** Buy a roll of 10-ounce jute webbing from an upholstery supply store; 6 yards will reweb an average chair. Tack, stretch and secure the new webbing *(left)*, following the procedure outlined on pages 71 and 72, steps 3 through 8. Position and weave the replacement webbing in the same pattern as the webbing you removed. Make sure that the strips sit squarely on the top coils of the springs, so you can sew the webbing to the springs *(next step)*.

RETYING COIL SPRINGS AND REPLACING WEBBING (continued)

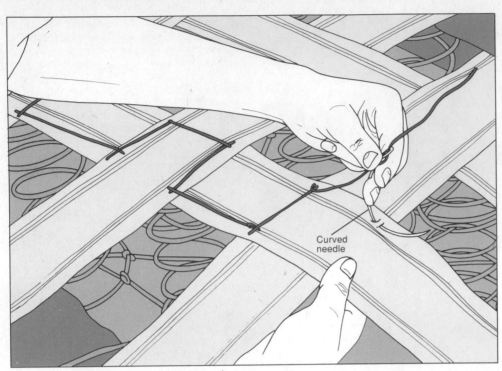

Curved needle

4 **Sewing the webbing to the springs.** To anchor the springs to the intersecting strips of webbing that cover them, thread a curved needle with about 3 feet of jute twine. To begin, insert the needle through two layers of webbing on the inside of a spring coil near the frame, and bring it up through the webbing on the outside of the coil. Pull the thread most of the way through the webbing and tie its end securely. To sew the spring to the webbing, use the curved needle to loop the twine around the top coil of the spring at each corner formed by the intersecting webbing. Continue stitching, forming a square pattern of four stitches over each spring *(left)*, until all springs are secured to the webbing. After the last stitch, tie the twine and snip it near the knot. Retack the dust cover, following the instructions on page 72, step 9.

RETYING CONICAL SPRINGS

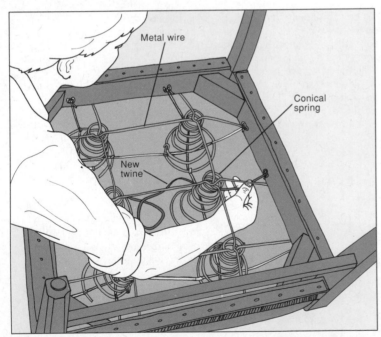

Metal wire

Conical spring

New twine

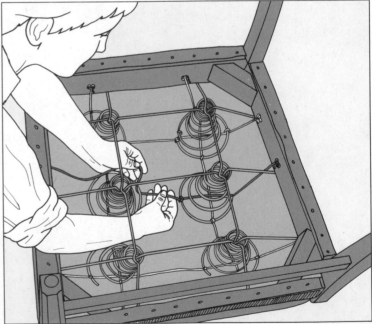

Renewing the link. Place the chair or sofa upside down on a work surface and remove the dust cover *(page 70, step 1)*. Rows of twine hold the springs in place where they rest against the underside of the seat. If the twine breaks in one spot, causing the springs to shift, cut away the broken piece of twine and pry up the tacks that hold it on the frame. Cut a new piece of twine 1 1/2 times longer than the width of the frame. Tap a tack halfway into the frame at the point where you removed the old twine, then loop one end of twine around the tack and drive in the tack. Tap in a second tack beside the first tack and loop the twine in the opposite direction, forming a figure eight *(page 73, step 2)*. Drive in the second tack. Pull the twine firmly toward the first spring in the row *(above, left)*. Loop the twine around the closest part of the coil and pass the twine through the loop, pulling it tight. Slip the twine between the spring and the seat, loop it around the other side of the coil and pass the twine through the loop. Pull the twine tight *(above, right)* and continue to the next spring in the row. When the twine reaches the opposite side of the frame, anchor it to the frame with two tacks as described above. Replace all worn twine the same way. When finished, retack the dust cover.

ANCHORING ZIGZAG SPRINGS

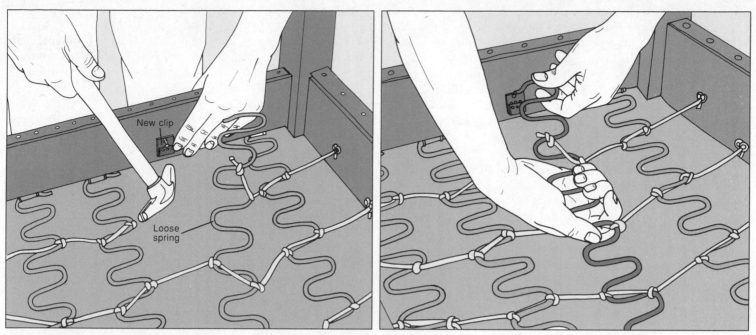

1 **Reconnecting a spring.** Zigzag springs stretch across the bottom of the seat and are held to the frame with metal clips. If a clip breaks or a spring works out of the clip, the seat will sag. Invert the chair or sofa on a work surface *(page 70, step 1)*. Buy a replacement clip and nails to secure it at an upholstery supply store. Set the new clip on the inside of the frame close to the old clip, the single-hole side up and the looped end as close to the edge of the seat rail as possible. Secure the clip by driving a nail into the single hole *(above, left)*. Pull forcefully on the unattached end of the spring and thread the hooked end into the loop of the clip *(above, right)*. To stretch a heavy zigzag spring, use locking pliers as a handle. Drive nails through the three remaining holes in the clip to close it against the spring.

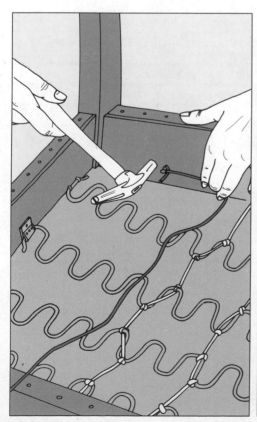

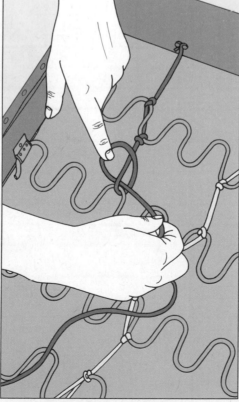

2 **Tying the springs.** When a spring snaps loose, it may tear the twine that links the springs. Untie the broken twine from the springs and pry up the tacks that hold it on the frame. Measure the width of the frame and cut heavy twine 1 1/2 times longer than this width. To anchor the new twine, tap a tack halfway into the spot on the frame where the old twine was anchored. Loop one end of the twine around it and tap the tack all the way in *(far left)*. Next, partially tap in a second tack beside the first, loop the twine around it and drive in the tack the rest of the way *(page 73, step 2)*. Pull the twine firmly to the first spring and tie it around the closest loop and the loop beside it. Then pull it to the next spring and tie it *(near left)*, without pulling the springs out of position. Continue tying the twine to each row of springs until it reaches the opposite side of the frame. Anchor the twine to this side of the frame with two tacks, as described above.

OUTDOOR FURNITURE

Climate and lifestyle dictate our choice of outdoor furniture. Short, active summers call for easy-to-store styles; in warmer regions, less portable furniture graces porches and patios year-round. Pictured at right are four very different designs.

A sturdy, popular style features narrow vinyl straps on a tubular aluminum frame. A broken strap can be replaced using a roll or strapping purchased at a hardware store. Wash soiled straps with a solution of vinegar, ammonia and water. To prevent rust, touch up nicks in the frame's acrylic coating with enamel paint.

A favorite since the 1950s, the portable, packable web chair has wide nylon webbing woven across a folding aluminum frame. Torn or frayed webbing can be replaced using a rewebbing kit. First, inspect the soundness of the frame. Also compare the cost of a new chair to the cost of a rewebbing kit; you may prefer to replace rather than reweb an inexpensive chair. If you do reweb, do the entire chair rather than a single strap. To brighten an unpainted frame, scrub it with a non-abrasive scouring pad dipped in kerosene or commercial aluminum brightener, then rinse with warm water and dry well.

A light coat of car wax will keep the frame shiny and protect it from corrosion.

Wicker is a general term for furniture woven of pliable plant fibers. Fine old wicker was made of willow woven around a wood frame; most modern wicker is woven from strips of the rattan palm. Wickerwork of twisted paper, fiber rush or sea grass is not usually suitable for outdoor use because water unravels the strands. Exposure to the elements can cause wicker fibers to snap or come unglued—typically, a woven seat will break through. With replacement fibers available at craft stores, and a bit of patience, you can restore wicker at home. Outdoor wicker furniture should be painted with exterior latex enamel. Wipe it clean from time to time with a soft, damp cloth.

The Victorian elegance of cast-iron furniture is created by ornate pieces of iron bolted together and painted. Keep rust at bay by regularly touching up chipped spots with rust-resistant metal spray paint; apply a commercial rust remover to any rust spots. To reveal hidden detail, strip the piece with a chemical paint remover, then repaint with rust-resistant enamel.

TROUBLESHOOTING GUIDE

SYMPTOM	POSSIBLE CAUSE	PROCEDURE
VINYL STRAP		
Frame and strapping dirty	Exposure to weather	Wash with a solution of vinegar, ammonia and water
Straps stretched or broken	Heat from sun and stress on seat	Replace damaged straps (p. 78) □●
WEB		
Frame joints stiff	Joints need lubrication	Spray joints with silicone lubricant and wipe with dry cloth
	Frame corroded or dirty	Scrub with non-abrasive scouring pad dipped in kerosene or aluminum brightener, rinse and dry, then polish with car wax
Webbing dirty	Exposure to weather	Wash with detergent-and-water solution and scrub brush
Webbing frayed or broken	Wear and tear; exposure to sun	Remove webbing and reweave chair (p. 79) ▣●
WICKER		
Finish dirty	Exposure to weather	Wash willow or rattan with a mild detergent-and-water solution. Do not soak twisted-fiber (sea grass or fiber rush) furniture
Binding cane unraveled from framework	Glue bond or binding cane broken	Reglue or replace binding cane (p. 80) □○
Seat broken	Fibers weakened by wear and tear and exposure to weather	Remove old fibers and weave a new seat (p. 80) ■●
Paint worn	Wear and tear; exposure to weather	Sand, clean and repaint (p. 82) ▣●
CAST IRON		
Finish rusted in spots	Exposure to weather or water	Remove rust with rust remover or steel wool and touch up with spray paint
Finish badly rusted	Exposure to weather or water	Strip and repaint (p. 83) ▣●
Bolt at joint rusted	Exposure to weather or water	Replace with corrosion-resistant nut and bolt (p. 83) □○

DEGREE OF DIFFICULTY: □ Easy ▣ Moderate ■ Complex
ESTIMATED TIME: ○ Less than 1 hour ● 1 to 3 hours ● Over 3 hours *(Does not include drying time)*

VINYL-STRAP CHAIR

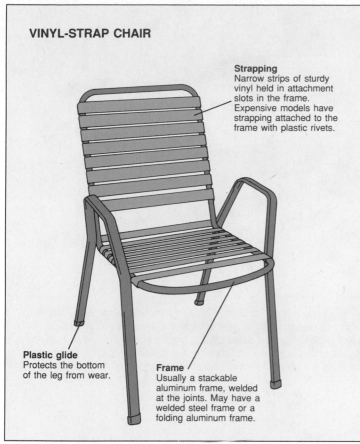

Strapping
Narrow strips of sturdy vinyl held in attachment slots in the frame. Expensive models have strapping attached to the frame with plastic rivets.

Plastic glide
Protects the bottom of the leg from wear.

Frame
Usually a stackable aluminum frame, welded at the joints. May have a welded steel frame or a folding aluminum frame.

WEB CHAIR

Webbing
Interwoven strips of nylon or vinyl attached to the frame with screws or metal clips.

Frame
Lightweight aluminum frame folds for carrying and storage. Joints held together by screws and rivets.

WICKER CHAIR

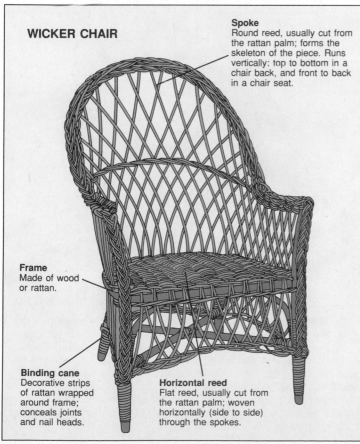

Spoke
Round reed, usually cut from the rattan palm; forms the skeleton of the piece. Runs vertically: top to bottom in a chair back, and front to back in a chair seat.

Frame
Made of wood or rattan.

Binding cane
Decorative strips of rattan wrapped around frame; conceals joints and nail heads.

Horizontal reed
Flat reed, usually cut from the rattan palm; woven horizontally (side to side) through the spokes.

CAST-IRON CHAIR

Joint
Nut and bolt join a leg to the seat and the seat to the chair back. Tighten a loose bolt with a screwdriver and wrench.

REPLACING VINYL STRAPPING

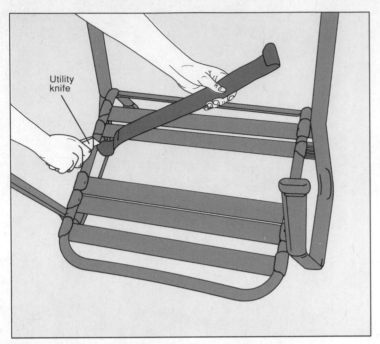

Utility knife

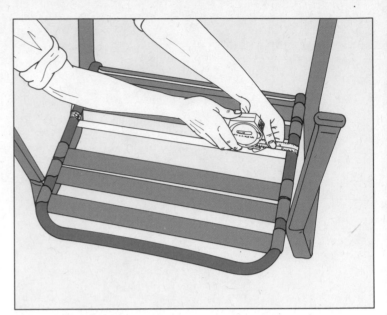

1 **Cutting away the damaged strap.** To remove a stretched or broken vinyl strap, set the chair upside down, then with a utility knife slice the strap where it enters the attachment slot *(above)*, taking care not to nick the frame's coating. The piece of strap inside the hollow frame will fall loose, leaving the slot clear. Cut away the strap on the opposite side, if it is not already detached. (On a chair with plastic rivets, pry out the rivets with a screwdriver.)

2 **Measuring for a new strap.** At a hardware store, buy a roll of replacement vinyl strapping the same width and color as the worn strap. To calculate the length of the new strap, measure the distance from one attachment slot to the other, as shown, then subtract 1 inch so the strap will stretch taut when secured to the frame.

Awl

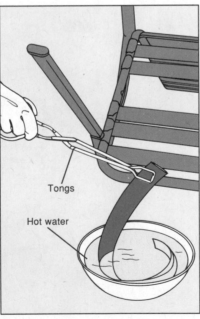

Tongs

Hot water

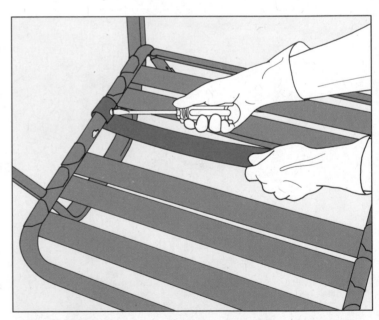

3 **Preparing the new strap.** Use scissors to cut the new strap to the required length. With an awl, pierce a hole 1/4 inch from each end in the center of the strap *(above, left)*. To soften the strap so you can stretch it tightly across the seat, soak it in boiling water for 10 minutes. Wearing rubber gloves to protect your hands from the hot vinyl, use tongs or pliers to pull the strap out of the water *(above, right)*. Work quickly to install the strap while it is still hot and pliable *(next step)*.

4 **Installing the new strap.** Push a sheet-metal screw through the hole at each end of the strap. Use a screwdriver to drive the screw into an attachment slot in the frame, as shown. (If attaching the strap with plastic rivets, insert the rivet through the hole in the strap and tap it into the frame with a rubber mallet.) Have a helper hold the chair while you pull hard on the strap, stretching it around the frame until the second screw reaches the opposite attachment slot. Tighten the screw in the slot to secure the strap to the frame. Repeat the procedure for any other worn straps.

INSTALLING NYLON WEBBING

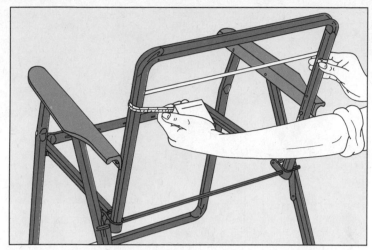

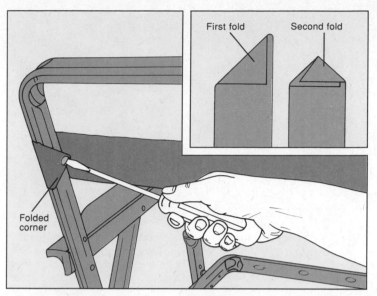

1 **Measuring for the horizontal webbing.** Working at the back of the chair, use a screwdriver to remove the screws or pry off the metal clips holding the webbing to the back frame. Loosen rusty screws by applying a few drops of penetrating oil. Turn the chair upside down and remove the screws or metal clips holding the webbing to the seat frame. Pull away the old webbing. At a hardware store, buy a kit that includes a roll of webbing and screws, or webbing and a package of metal rewebbing clips. To determine the length to cut the horizontal straps, measure the distance from the attachment slot on one side of the frame to its mate on the opposite side *(above)*, then add 3 inches if you are attaching the webbing with screws and 1 1/2 inches if you are attaching the webbing with clips. Cut the replacement webbing with scissors. To install the webbing with screws, go to step 2; to install it with rewebbing clips, go to step 3.

2 **Attaching the horizontal webbing with screws.** Fold one end of the first strap twice to form a point *(inset)*, then use an awl or large nail to pierce a hole 1/2 inch from the tip of the point. Set a screw in the hole in the new webbing and drive the screw into the attachment slot at the top of the chair frame *(above)*. Pull the webbing across the frame and repeat the procedure to secure the webbing on the opposite side. Install each horizontal strap the same way, working down the back and the seat, then go to step 4.

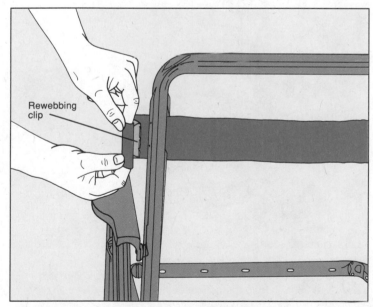

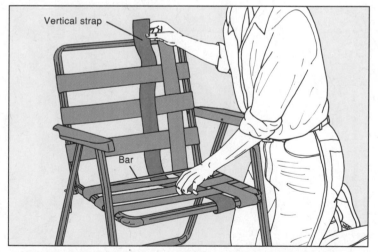

3 **Attaching the horizontal webbing with metal clips.** Wrap 3/4 inch of webbing over the smooth edge of the rewebbing clip. Snap the clip onto the frame, covering an attachment slot at the top of the chair *(above)*. Pull the webbing across the frame and repeat the procedure on the opposite side. Install each horizontal strap the same way, working down the back and the seat, then go to step 4.

4 **Weaving in the vertical webbing.** To determine the length to cut the vertical straps, measure the distance from the attachment slot at the top of the frame back to its mate at the chair seat. Add 3 inches if attaching the strap with screws and 1 1/2 inches if attaching it with metal clips. Use scissors to cut the replacement webbing into straps. Fasten the first vertical strap to the seat frame, using a screw *(step 2, above)* or a rewebbing clip *(step 3, left)*. Weave the vertical strap alternately over and under the horizontal webbing on the seat, pass the strap behind the bar at the seat back, then weave it over and under the horizontal webbing on the chair back. Attach it at the top with a screw or rewebbing clip. Install each vertical strap the same way, alternating the weaving pattern.

REWRAPPING A WICKER LEG

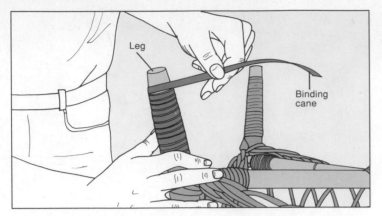

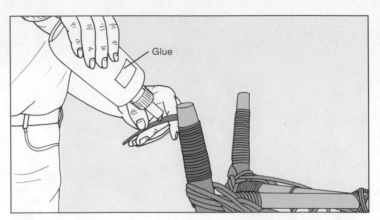

1 **Wrapping new binding cane.** To remove broken binding cane from a leg, turn the chair upside down, peel off the damaged cane and cut it off with tin snips. Take the old piece to a craft supply store and buy binding cane of the same width and thickness; a length of 2 feet per leg should be adequate. Hold the new cane under warm running water to make it pliable. With a tack or small nail, secure the end of the cane to an inconspicuous spot on the inside of the chair leg, near the joint. Wrap the cane around the leg once so that it covers the nail and the cut end of the old cane, then continue wrapping it snugly around the leg, overlapping it in a spiral pattern *(above)*. Stop 1/2 inch from the foot.

2 **Attaching the binding cane.** Dab the unattached end of the binding cane with yellow glue *(above)*, then wrap it around the leg once and secure it to the inside of the leg with a tack or small nail. Use tin snips to trim the cane 1/8 inch from the nail. Wrap masking tape around the end of the cane to hold it down while the glue sets. Wait three to four hours, then carefully peel off the masking tape. Paint the new binding cane with a coat of white glue diluted with an equal amount of water to seal the finish, then spray-paint the leg *(page 82)* to match the rest of the chair.

WEAVING A WICKER SEAT

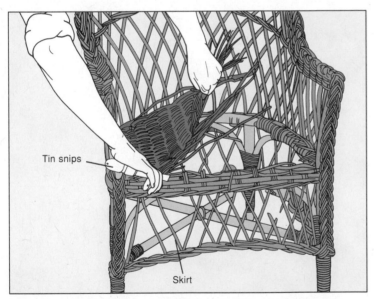

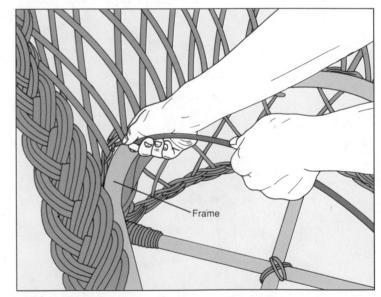

1 **Cutting away the damaged seat.** To guide you when reconstructing the pattern of the original seat, take a reference photo or draw a sketch before removing the damaged wicker. Count the spokes—round reeds that run front to back on the seat—and note the path they follow. Use a nail puller *(page 114)* to extract any nails holding the spokes to the frame. Clip out the broken seat with tin snips *(above)*. Use pliers to pull out stubborn bits that remain in the frame. If the spokes extend into the skirt, and it is also broken, cut it away as well. Take one of the round-reed spokes and one of the flat reeds to a craft supply store to match the wicker fibers; a one-pound coil of each fiber should be plenty to weave a new seat.

2 **Inserting a new spoke.** To determine the length to cut the new spokes, measure the distance from the seat back to the seat front, then to the bottom of the skirt if you are reweaving it, and add 4 to 5 inches. With tin snips, cut the round reed into spokes of this length, then immerse the spokes in a large bucket of tepid water until they are pliable. Soak round reed at least 10 minutes but no more than 30 minutes; oversoaking will cause the fiber to split and fray. Pull a spoke from the water, then use tin snips to nip each end into a point. Slide a sharpened end into a gap between the frame and the horizontal weave at the back of the seat *(above)*. If you wedge the spoke firmly, gluing should not be necessary.

WEAVING A WICKER SEAT (continued)

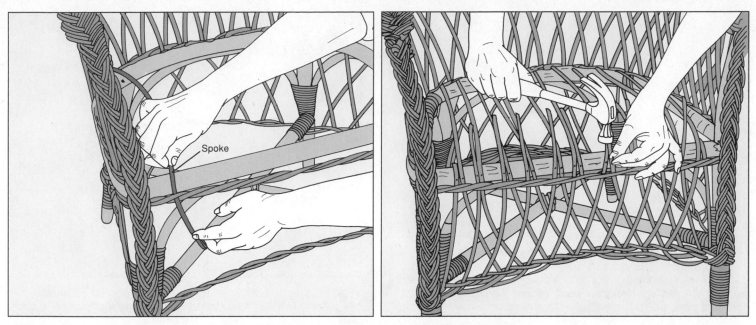

3 **Securing the spoke.** Consult your reference photo or sketch to determine the exact pattern in which the spokes were woven. On a chair of the style pictured here, run the first spoke to the front of the seat, then bend it down around the frame and insert it through the horizontal weave of the skirt *(above, left)*. Following the original pattern, curve the spoke down and insert the free end through the weave at the bottom edge of the skirt, then curve the spoke back up toward the seat. Install each spoke to correspond to the original pattern. While the spokes are still damp, secure them to the frame at the front of the seat with small nails *(above, right)*.

4 **Weaving in the flat reeds.** Cut the flat reeds into lengths of 2 to 3 feet. To ensure flexibility, soak each reed in warm water for a maximum of five minutes. Wedge the end of the first reed into the front right corner between the arm and the seat frame. Weave the reed to the other side of the seat, duplicating the pattern of the original; in this case passing the reed over the frame, under the first spoke and over the next. Continue the over-and-under weave, using one hand to feed and the other to guide *(above, left)* until you reach the opposite side of the seat. At the end of the row, loop the reed around the seat frame and use it to start a new horizontal row, alternating the over-and-under pattern *(above, right)*. Spray the reeds with an atomizer from time to time to keep them supple. At the end of a reed, start a new reed, overlapping it with the previous reed for two or three spokes. When the seat is complete, stick the final reed down through the seat, weave it under two or three spokes to secure it, then cut it off. Seal and paint the new wicker *(page 82)*.

REPAINTING A WICKER CHAIR

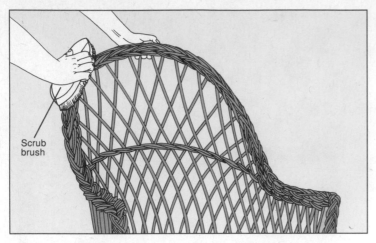

1 Cleaning the surface. Wearing goggles to protect your eyes from flying paint chips, remove flaking paint with a wire brush. Use fine sandpaper to smooth uneven areas, then rub the entire surface with medium (1/0) steel wool. Vacuum the chair to get rid of dust and loose paint. To clean willow or rattan, scrub it with a soft brush dipped in a mild detergent-and-water solution *(above)*, then rinse it with a garden hose and wipe it dry.

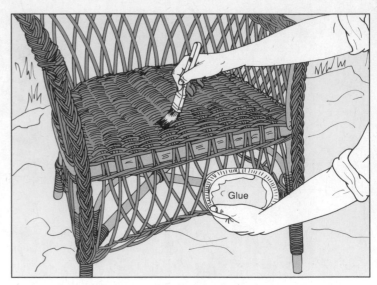

2 Sealing new wicker. To seal new, unfinished wicker and strengthen the weave before painting, use a paintbrush to apply a thin coat of white glue mixed with an equal amount of water *(above)*. Allow three or four hours for the glue to dry completely.

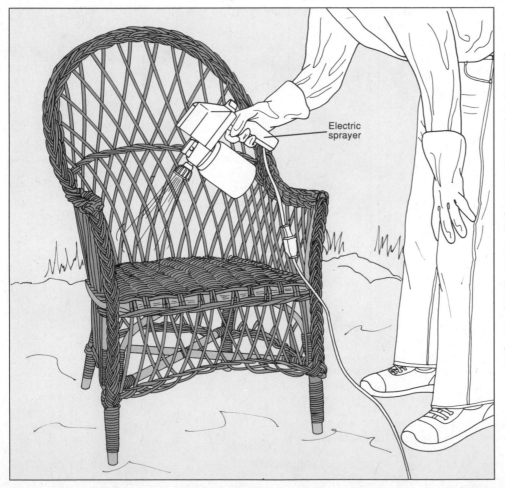

3 Spraying on the paint. Buy an exterior latex enamel paint; a gallon should provide enough paint to apply two or three coats. Rent an airless electric paint sprayer from a tool rental company. Stretch a double layer of cheesecloth over a paint bucket and strain the paint into the bucket. Pour about eight ounces of paint into the sprayer's reservoir and screw the reservoir onto the gun. Plug in the gun and set the pressure gauge to medium. To ensure even application, use cardboard or scrap wood to test the sprayer; holding the nozzle 12 inches from the surface, push the trigger and move the sprayer from side to side. Examine the band of paint on the practice piece and readjust the setting until it produces an even coating. It is best to spray paint outdoors. If you must spray inside, work in a well-ventilated room. Protect the area under and around the chair with a drop cloth or newspapers. Wearing goggles and a respirator with a spray paint filter *(page 114)*, spray the underside of the piece first, then turn it upright and spray the back, arms, seat and legs *(left)*. Wait three to four hours for the paint to dry completely, then apply a second coat. Apply a third coat if necessary.

REFINISHING A CAST-IRON CHAIR

Wire brush

Wrench

1 Stripping the old finish. Work outside, and protect your lawn or patio with a drop cloth or sheets of cardboard. Wearing rubber gloves, goggles and a respirator with an organic vapor cartridge, spread chemical paint stripper on the chair with an old paintbrush. Wait a few minutes, then test the paint with a putty knife; when it peels off easily, scrape the surface with a stiff wire brush *(above)*. Clean out ornamentation and corners with an old toothbrush. Use a garden hose to rinse away the debris. Apply rust remover jelly on the rusted areas with the paintbrush, working the jelly into pitted spots, then scrape away the rust with a toothbrush. Rinse the piece again, then wipe it dry. Scrub stubborn rust spots with steel wool to reveal clean cast iron. Apply rust-resistant paint within an hour.

2 Replacing a rusted bolt. Before repainting the cast-iron chair, inspect the hardware at the joints. If a bolt and nut are rusted together, lay the chair on its side and spray on penetrating oil to loosen them. Wait 10 minutes, then use a wrench and screwdriver to remove the bolt and nut *(above)*. Install corrosion-resistant replacements made of stainless steel or galvanized metal.

3 Painting the chair. Buy rust-resistant exterior enamel paint; one quart should be enough for two or more coats. A few brands of paint still require a primer undercoat; read the manufacturer's instructions before choosing the paint. Set the chair upside down and, with a paintbrush, apply a thin coat of enamel to the underside of the chair, making sure to cover all unseen parts to protect them from rust. Set the chair upright and paint the rest of the chair, from top to bottom *(left)*. Apply two or three coats of paint, waiting at least four hours between coats to allow the paint to dry.

REPAIRING SURFACES

Furniture surfaces are vulnerable to damage simply through everyday use; sharp objects, food and drink, hot dishes, wet glasses, burning cigarettes, and moving days are common enemies. Although serious or extensive damage may require the services of a professional refinisher, the homeowner can successfully tackle many surface flaws.

The repairs in this chapter range from simple methods for removing accumulated grime and wax to more complicated filling and patching techniques. Before jumping into a repair, practice on a piece of scrap wood, then test any cleaning or patching products on a hidden area of the finish. As you become proficient at spot repairs, you may begin to undertake specialized jobs that require professional supplies. Wood restoration products, such as shellac sticks or specially formulated dyes, are often not available at neighborhood hardware stores; look in the telephone book to find woodworking stores that stock them, or ask about mail-order supply houses.

The chapter provides alternate solutions for certain repair problems such as filling gouges, which can be done with a shellac stick, wax stick or wood putty. To disguise a shallow scratch, you can use furniture dye, an artist's brush and colors or a touch-up marker, depending on what you have at your disposal. Or you can color the scratch with a cotton swab dipped in shoe polish or iodine. Test the color on a hidden area before treating the scratch. Start with a color slightly lighter than the finish, and darken it with repeated applications.

Wood veneer suffers many of the ailments that beset solid wood; in addition, heat and moisture can make it peel off or blister. Damaged wood veneer may require patching (page 94). Plastic laminate, a nonporous, easy-to-clean surface

TROUBLESHOOTING GUIDE

SYMPTOM	POSSIBLE CAUSE	PROCEDURE
Finish yellowed or sticky	Wax buildup	Dissolve wax buildup (p. 86) □○; oil or wax and buff (p. 87) □○
Finish dirty or darkened	Layers of grime and wax	Revive the finish (p. 86) ◨◕; oil or wax and buff (p. 87) □○
Finish dull but undamaged	Polish worn off	Apply new oil or wax and buff (p. 87) □○
Hairline crack in finish	Exposure to direct sunlight or heat; aging	Wax with steel wool and buff (p. 87) □○
Finish alligatored (network of tiny cracks)	Exposure to direct sunlight or heat; aging; finish not applied correctly	Strip and refinish surface (p. 96) ■●
Shallow scratch in finish	Wear and tear; bottom of knickknack or display item not padded	Polish with oil or furniture polish (p. 87) □○; disguise scratch with furniture dye, artist's colors or touch-up marker (p. 88) □○
Candle wax stuck to finish	Dripping candles not shielded; vent blowing on candles	Harden wax with plastic-wrapped ice cube, then pry it off carefully with a blunt knife; wipe off remainder with mineral spirits
Paper stuck to finish	Moisture or heat and pressure against paper	Soak paper with mineral oil, then peel it off; remove residue with 4/0 steel wool dipped in mineral oil
Stain or mark on finish	Spill not cleaned immediately	Lift stain (p. 88) □○
	Hot or wet object placed on finish has left white mark or ring	Lift white mark or ring (p. 88) □○
	Water has soaked through finish and penetrated wood	Strip, bleach and refinish surface (p. 96) ■●
Bare spot on surface	Finish and stain worn through	Refinish spot (p. 92) ◨○; refinish surface (p. 96) ■●
Crack, gouge or deep scratch in surface	Wear and tear; accidental blow	Fill damaged area with shellac stick (p. 89) ◨◕, wax stick (p. 90) □○, or wood putty (p. 90) ◨○
Burn in surface	Lit cigarette	Remove charred wood and fill depression (p. 91) ◨◕
Surface dented	Accidental blow; falling object	Lift dent with water or steam (p. 91) ◨○
Veneer blistered	Veneer expanded by heat or moisture	Slit blister and reglue veneer (p. 93) ◨○
Veneer gouged or burned	Accidental blow; lit cigarette	Patch veneer (p. 94) ■◕
Veneer or plastic laminate lifted	Wear and tear; heat and moisture have weakened glue bond	Reglue veneer or plastic laminate (p. 93) ◨○
Plastic laminate dirty or stained	Daily wear; minute scratches caused by abrasive cleaner	Clean laminate (p. 95) □○
Marble dirty or stained	Daily wear; surface corroded by acid or abrasive cleaner	Wash marble, or apply poultice to remove stain (p. 95) □○

DEGREE OF DIFFICULTY: □ Easy ◨ Moderate ■ Complex
ESTIMATED TIME: ○ Less than 1 hour ◕ 1 to 3 hours ● Over 3 hours

found on tables and cabinets, can also lift. If it does, glue it down with contact cement. Treat marble with care; do not use alcohol, acid or coarse abrasives to clean it, and do not apply acetone to synthetic marble.

You can save money by performing spot repairs, but keep in mind that a more successful and longer-lasting result is sometimes achieved by stripping and refinishing the entire surface *(page 96)*. When deciding whether to repair the surface or strip it and start afresh, consider the extent of the damage and compare the cost in time, energy and money for a spot repair. You can probably handle one or two small repairs, but many sizable gouges and cracks in the finish may call for refinishing. However, if the furniture is a valuable antique, refinishing may decrease its value; have the piece assessed by a professional furniture restorer.

To maintain the allure of a fine wood finish, dust it regularly with a soft, dry, lint-free cloth. To bring up the sheen, buff it occasionally by rubbing along the grain using a cloth moistened with furniture polish. Keep wood furniture away from heat sources, such as direct sunlight and radiators, and try to maintain an even temperature of 65°F to 70°F, and a humidity level of 50 percent.

The tools and supplies for surface repairs *(below)* can be hazardous. Wear chemical-resistant rubber gloves and work in a well-ventilated area when using solvents or finishes of any kind. Treat solvent-soaked rags with great care. Before throwing them away, stretch them outdoors on a clothesline to allow the solvent to evaporate. Do not pile up oil-soaked rags to await a weekly cleanup. Instead, soak the rags with water and place them inside tightly sealed glass jars or metal cans.

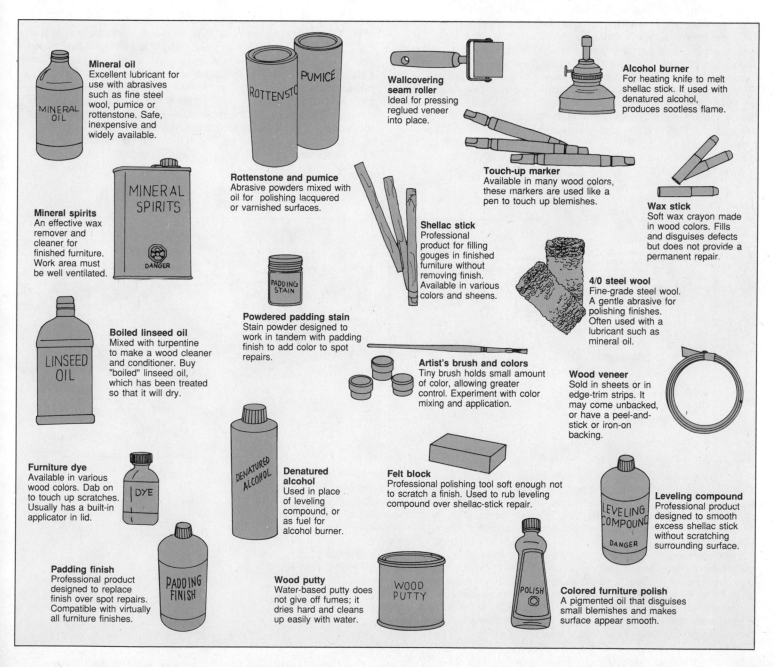

Mineral oil
Excellent lubricant for use with abrasives such as fine steel wool, pumice or rottenstone. Safe, inexpensive and widely available.

Mineral spirits
An effective wax remover and cleaner for finished furniture. Work area must be well ventilated.

Boiled linseed oil
Mixed with turpentine to make a wood cleaner and conditioner. Buy "boiled" linseed oil, which has been treated so that it will dry.

Furniture dye
Available in various wood colors. Dab on to touch up scratches. Usually has a built-in applicator in lid.

Padding finish
Professional product designed to replace finish over spot repairs. Compatible with virtually all furniture finishes.

Rottenstone and pumice
Abrasive powders mixed with oil for polishing lacquered or varnished surfaces.

Powdered padding stain
Stain powder designed to work in tandem with padding finish to add color to spot repairs.

Denatured alcohol
Used in place of leveling compound, or as fuel for alcohol burner.

Wood putty
Water-based putty does not give off fumes; it dries hard and cleans up easily with water.

Wallcovering seam roller
Ideal for pressing reglued veneer into place.

Shellac stick
Professional product for filling gouges in finished furniture without removing finish. Available in various colors and sheens.

Artist's brush and colors
Tiny brush holds small amount of color, allowing greater control. Experiment with color mixing and application.

Felt block
Professional polishing tool soft enough not to scratch a finish. Used to rub leveling compound over shellac-stick repair.

Touch-up marker
Available in many wood colors, these markers are used like a pen to touch up blemishes.

Alcohol burner
For heating knife to melt shellac stick. If used with denatured alcohol, produces sootless flame.

Wax stick
Soft wax crayon made in wood colors. Fills and disguises defects but does not provide a permanent repair.

4/0 steel wool
Fine-grade steel wool. A gentle abrasive for polishing finishes. Often used with a lubricant such as mineral oil.

Wood veneer
Sold in sheets or in edge-trim strips. It may come unbacked, or have a peel-and-stick or iron-on backing.

Leveling compound
Professional product designed to smooth excess shellac stick without scratching surrounding surface.

Colored furniture polish
A pigmented oil that disguises small blemishes and makes surface appear smooth.

REVIVING THE FINISH

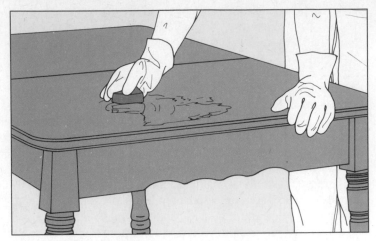

1 **Washing off dirt and grime.** To clean a varnished or painted surface, first try washing it with a solution of mild dishwashing detergent and warm water (or use oil soap, which is specially formulated for wood furniture and paneling). Since water tends to cloud shellac and lacquer, spot test the finish by dipping a soft, clean cloth or sponge in the solution and wiping it on an inconspicuous surface. Rinse away the detergent with a fresh cloth dipped in clear water, then rub the spot dry with another clean cloth. If the finish turns white or cloudy, clean the surface with mineral spirits instead *(step 2)*. If the finish does not change color, continue washing, rinsing and drying one small area at a time *(above)*, taking care not to soak the surface. To remove a stubborn wax buildup, go to step 2; to polish the cleaned surface, go to page 87.

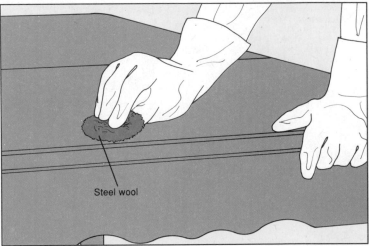

2 **Dissolving old wax buildup.** To dissolve wax buildup or wash a shellac or lacquer finish, use mineral spirits, a solvent. Wearing rubber gloves and working in a well-ventilated area, moisten a clean cloth with mineral spirits and wipe the solvent sparingly onto a small area of the finish at a time. Rub firmly to loosen wax and dirt, then wipe with a clean, dry cloth. Remove old wax from turnings with a tongue depressor or an ice-cream stick wrapped in a solvent-soaked rag *(above)*. Use a toothbrush soaked in mineral spirits to clean fine details and carvings. Polish the cleaned surface *(page 87)*; if the finish has dulled with age, condition it *(step 3)*.

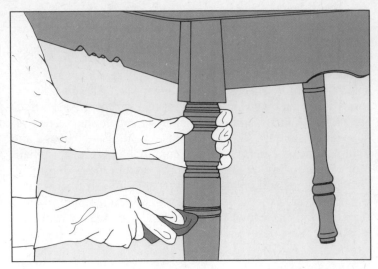

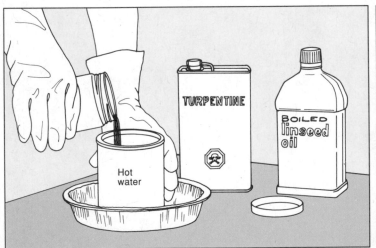

Steel wool

3 **Cleaning and conditioning the finish.** Work outside or in a well-ventilated area. Wearing rubber gloves, mix one part turpentine with three parts boiled linseed oil in a glass jar with a lid. Shake the jar well to mix the solution. Set a wide-mouth container on a metal pie plate and fill the container with boiling water. Slowly pour the boiled linseed oil solution into the container of hot water *(above, left)* until the solution forms a 1/4-inch film on the water's surface. Do not stir. Dip a clean cloth or, for deep cleaning, grade 3/0 steel wool, into the oily film and rub the mixture onto a small area of the finish, stroking gently in the direction of the grain *(above, right)*. Immediately wipe off excess conditioner with a warm, moist cloth, then wipe it with a dry cloth. Repeat the procedure until the entire surface has been treated. As the mixture cools, pour it into a metal or glass container for later disposal, and mix more conditioner in the same manner. Finally, use a clean, dry cloth to rub the entire surface along the grain. Soak used rags in water and dispose of them in a sealed container to prevent them from igniting spontaneously. If the surface is still dull or dry, wax it *(page 87)*.

ADDING LUSTER WITH OIL

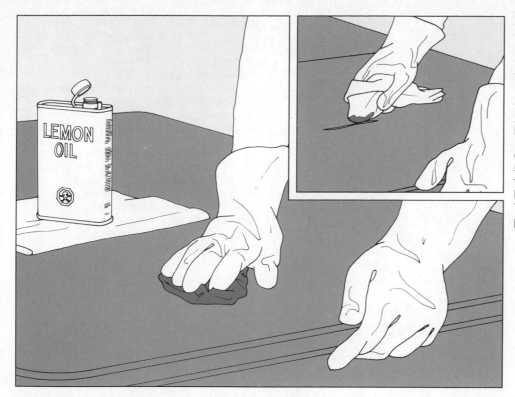

Achieving a quick polish. To restore luster to the finish and emphasize the wood grain, smooth on a coat of furniture polish, such as lemon oil. Avoid polishes that contain silicone, which leaves a deposit that makes later refinishing more difficult. Do not apply polish over a dirty or waxed surface; first remove any build-up *(page 86)*. Dampen a soft, clean cloth with polish and wipe it on the finish, along the grain *(left)*. When using a "scratch-removing," or colored, furniture polish, force polish into the scratches *(inset)* before applying the polish to the entire surface. Buff with a clean cloth if buffing is recommended by the manufacturer. To increase the sheen, you can buff with a power drill and lamb's wool pad *(below)*.

ADDING WAX FOR A PROTECTIVE SHEEN

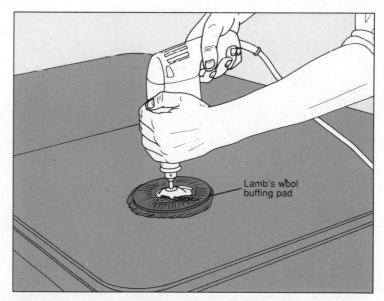

Lamb's wool buffing pad

1 **Applying wax.** Clean the surface by dissolving old wax with mineral spirits *(page 86)*. Spoon a small amount of high-quality furniture paste wax onto a soft, clean cloth *(inset)*, then fold the cloth around the wax. Or, to work wax into the wood grain, dip a pad of 4/0 steel wool into the wax. Apply the wax on one small area at a time *(above)*. Use a clean cloth to wipe away the excess, rubbing along the grain. When the surface is covered, allow the wax to dry, following the manufacturer's directions for drying time.

2 **Buffing the wax.** Achieve a good sheen by rubbing the wax vigorously by hand with a soft, clean cloth. Alternatively, use a lamb's wool buffing pad attached to a drill. Tie the pad securely to its mount on the drill and tuck in the loose strings. Hold the drill perpendicular, and steady it with the other hand to maintain an even pressure. Move the pad slowly along the grain of the wood *(above)*. Press lightly to avoid marring the surface, and angle the pad upward as you approach the edges to avoid burning them.

LIFTING STAINS AND WHITE RINGS

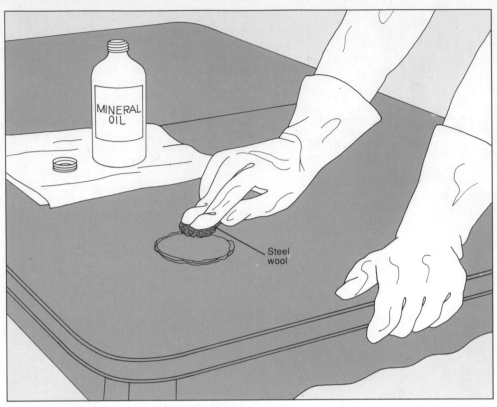

Removing a stain with abrasives. Light abrasion, in combination with a lubricant, will erase a stain without damaging the finish. First try dampening grade 3/0 steel wool or a coarse cloth with mineral oil, and rub the ring or spot gently *(left)*, along the grain if possible. Remove excess oil with a clean cloth. If the oil alone is not effective, mix rottenstone with mineral oil to form a soft paste, dip grade 3/0 steel wool into the paste and gently rub the entire area along the grain. Check your progress after each light stroke. If, after several strokes, the stain is not fading, slightly increase the pressure of the stroke. Once the mark is lifted, wipe off the excess paste with a damp cloth, then dry the area with a soft, clean cloth. If the treatment has left a dull spot on the finish, polish the surface *(page 87)*.

DISGUISING SCRATCHES

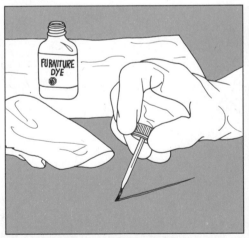

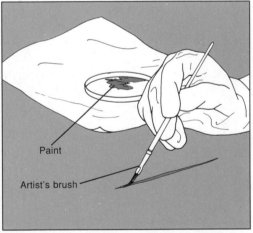

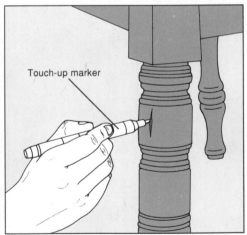

Matching the finish color. Furniture dye, artist's colors or a furniture touch-up marker can be used to color a scratch that has cut through the finish but not into the wood. Before applying color, test the match on scrap wood or an inconspicuous area of the furniture. To use furniture dye, begin with a light-colored stain and darken the color by adding coats as necessary. Dip the applicator brush into the dye and wipe off the excess on the edge of the bottle, making sure there is very little dye on the applicator. Use the tip of the brush to spread the dye along the scratch *(above, left)*, wait a few seconds to allow the color to soak in, then blot up excess dye with a cotton swab or the tip of a clean cloth. If you are using an artist's brush, blend the paint or stain until you have the desired shade. Wet the artist's brush with a very small amount of stain, then stroke on the color *(above, center)*, as described for furniture dye application. For scratches in less visible areas, draw on color with a furniture touch-up marker *(above, right)* or a pen or pencil of the appropriate color.

PATCHING GOUGES AND CRACKS WITH A SHELLAC STICK

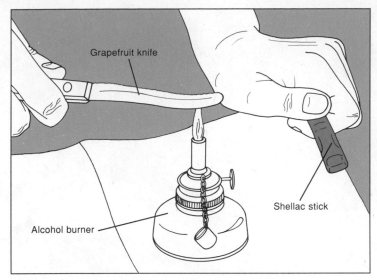

1 **Heating the knife.** Shellac sticks, used by professional furniture restorers, are particularly useful for filling small, deep cracks and gouges on highly visible finished surfaces. Shellac sticks come in a wide variety of colors; buy a stick the same color or slightly darker than the shade of the finish, and specify high-gloss or satin when ordering. Other supplies needed for this repair are a small alcohol burner, a felt block, leveling compound and denatured alcohol, all available from a furniture refinishing supplier. Practice this repair on scrap wood before attempting it on your furniture. Carefully scrape the damaged area clean with a shop knife. Fill the alcohol burner with denatured alcohol—which produces a sootless flame—adjust the height of the wick and light it. Heat a grapefruit knife with a curved, flexible blade, or a palette knife, by holding it over the flame for approximately 30 seconds *(above)*.

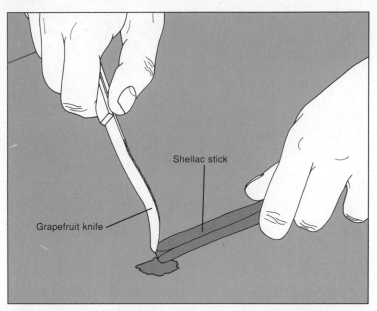

2 **Dripping the shellac.** Hold the shellac stick with its tip pointed toward the area to be filled. Press the end of the heated knife against the tip of the shellac stick *(above)*. Keep the knife pressed against the stick long enough for the shellac to melt and drip into the gouge or crack, overfilling it slightly. Wet the tip of your finger and press the shellac into the depression to remove any trapped air.

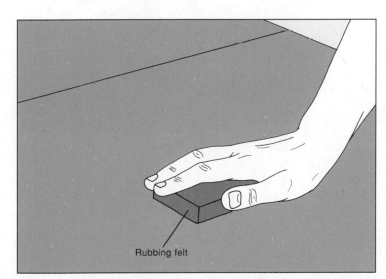

3 **Leveling the patch.** Reheat the knife and wipe it across the hardened shellac to level its surface, taking care not to touch the surrounding finish. Wipe the knife clean with a rag after each stroke. Allow the shellac to harden for a few minutes, then use a single-edged razor blade carefully to shave off any excess. Moisten one side of a thick block of rubbing felt with leveling compound or denatured alcohol. Rub the felt block back and forth across the patch to smooth it flush with the surrounding surface *(above)*. Wipe off the excess leveling compound with a clean cloth.

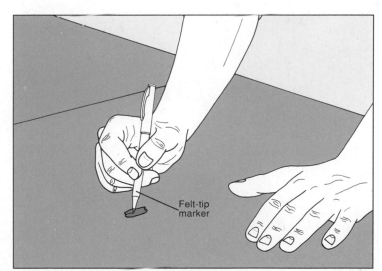

4 **Drawing fake grain.** Use an ordinary felt-tip marker, a professional graining marker, or an artist's brush and paint to draw grain lines on the patch. Practice first on a piece of scrap wood. Make sure the color of the marker matches that of the wood grain. Draw lines across the patched area, extending the grain pattern of the surrounding wood *(above)*. If the new grain lines are too sharp, smudge them by rubbing gently with your finger or a cloth.

PATCHING WITH A WAX STICK

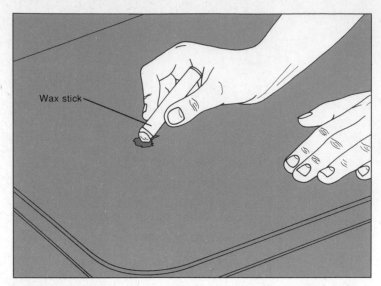

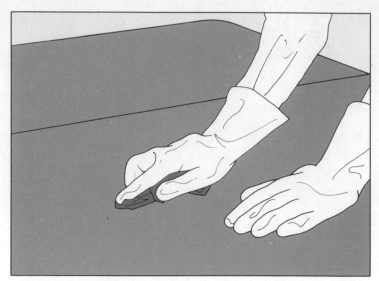

1 **Rubbing in the wax stick.** Crayon-like wax sticks are available at hardware stores in a variety of wood colors. They are useful for quick—though temporary—repair of scratches, gouges and dents. First, scrape the depression clean with the tip of a knife. Soften the tip of the wax stick in your fingers, then rub it from side to side across the depression *(above)*, pressing firmly to fill it in.

2 **Smoothing the patch.** Use your finger or a soft cloth to press the wax deeply into the depression. Add more wax as you did in step 1; rub until the depression is flush with the finish surface. To clean excess wax from the surrounding finish, lightly dampen a clean, soft cloth with mineral spirits and wipe sparingly around the patch *(above)*. Allow the patch to harden for one hour and buff it to luster.

PATCHING WITH WOOD PUTTY

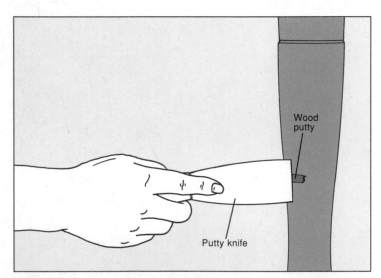

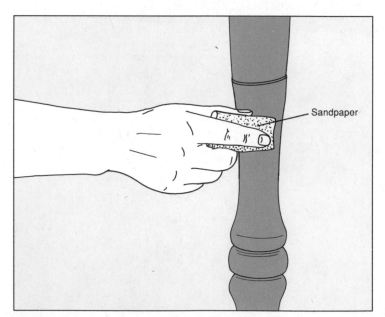

1 **Filling a crack or gouge.** Wood putty comes in premixed or powdered form; some are pre-colored, while others are creamy white and can be stained before or after application. Because it is hard to disguise a wood putty patch, this material is recommended for repairs to less visible surfaces. Following the manufacturer's instructions, mix the putty if necessary, and add stain if desired. Use a narrow putty knife to spread wood putty from side to side across the defect *(above)*. Press in the putty firmly and overfill the area slightly to allow for shrinkage. Allow the putty to dry, following the directions on the container. If the patch shrinks below the surface, smooth more putty over it.

2 **Leveling the patch.** When the patch is dry, use medium-grit sandpaper to smooth it, working in the direction of the grain. Hand sand a contoured surface *(above)*; use a sanding block on a flat surface. Wipe away the dust with a rag. To add stain to an uncolored patch or to touch up the finish, go to page 92.

REMOVING A CIGARETTE BURN

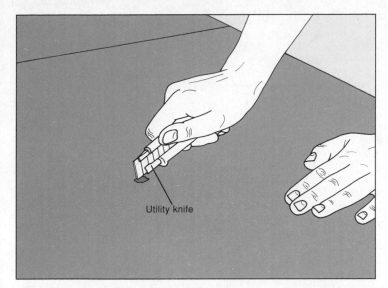

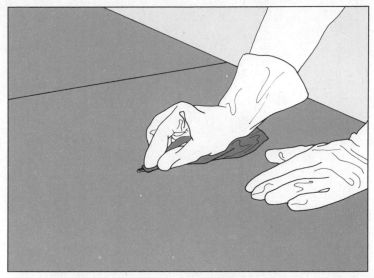

1 **Scraping away the charred wood.** To treat a cigarette burn in a wood surface, first use the tip of a utility knife to loosen charred material in the burned area *(above)*. Scrape out as much of the charred wood as possible, taking care not to damage the surrounding finish. Wipe away the loose fragments.

Utility knife

2 **Cleaning the depression.** To bleach the burned area, dampen a clean cloth with denatured alcohol and sponge it lightly. Apply more alcohol until the gouged area lightens to match the surrounding wood. When the gouge is clean, fill it using one of the techniques shown on pages 89 and 90.

RAISING DENTS

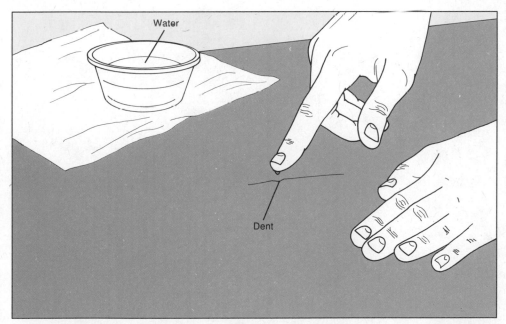

Water

Dent

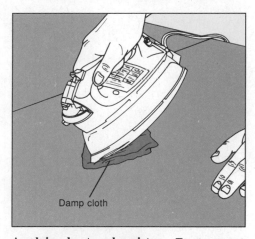

Damp cloth

Applying heat and moisture. To steam out a depression, fold a clean, damp cloth into a small square and lay it over the dent. Press the tip of a hot iron against the cloth *(above)*, allowing the steam to penetrate the wood. Do not allow the iron to touch the bare finish. Check the results, and repeat the procedure several times until the dent is raised.

Soaking a dent with water. To cure a shallow dent or compressed area in the wood surface, add water to make the wood fibers swell to their original shape. Since water tends to produce white spots on shellac and lacquer, first test the finish by touching water to a hidden spot. If the finish becomes clouded, do not proceed with this repair. If the finish does not turn white, clean grime and wax from the dented area *(page 86)* to allow the water to penetrate. Dip your finger in water and allow several drops to fill the dent *(above)*. Let the wood absorb the water. If the wood does not swell enough to eliminate the dent, prick a few minute pinholes into the depression with a fine needle. Apply the water again and allow it to soak into the wood.

SPOT REFINISHING

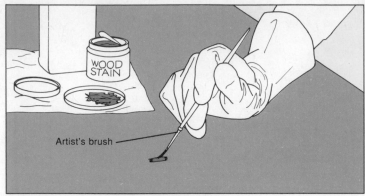

Artist's brush

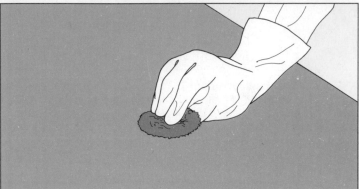

1 **Reapplying the original finish.** The trick to touching up bald spots and unfinished patches is to match the color and sheen of the original surface. If you do not have the finishing product that was originally used on the surface, apply one of the commercial spot refinishing products that are compatible with virtually all finish types *(step 2)*. If you do have the original finishing product, first select and prepare a stain to match the color of the surrounding surface, following the instructions on page 104. When you have achieved the desired color, dip an artist's brush into the stain, then wipe the tip against a piece of paper to remove the excess. Stroke or tap the stain sparingly onto the repaired area *(left, top)*, avoiding color buildup near the edges. Consult the chapter on refinishing for instructions on wiping on penetrating finish *(page 109)*, brushing on varnish or shellac *(page 110)* and spraying on lacquer *(page 111)*. To blend the new finish with the existing finish, dip a piece of 4/0 steel wool in mineral oil and polish the edges of the newly finished area along the grain, in one direction only *(left, bottom)*.

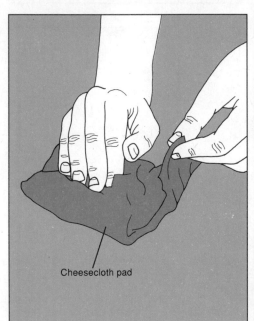

Cheesecloth pad

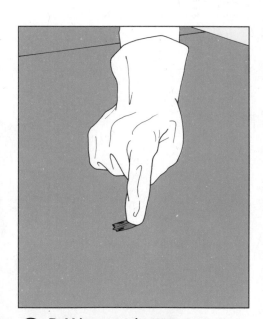

2 **Applying padding finish.** Specialized padding finishes and powdered stains, available from a furniture refinishing supplier, are designed to touch up all types of finishes. The term "padding" describes the technique of using a tightly rolled pad to sweep finish onto a surface. To make a pad, cut out a 1-foot-square piece of cheesecloth or cotton, fold each corner of the square so that all four corners meet in the middle *(above, left)*, then fold the new corners into the center until you have formed a tight wad with one smooth side. Holding the pad by the folded corners, moisten the smooth side lightly with the padding finish. Sweep the pad three or four times across the repaired area using a quick, back-and-forth motion *(above, right)*. To tint the spot, rub on stain before the finish dries *(step 3)*. If stain is not needed, allow the finish to dry, then cut the gloss, if necessary, by smoothing the spot with 4/0 steel wool.

3 **Dabbing on stain.** While the finish is still wet, dip your finger into a powdered stain that matches the surrounding surface and rub a tiny amount into the repaired area *(above)*. Continue applying padding finish and stain until the desired color is achieved. Allow the stained finish to dry, then smooth it as in step 2.

STICKING DOWN VENEER OR PLASTIC LAMINATE

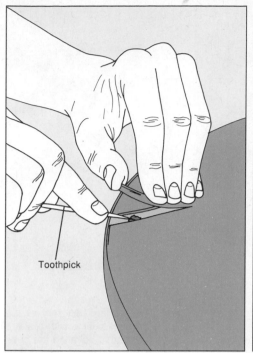

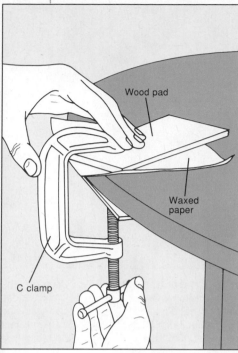

Wood pad

Waxed paper

C clamp

Toothpick

A quick fix for loose edges. Lift the loose edge gently and scrape out old glue with a sharp knife, working along the grain, if possible. Use a straw to blow out the loose debris. With a toothpick or other pointed tool, spread white or yellow glue on the gluing surfaces of the wood *(far left)*. For a plastic laminate, brush on contact cement *(page 121)*. Press the lifted piece into place and wipe off excess glue. Secure the repair with a C clamp, inserting pads of wood or cork in its jaws to protect the furniture finish. To avoid gluing the pads to the surface, slip a piece of waxed paper under each pad. Tighten the clamp *(near left)*. Wait 24 hours for the glue to set, then release the clamp. In the case of wood veneer, sand the repair lightly with very fine sandpaper, and refinish the area. For plastic laminate, wash and wax the repaired area *(page 95)*.

FLATTENING BLISTERED VENEER

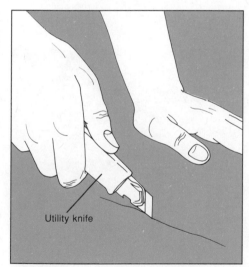

Utility knife

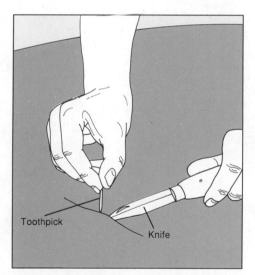

Toothpick

Knife

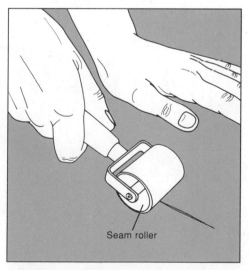

Seam roller

1 Slitting the blister. Heat and moisture can cause a veneered surface to bubble. If the raised veneer is broken, repair it with a patch *(page 94)*. Use a utility knife or single-edged razor blade to slice through the center of the blister in the direction of the grain *(above)*. Gently insert the blade of a shop knife under the veneer and scrape out loose glue particles. Dampen the underside of brittle veneer with a drop of warm water, then press the blister flat to test its fit. Use the utility knife to slice slivers off the edges of the slit until they butt together, or sand one edge lightly with an emery board.

2 Applying glue. Holding one side of the blister open with the blade of a knife, use a toothpick to spread white or yellow glue on the back of the veneer and the surface of the wood *(above)*. Alternatively, inject glue with a glue syringe *(page 121)*. Repeat the procedure for the other side of the blister. Press both sides of the blister into place and wipe away excess glue with a damp cloth.

3 Leveling the blister. Use a seam roller to flatten the veneer and distribute the glue. Run the roller along the seam, parallel to the wood grain, in one direction only *(above)*. After each stroke, wipe excess glue from the veneer and the roller with a damp cloth. When the blister lies flat, set a sheet of waxed paper over it, then place heavy books or other weights on top. Allow the glue to set for 24 hours. Refinish the repaired area *(page 92)*.

PATCHING DAMAGED VENEER

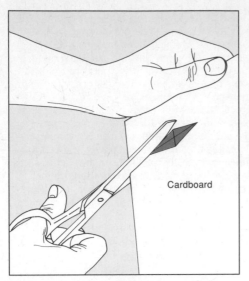

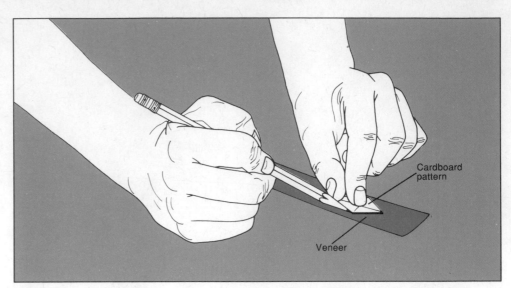

1 **Cutting a pattern for the patch.** Mend a badly damaged area of the veneered surface with a patch cut from new veneer. A diamond-shaped patch along the grain will best blend into the surrounding grain. Make a pattern for the patch on a piece of stiff cardboard, drawing a diamond shape slightly larger than the damaged area. Use scissors to cut out the pattern *(above)*, then place it over the damaged area to make sure that it is covered completely.

2 **Tracing the patch.** Buy a piece of unbacked veneer larger than the patch, of the same thickness and wood type as the damaged veneer. Lay the new veneer over the damaged surface and align it so that their grain lines run parallel. Set the cardboard pattern over the new veneer with the length of the diamond parallel to the grain, and trace its outline with a sharp pencil *(above)*. Use a utility knife and straightedge to cut out the veneer patch, beveling the cut slightly toward the center.

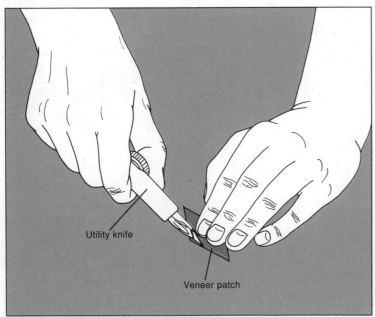

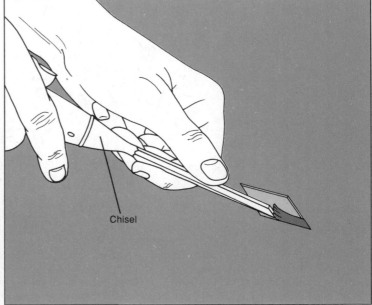

3 **Removing the damaged veneer.** Place the veneer patch over the damaged area, aligning their grain patterns. Use a utility knife to score the outline of the patch in the damaged veneer *(above, left)*, then set aside the patch and slice along the scored lines, cutting with the same inward slant as in step 2. Use a small wood chisel to clean out the damaged veneer *(above, right)*, working from the center out toward the cut outline. Take care not to gouge the wood beneath.

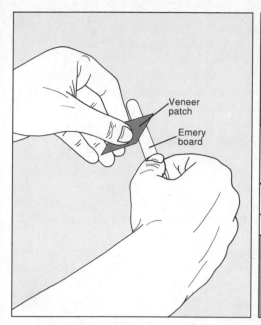

Veneer patch

Emery board

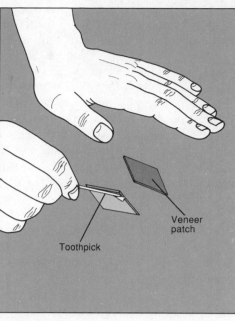

Toothpick

Veneer patch

4 **Setting the patch in place.** Insert the veneer patch, unglued, into the cleaned-out area. If the patch does not fit snugly, use an emery board to sand the edges slightly in the direction of the grain *(far left)*, making sure to retain the bevel. Use a toothpick to spread a thin layer of white or yellow glue onto the cleaned-out surface and the underside of the patch *(near left)*. Press the patch into place and wipe away excess glue with a damp cloth. Use a seam roller to flatten the veneer *(page 93)*, set a sheet of waxed paper over the repair and place heavy books or other weights on top. Wait 24 hours for the glue to set, then add stain and finish to the patch *(page 92)* or refinish the entire surface *(page 96)*.

REVIVING PLASTIC AND MARBLE SURFACES

BAKING SODA

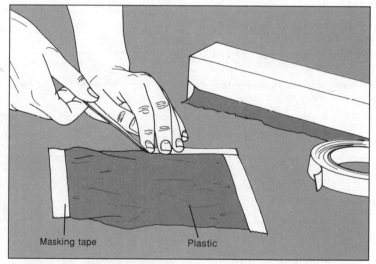

Masking tape

Plastic

Cleaning plastic laminate. For day-to-day cleaning of plastic laminate, use a mild detergent-and-water solution and a soft cloth or sponge. Do not apply abrasives to a plastic surface; abrasives leave minute scratches where dirt and stains can lodge. To remove stains, sprinkle on a generous amount of baking soda and rub it gently with a damp cloth *(above)*. Wash the surface with a cloth dipped in clean water. To fade stubborn stains, mix a thick paste of baking soda and water, smooth it over the stain and leave it on until it dries. Scrub it away with a clean cloth and water. To provide an ideal protective coating for plastic laminate, apply automotive wax, following the instructions on the label.

Caring for a marble surface. To remove scratches or ring marks in a polished marble surface, sand with the finest wet-or-dry emery paper, using water as a lubricant. Rub gently in a circular motion until you obtain a satin finish. Then sprinkle the surface with water and tin oxide powder (marble polishing powder, available from marble dealers) and polish it with a soft, clean cloth. Buff by hand or with a power drill and buffing pad *(page 87)*. To draw a stubborn stain from marble, apply a poultice. Mix talc, whiting (calcium carbonate) or plaster of paris with chlorine bleach or hydrogen peroxide to form a thick paste. For oily stains, mix the powder with acetone or lacquer thinner instead. Spread the paste thickly over the stain, then cover it with a sheet of plastic and tape down the edges *(above)*. This prevents the poultice from drying out before it has had time to work. Leave the poultice overnight, then gently scrape off the caked paste with a wood or plastic spatula and wipe the surface clean with a damp cloth.

REFINISHING

Few home repairs are as relaxing and satisfying as transforming an unsightly piece of furniture into a fine work. However, few repairs are as hazardous; many refinishing products are toxic, caustic or flammable.

Whether to strip an existing finish depends on its condition and the appearance you want. Test an old finish by scratching an inconspicuous surface with the edge of a coin. If it powders or flakes and bare wood is exposed, the finish must be taken off; if the finish doesn't lift, you may first try to revive it *(page 84)*. To apply a different type of finish, you will have to remove the existing finish.

Prepare furniture for refinishing by removing hardware, pulling out drawers and dismounting doors. Prop up the furniture, if necessary, so that each operation can be performed on one horizontal surface at a time, progressing from top to bottom and interior to exterior.

Proceed through each stage of refinishing as shown on the chair at right. Strip the finish *(page 98)* and identify the type of wood *(page 100)*. Stain *(page 104)*, bleach *(page 106)*, seal *(page 107)* or fill the wood *(page 107)*, if needed. Apply a penetrating finish, which soaks into the wood fibers, or a surface finish such as varnish, lacquer or shellac. After each stage of refinishing, clean up the work area *(page 112)*.

Furniture refinishing should be done in a place with excellent air circulation. Outdoors is ideal, away from direct sun, with the wind blowing fumes away from you. An alternative location is a garage or shed with large doors or windows and a spark-proof exhaust fan.

Follow the manufacturer's directions when using refinishing products, and read the safety tips in the Emergency Guide on page 8. Consult your physician if you suffer from heart trouble or a breathing ailment that can be aggravated by toxic fumes. Wear an organic vapor respirator, but remember: There is no cartridge rated to protect against methylene chloride. A simple dust mask will suffice while sanding.

Most solvents are flammable or combustible. Do not smoke or cause sparks in the work area. Dispose of soaked rags with care *(page 112)*. Avoid skin contact with chemicals by wearing long pants, a long-sleeved shirt, a shop apron, rubber gloves and safety goggles.

TROUBLESHOOTING GUIDE

SYMPTOM	POSSIBLE CAUSE	PROCEDURE
Furniture has no finish; areas of bare wood exposed	New furniture purchased unfinished	Finish the wood *(p. 108)* ⬓●
	Oil finish has soaked into wood or worn off	Finish the wood *(p. 108)* ⬓●
Finish cracked, chipped or peeling	Finish improperly applied; wear and tear	Strip old finish and apply new finish *(p. 98)* ■●
Finish hazy or cloudy	Moisture has penetrated finish	Attempt spot repair *(p. 84)* □○; if damage is extensive, strip old finish and apply new finish *(p. 98)* ■●
Finish has streaks or dull patches	Buildup of old wax or polish	Revive finish *(p. 86)* □○
	Wear and tear	Strip old finish and apply new finish *(p. 98)* ■●
Finish scratched, dented or gouged	Wear and tear; finish softened with age	Attempt spot repair *(p. 84)* □○; if damage is extensive, strip old finish and apply new finish *(p. 98)* ■●
Finish difficult to strip	Stripper scraped off surface too early; finish very thick	Reapply stripper *(p. 98)* ⬓○
Stripped wood feels rough to the touch	Wood fibers raised by stripping, filling or staining	Smooth the surface *(p. 102)* □◒
Stripped wood not smooth after sanding	Wood fibers raised by excessive humidity	Lower the humidity level and wait for the wood to dry; resand
	Wood has an open grain	Fill the wood, or apply sealer to stiffen fibers *(p. 107)* □○; smooth the surface *(p. 102)* □◒
Stripped wood too dark	Stain or filler has penetrated wood pores	Smooth the surface *(p. 102)* □◒; bleach the wood *(p. 106)* □○
Stripped wood reveals dark blemishes	Imperfections in wood grain; liquid spill has penetrated wood pores	Smooth the area *(p. 102)* □◒; bleach the wood *(p. 106)* □○
Wood too light or not desired color	Wood not stained	Stain the wood *(p. 104)* ⬓◒
Wood doesn't accept stain or finish uniformly	Coarse, open grain	Identify wood type *(p. 100)*, then fill wood, if necessary, before applying stain or finish *(p. 107)* □○
Stain penetrates too deeply into wood or bleeds into finish	Sealer required	Apply sealer *(p. 107)* □○

DEGREE OF DIFFICULTY: □ **Easy** ⬓ **Moderate** ■ **Complex**
ESTIMATED TIME: ○ **Less than 1 hour** ◒ **1 to 3 hours** ● **Over 3 hours**

Painted chair. Years of accumulated paint have hardened on this pressed-back chair. To restore the chair and reveal the wood grain, the paint must first be removed.

Stripped chair. The paint has been stripped away *(page 98)* and the wood surface smoothed *(page 102)*, revealing oak with a handsome grain *(page 100)*. Now is the time to inspect the joints and do any necessary structural repairs.

Refinished chair. Golden oak stain has been applied to enhance the wood grain *(page 104)*. Since oak has an open grain, a filler was applied first *(page 107)*. Finally, two coats of lacquer were sprayed on *(page 112)*, with a light sanding between coats, to protect the wood and restore its beauty.

STRIPPING THE OLD FINISH

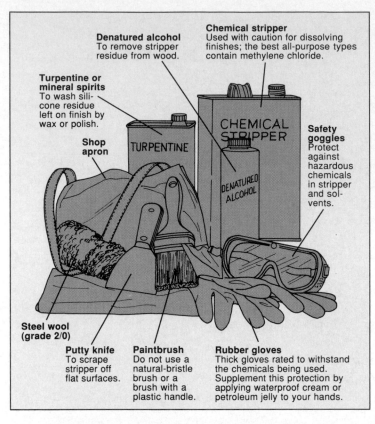

Denatured alcohol
To remove stripper residue from wood.

Chemical stripper
Used with caution for dissolving finishes; the best all-purpose types contain methylene chloride.

Turpentine or mineral spirits
To wash silicone residue left on finish by wax or polish.

Shop apron

Safety goggles
Protect against hazardous chemicals in stripper and solvents.

Steel wool (grade 2/0)

Putty knife
To scrape stripper off flat surfaces.

Paintbrush
Do not use a natural-bristle brush or a brush with a plastic handle.

Rubber gloves
Thick gloves rated to withstand the chemicals being used. Supplement this protection by applying waterproof cream or petroleum jelly to your hands.

1 Setting up for stripping. Chemical strippers soften a finish so that it can be scraped off the wood surface. Strippers pose serious health and safety risks; to avoid these hazards entirely, have the piece stripped by a professional. If you decide to do the job yourself, work cautiously and follow the manufacturer's directions. Round up the tools and supplies at left, as well as newspapers to protect the work area and a plentiful supply of clean, lint-free cloths. Also useful are old jars for solvents, pie tins for catching run-off stripper, and toothpicks and cotton swabs for cleaning out carvings. For reliable results, use an all-purpose stripper containing methylene chloride; on surfaces that must be kept vertical, a paste formula will grip better than a liquid. Avoid strippers that require a water wash to remove the residue—water raises the wood fibers. Do not use lye and oxalic acid as strippers; they are harsh and their action is difficult to control.

Work outdoors, away from direct sun. There is no respirator cartridge rated to protect against methylene chloride; if you must work indoors, set up in an extremely well-ventilated area with a spark-proof fan aimed outside. Avoid skin contact with chemicals by wearing long pants, a long-sleeved shirt, a shop apron and rubber gloves; protect your eyes with safety goggles.

Most furniture polishes contain silicone; to remove the silicone, wash the finish with a cotton cloth dipped in turpentine or mineral spirits and sprinkled with powdered detergent. Scrub gently along the grain, changing to a new cloth often to prevent reapplying the silicone taken off. Rinse the finish with fresh turpentine to remove remnants of detergent.

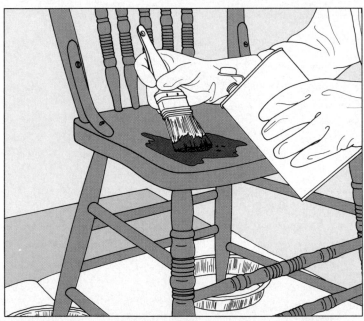

2 Applying a chemical stripper. Use newspapers, anchored with masking tape if necessary, to protect the floor or work surface from the stripper. Set an old metal pan or pie plate under each leg to catch run-off stripper. Turn or prop the furniture as necessary and, starting at one end of a horizontal surface, use a paintbrush to pat on a thick, even coat of stripper *(above)*. Spread the stripper in one direction over an area that can be coated in about 5 to 10 minutes—the time that it usually takes for the finish to start lifting. Avoid over-brushing or trying to work in the stripper, since this hampers rather than speeds its effectiveness.

3 Lifting off the old finish. Allow the stripper to sit on the finish 10 to 15 minutes or until it stops bubbling, a sign that the finish is softening and lifting. To test the reaction of the stripper, use a gloved fingertip *(inset)* or the tip of a putty knife to rub the surface. If your fingertip works through one or more layers of finish, the surface is ready for scraping. Avoid letting the dissolved finish reharden on the surface. Slide the blade of a putty knife along the grain, lifting off the sludge *(above)*; use short, light passes to avoid gouging the wood. Clean off the blade by scraping it across the lip of a container or by wiping it on newspaper. Leave any finish that does not readily lift off for a subsequent application of stripper.

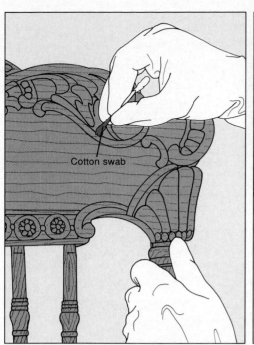

Cotton swab

Steel wool

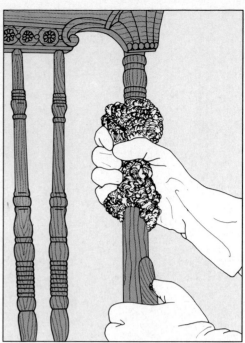

4 **Cleaning out carvings, contours and turnings.** To remove the stripper and dissolved finish from tight corners, special care and a little ingenuity are needed. A cotton swab *(above, left)* or a toothpick can be used to clean an intricate carving without risk to the wood. On a contoured edge, use grade 2/0 steel wool or a nylon pot scrubber, gently rubbing in the direction of the wood grain, if possible. Place a small wad of steel wool on the eraser end of a pencil to reach a tight contour *(above, center)*. To clean a spindle, wrap steel wool around it and rotate it *(above, right)*. Short lengths of jute twine or rope can be used shoeshine-style to clean out circular grooves or turnings. Work slowly, applying light pressure; surfaces coated with stripper usually soften, making them more prone to damage.

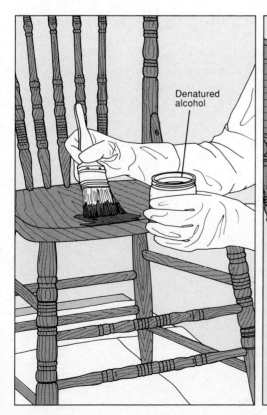

Denatured alcohol

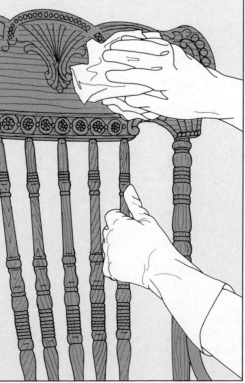

5 **Washing the wood.** Repeat steps 2, 3 and 4 as often as necessary to strip the finish to bare wood. To clean off stripper residue and prevent adhesion problems with subsequent finish coats, wash the wood with a solvent. Unless another solvent is indicated by the stripper manufacturer, use denatured alcohol. Pour a small amount into a wide-mouth container. Working along the grain, apply the solvent with a paintbrush *(far left)* or a rag, rub it in along the grain with grade 2/0 steel wool and wipe the wood clean using a cotton cloth *(near left)*. Repeat the detergent-and-turpentine wash described in step 1. Safely store or dispose of all tools and supplies *(page 112)*. Make any necessary repairs to the furniture surface and structure. Identify the wood using the chart on pages 100 and 101. Sand the surface smooth *(page 102)*, then bleach *(page 106)*, fill *(page 107)*, seal *(page 107)* or stain *(page 104)* if necessary. Select a finish from among those listed on page 108.

IDENTIFYING THE WOOD

Pine Country and modern furniture; may be used for moldings, drawer sides and cabinet framing. White to pale brown; often with red streaks. Fine, even, close grain; straight pattern. Moderately light and soft. Can be stained; rarely bleached. Needs no filler.

Ash Country and contemporary furniture; often used for table tops, chairs, bent parts and turnings. White to dark brown. Coarse, uneven, open grain; vivid, straight pattern similar to oak. Heavy and hard. Can be stained or bleached. Filler required.

Oak Traditional and high-quality modern furniture; often used for table tops; may be figured veneer. Pale gray to reddish brown. Coarse, even, open grain; flecked, straight pattern. Heavy and very hard. Can be stained; easy to bleach. Filler required.

Elm Usually country furniture; used for table tops, chair seats and bent parts. Light to dark brown; may have hints of red. Coarse, uneven, open grain; irregular pattern. Moderately hard and heavy. Can be stained; easy to bleach. Filler can be used.

Teak Modern furniture; often veneer. Medium to dark brown with hints of yellow. Coarse, even, open grain; straight pattern. Heavy and very hard. Rarely stained or bleached. Filler can be used. An oily wood best suited to an oil finish.

Butternut Usually old furniture; may be used for carvings; often veneer. Pale to dark brown; may have black streaks. Coarse, even, open grain; straight pattern. Moderately heavy and soft. Can be stained; rarely bleached. Filler required.

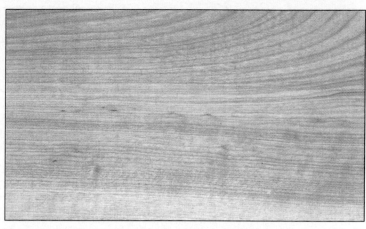

Maple High-quality furniture; often used for table tops, chair seats and turnings; may be veneer. White to pale reddish brown. Fine, even, close grain; straight, bird's-eye or burl pattern. Heavy and hard. Can be stained or bleached. Needs no filler.

Birch Country and modern furniture; often used for chair legs, bent parts, turnings and imitating other woods. White to pale brown. Fine, uneven, close grain; straight or wavy pattern. Heavy and hard. Can be stained; easy to bleach. Filler can be used.

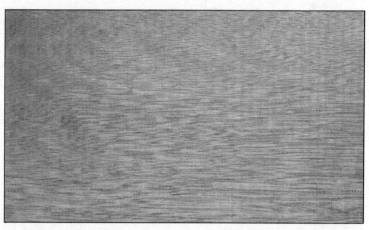

Cherry High-quality furniture; often used for table tops; may be veneer. Pale to dark reddish brown; may have hints of green. Fine, even, close grain; straight pattern. Moderately heavy and hard. Can be stained; rarely bleached. Filler can be used.

Mahogany High-quality furniture; often used for table tops and turnings; may be veneer. Brown to dark reddish brown. Fine, even, open grain; vivid, flecked, straight pattern. Heavy and moderately hard. Can be stained or bleached. Filler required.

Walnut High-quality furniture; often used for table tops and carvings; may be veneer. Grayish to dark brown; may have hints of purple. Coarse, even, open grain; straight pattern. Moderately heavy and hard. Can be stained or bleached. Filler required.

Rosewood High-quality furniture; usually veneer. Dark brown to black with hints of dark purple or orange streaks. Coarse, uneven, open grain; highly figured pattern. Heavy and hard. Rarely stained or bleached. Oily wood best suited to an oil finish. Filler can be used.

SMOOTHING THE WOOD

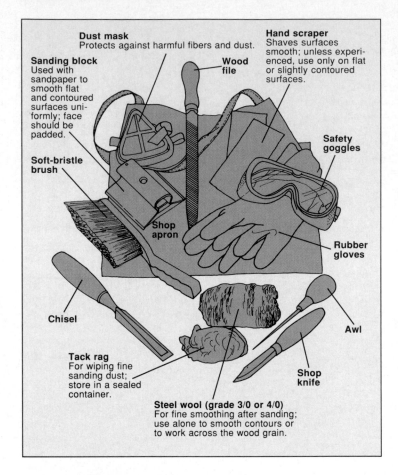

Dust mask
Protects against harmful fibers and dust.

Sanding block
Used with sandpaper to smooth flat and contoured surfaces uniformly; face should be padded.

Soft-bristle brush

Wood file

Hand scraper
Shaves surfaces smooth; unless experienced, use only on flat or slightly contoured surfaces.

Safety goggles

Shop apron

Rubber gloves

Chisel

Awl

Tack rag
For wiping fine sanding dust; store in a sealed container.

Shop knife

Steel wool (grade 3/0 or 4/0)
For fine smoothing after sanding; use alone to smooth contours or to work across the wood grain.

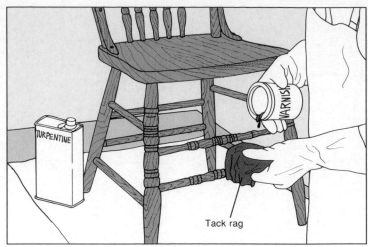

Tack rag

1 Getting ready for smoothing. To ensure a satiny finish, sand the wood each time the fibers are raised—after stripping, after bleaching, after sealing and between coats of finish. Gather together the equipment shown at left. Buy or make a sanding block *(page 117)* for flat surfaces; for rounded or curved surfaces, wrap medium-grit sandpaper around a dowel. Buy a tack rag at a hardware store or make your own. To make a tack rag, dip cheesecloth in warm water, wring it out, then saturate it with turpentine and shake it out. Drip varnish evenly over the cloth *(above)*. Fold it up and knead it until it turns uniformly sticky. Store the tack rag in a sealed glass container for later use. When smoothing wood, work in a well-ventilated, well-lit area. Wear long pants, a long-sleeved shirt, a shop apron, rubber gloves, safety goggles and a dust mask.

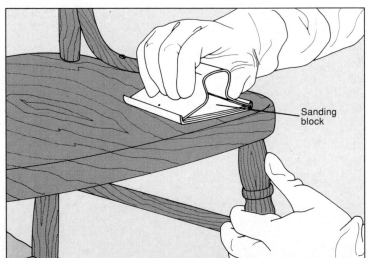

Sanding block

2 Smoothing flat surfaces. Smoothing the wood is a slow and painstaking procedure. Work evenly over one surface at a time. For initial smoothing, use sandpaper rather than steel wool; steel wool has a polishing effect and may close the wood pores. Using a sanding block with medium-grit sandpaper, stroke along the wood grain, applying moderate, even pressure in short, straight passes *(above)*. Replace the sandpaper strip as soon as it clogs. Use your fingertips as well as your eyes to determine whether a surface is sufficiently smoothed: a barely visible blemish will be magnified by a new finish. To spot blemishes, examine the wood under natural light if possible; fluorescent light may hide blemishes. Use a soft-bristle brush to whisk sanding particles off the surface.

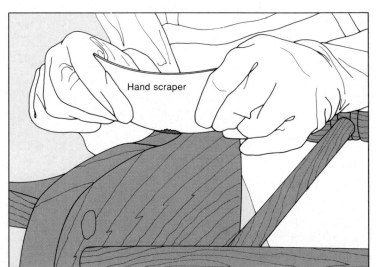

Hand scraper

3 Smoothing edges. Although it requires practice to master, a hand scraper is especially useful for smoothing edges with end grain. Bend the hand scraper, as described on page 117, and push it along the edge *(above)*. Wipe and resharpen the hand scraper *(page 118)* as often as necessary. You can also smooth surfaces with a small sanding pad, made by twice folding a quarter sheet of medium-grit sandpaper. Set the pad on the edge of the wood, apply pressure with your thumb and slide the pad along the grain in short passes, lifting the underside of the pad to avoid rounding off a flat edge. Change sanding pads often. Brush off the edge with a soft brush.

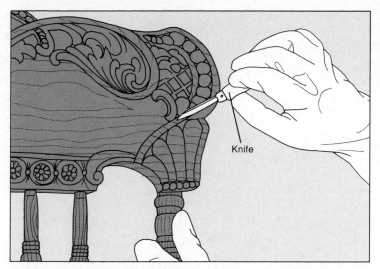

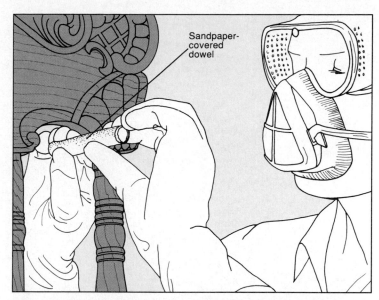

4 **Detailing carvings.** Smoothing the wood around intricate carvings may require the use of sharp-edged tools, steel wool and small sanding pads. Slip the tip of a knife, for example, into a carved line and run it lightly from one end to the other, lifting out any lingering particles of finish or stripper *(above)*. For an especially fine or delicate carving, stroke gently with the tip of an old awl or a nail. Follow up with a small sanding pad, if possible, or grade 3/0 steel wool. Abrasive tapes and cords, available at hardware stores, are also excellent for cleaning out hard-to-reach areas. At one end of a carved line, work in an abrasive tape or several intertwined strands of steel wool; pull it slowly along the route of the carving, taking care not to scratch the bordering surfaces. Brush off the carving with an old toothbrush, then a soft brush.

5 **Cleaning out contours.** To smooth contours that are gently rounded or curved, wrap sandpaper around a dowel. Set the sandpaper-covered dowel against the contour and twist it slowly and evenly *(above)*. Replace the sandpaper as soon as it clogs and cannot be cleared by tapping on a hard surface. Smooth the wood of an acutely rounded or curved contour using a sharp-edged tool, steel wool or a sanding pad. If using a file or chisel, work carefully to prevent gouging or tearing the wood. Dust off the surface with a soft brush.

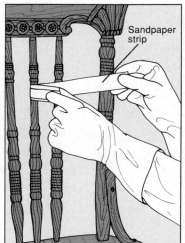

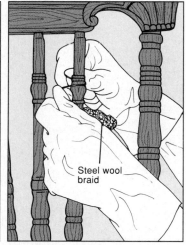

6 **Getting at turnings.** Strips of medium-grit sandpaper, a sharp-edged tool and steel wool are useful for smoothing turnings. Cut a narrow strip from the length of a sandpaper sheet and reinforce the back with masking tape. Wrap the strip snugly around the turning, grip it at each end, then draw the strip back and forth shoe-shine-style *(above, left)*. Clean finely detailed areas first with the tip of a rasp or an awl. Then braid a cord of grade 3/0 steel wool strands, fit the cord tightly into the detail without touching any bordering surface, and use the motion described above to smooth the detail *(above, right)*. A commercial abrasive tape or cord may also be used. Brush particles from the surface as you work.

7 **Cleaning the surface.** Follow the initial smoothing by thoroughly cleaning the wood. Working along the grain, first dust off the wood with a soft brush, then vacuum it. Finally, wipe the surface with the tack rag you made in step 1. Clean your work area to prepare for the next steps; refinishing must be done in a dust-free area. To determine the next steps, consider the type of wood you are refinishing *(page 100)*, along with its age and condition. To change the color of the wood, it may be necessary to bleach it *(page 106)* or stain it *(page 104)*. If no bleaching or staining is needed, the next steps depend on the type of wood; apply a finish to a close-grained wood, such as pine, maple or cherry; fill an open-grained wood, such as ash, oak or mahogany. If you intend to apply a penetrating finish, leave the grain open to absorb the oil.

STAINING FOR RICH COLOR

STAINS

Penetrating stains		Characteristics	Uses
Stains containing dyes that are absorbed into the wood fiber	Oil-based stain	Does not fade or bleed; does not raise grain. Easy to apply, dries in 24 hours.	Gives rich tones to coarse-grained woods such as mahogany, oak, rosewood, walnut, and light-colored hardwoods such as cherry, birch, ash and beech. Not recommended for softwoods such as pine, since it may over-emphasize grain.
	Alcohol-based stain	Fades in direct sunlight; does not raise grain; does not accept shellac finish. Requires skill to apply; dries in 15 minutes.	Highlights green tints in ash and oak; suited to close-grained woods such as birch, maple or beech.
	Water-based stain	Does not fade or bleed; raises grain. Easy to mix and apply; dries in 24 hours.	Best on mahogany, cherry and walnut.
	Solvent-based stain (non-grain-raising or NGR)	Does not fade or bleed; does not raise grain. Requires skill to apply; dries in an hour.	Best on woods with an attractive grain. Not recommended for softwoods such as pine.

Non-penetrating stains		Characteristics	Uses
Stains containing dyes that coat the surface of the wood	Oil-based stain	Does not fade or bleed; does not raise grain; conceals grain pattern; makes different types of wood look alike. Easy to apply; dries in 12 to 24 hours.	Emphasizes pattern of close-grained woods such as birch, maple and beech. Can be used to darken softwoods. Not recommended for open-pored hardwoods such as walnut and oak.

1 **Choosing the right stain.** Many stains are available to enhance wood grain, change its color, or disguise the wood entirely. To emphasize the pattern of wood with an open grain such as ash, oak, mahogany or walnut, use stain that has a penetrating oil base. If you wish to apply a shellac finish, use stain that does not have an alcohol base, since it dissolves shellac. Use the chart at left to help you choose an appropriate stain. After deciding on a stain type, select the color. Keep in mind that a stain color will vary depending on the solvent base and the manufacturer; also, a stain will vary in its effect on different types of wood. The chart on page 105 illustrates how stains change the color and enhance the grain of five common woods. To reduce stain penetration into the wood and to keep resins in softwoods from bleeding into the stain, apply a sealer *(page 107)* before staining.

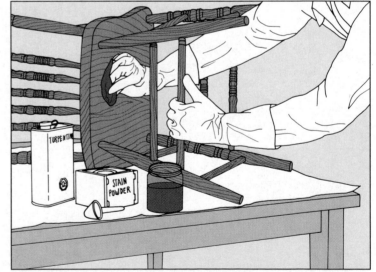

2 **Preparing the stain.** Follow the manufacturer's directions; while some stains are available ready-mixed and need only be stirred, others require mixing or must be diluted. If you cannot find a ready-mixed stain to your liking, use stain powder and add the recommended solvent—usually turpentine, denatured alcohol or water. Prepare the stain in a container made of glass or plastic—not metal, which may react with the solvent. Pour the solvent into the container and add the stain powder, stirring until it is dissolved *(above)*; in most instances, start with a quart of solvent and 2 or 3 tablespoons of stain powder.

3 **Getting the right color.** Experiment by mixing stain colors of the same solvent base to find the desired shade, noting any combinations that you may later want to duplicate. Settle for a color slightly lighter than the final shade desired; most stains darken as they dry and appear darker still under a finish. Using a pad of folded cheesecloth, apply a small test patch of the stain on an inconspicuous surface of the wood *(above)*. Wait until the test patch dries, then continue testing, adding stain to the mixture to darken it and solvent to lighten it. Coat the test patch with the finish you plan to use before judging its final color. If you are using a stain powder, strain the final mix carefully through cheesecloth to remove any undissolved particles. Go to step 4 to apply the stain.

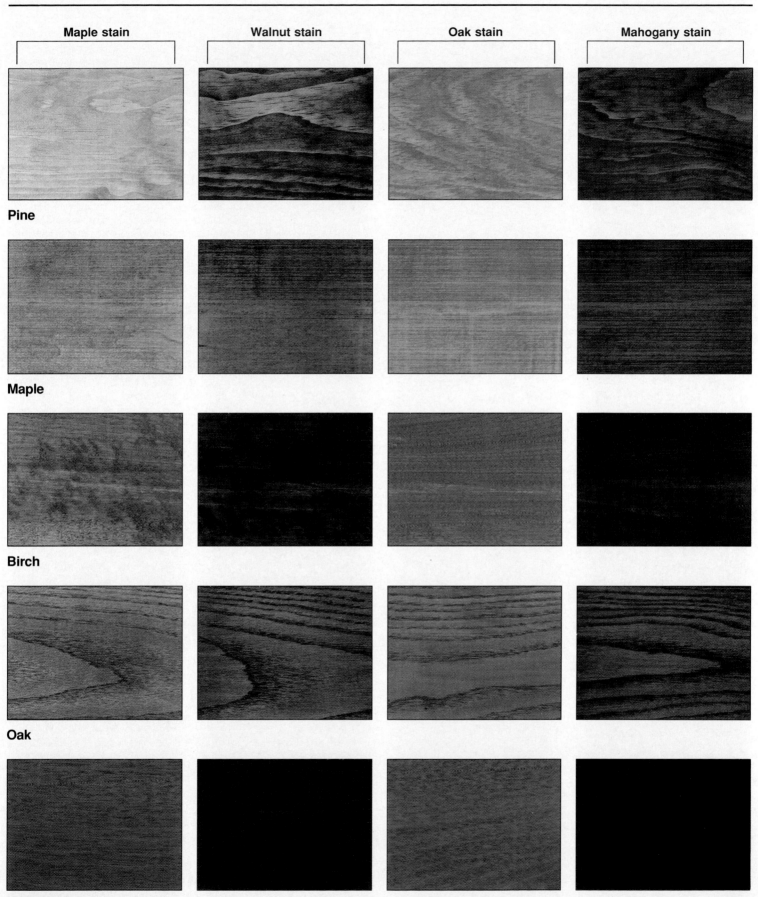

| Maple stain | Walnut stain | Oak stain | Mahogany stain |

Pine

Maple

Birch

Oak

Mahogany

STAINING FOR RICH COLOR (continued)

4 **Applying the stain.** To achieve a uniform color, apply stain to one entire surface of the furniture at a time, propping it so that the surface is horizontal, if possible. Wearing rubber gloves, dip a folded cheesecloth pad into the stain, leaving it damp, but not dripping. Wipe the stain onto the surface *(left)*, working in the direction of the wood grain. Overlap strokes to prevent streaks. Use a second pad to wipe off excess stain before it dries. If applying nonpenetrating oil stain, wait for the stain to dull slightly before wiping off the excess. If necessary, rub in the stain's base solvent to lighten any dark spots—for an oil stain, use turpentine. Wipe a sparing amount of stain on any surface with end grain, which is porous and absorbs stain faster. Allow the first application of stain to dry completely and repeat applications, if required, to build up color. Clean up the work area, safely storing or disposing of all tools and supplies used; if necessary, spread out fresh newspapers. After the final application is dry, fill the wood *(page 107)* with a filler that matches the color of the stain, then seal the surface *(page 107)*. If you want to apply a contrasting filler, seal first, then apply the filler.

BLEACHING TO LIGHTEN THE WOOD

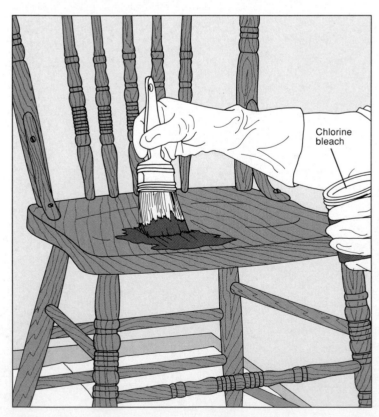

Chlorine bleach

Applying and neutralizing bleach. Bleaching, the process of lightening the wood by chemical means, can be accomplished using household products. Standard chlorine bleach, applied full strength, is excellent for removing discolorations, stains or water marks from bare wood. Wear rubber gloves and work in a well-ventilated area. Pour a small amount of chlorine bleach into a jar and use a paintbrush with synthetic bristles to apply the bleach evenly along the grain *(left)*. Apply bleach repeatedly until the wood has lightened to the desired shade. To stop the bleaching action, brush white vinegar onto the area. Hydrogen peroxide can be used in place of chlorine bleach for a slightly stronger bleaching action. To bleach the entire piece, a two-step procedure of peroxide and caustic soda is used; have the furniture bleached and neutralized by a professional, who will be equipped to work safely with these dangerous chemicals.

Rinse the wood with water, then wipe with it a cloth and allow it to dry overnight. Bleaching and neutralizing raise the wood fibers. Wearing a dust mask to avoid inhaling bleach-saturated particles, smooth the surface lightly with extra-fine sandpaper or grade 3/0 or 4/0 steel wool. Remove wood particles with a soft brush and a tack rag, then apply sealer *(page 107)* unless you plan to apply a penetrating finish.

FILLING THE WOOD

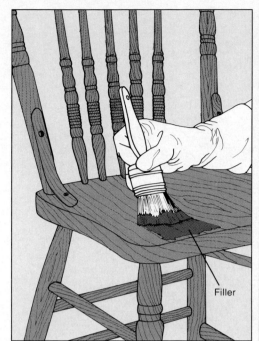

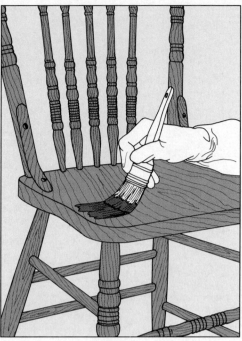

Filler

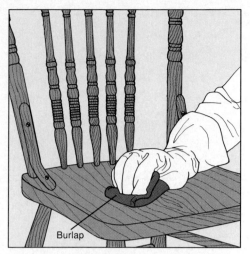

Burlap

1 **Pressing in the filler.** To provide a uniformly smooth surface on coarse-textured or open-pored wood, fill the pores with a paste or liquid filler before applying a finish other than penetrating finish. Use the chart on pages 100 and 101 to guide you in determining whether to fill the wood. Select a filler that is as close to the wood color as possible or, if the wood has been stained, tint a neutral filler by mixing in the same stain to the desired shade. Wear gloves, work in a well-ventilated area and wear a respirator if you are working with large quantities of solvent. Prepare the filler following the manufacturer's directions, thinning it with the required solvent—usually turpentine or mineral spirits. Using a stiff, short-bristle brush, press a thick layer of filler evenly into the wood pores; brush along the grain *(above, left)*, then across the grain *(above, right)*. Apply filler over an area that can be coated in about 5 to 10 minutes— the time that it usually takes for the filler to start drying.

2 **Padding the filler.** Let the filler set 5 to 10 minutes, until it loses its gloss and starts hardening, but not until it dries out completely. Rub in the filler across the grain with a pad of folded burlap, applying moderate pressure to force the filler into the pores and remove any excess *(above)*. Clean the surface by wiping lightly along the grain, taking care not to lift any filler from the pores. Let the filler dry for at least 24 hours. Shine a bright lamp across the grain to check the filler for a slight sheen. If you detect varying highlights or flat areas, apply the filler again and allow it to dry. Smooth the surface, following the procedures on page 102, but do not use any sharp tools. Clean the wood by gently wiping each surface with a tack rag, then apply sealer *(below)*. Safely store or dispose of used tools and supplies, and spread out fresh newspapers.

SEALING THE SURFACE

SEALERS

Stain	Sealer solution	Sealer application
Alcohol-based stain; non-grain-raising (NGR) stain	1 part shellac mixed with 8 parts denatured alcohol.	Brush onto surface before applying stain.
Oil-based stain	1 part boiled linseed oil mixed with 1 part mineral spirits.	Wipe onto surface before applying stain.

Finish	Sealer solution	Sealer application
Shellac; lacquer	1 part shellac mixed with 8 parts denatured alcohol.	Brush onto surface before applying finish.
Varnish	1 part varnish mixed with 1 part mineral spirits.	Brush onto surface before applying finish.

An undercoat for stain or finish. Sealers serve several useful functions in refinishing. Apply a sealer before staining or finishing to prevent resins in softwood from bleeding into the stain or finish. Applied before staining, a sealer reduces penetration of the stain into the wood; after staining, it prevents the stain from bleeding into the filler or finish. Apply sealer after filling to coat the filler, and before applying a finish to provide a base for the finish. The chart at left will help you choose the proper sealer. Apply one thin coat of sealer at each stage of refinishing, using a paintbrush or a cotton rag. Work on one horizontal surface at a time, progressing from top to bottom, interior to exterior. Let the sealer dry as recommended by the stain or finish manufacturer. Smooth the wood *(page 102)*, clean it thoroughly by brushing and wiping with a tack rag, then proceed with the next stage: staining *(page 106)*, filling or finishing. Safely store or dispose of used tools and supplies; if needed, spread out fresh newspapers.

APPLYING THE FINAL FINISH

FINISHES

Finish	Characteristics	Uses
Penetrating finish	Low resistance to water and alcohol; does not chip or peel. Enhances grain pattern and wood characteristics. Easy to apply and touch up; dries slowly. Must be reapplied once or twice a year.	Produces a soft, deep luster in wood. A good choice for large pieces of furniture and furniture with intricate carvings and turnings.
Shellac	Low resistance to water, alcohol and heat; moisture produces white marks on finish. Orange shellac imparts an amber hue to wood; white shellac dries to a clear finish. Easy to apply with good results; dries quickly.	A quick, clear, glossy finish that gives wood warmth. Not a durable finish for furniture that receives a lot of wear, such as table tops, but suitable for decorative wood items or dark cabinet woods.
Lacquer	Excellent resistance to water, heat, alcohol and daily wear. Difficult to apply; best results if sprayed; dries quickly, preventing dust particles on surface.	Intensifies wood grain and color. Produces a very hard, clear film on wood. For all indoor furniture.
Varnish	A tough finish that is waterproof, alcohol-proof and heat-resistant. Some varnishes have a slight yellow color, but most dry to a clear, transparent film on wood surface. Requires practice to apply well; dries slowly; difficult to avoid dust particles landing on surface. Polyurethane is the easiest to apply and the quickest-drying. Dries clear and will not darken with age or exposure to sunlight.	A highly durable finish that intensifies wood tones and imparts warmth to the wood. Suitable for indoor and outdoor furniture. Polyurethane varnish is especially durable and has a high resistance to abrasion.

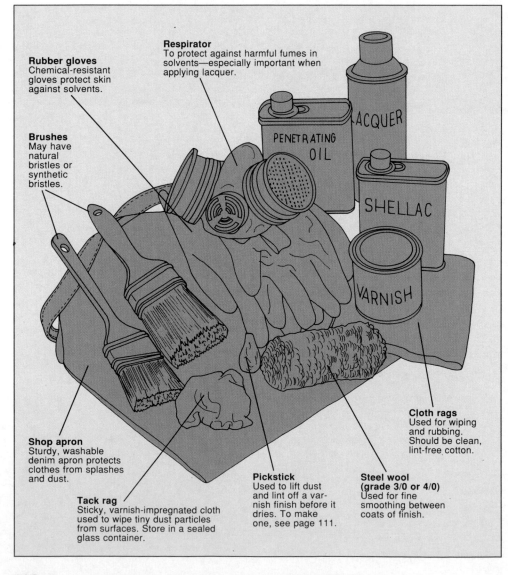

Rubber gloves
Chemical-resistant gloves protect skin against solvents.

Respirator
To protect against harmful fumes in solvents—especially important when applying lacquer.

Brushes
May have natural bristles or synthetic bristles.

Shop apron
Sturdy, washable denim apron protects clothes from splashes and dust.

Tack rag
Sticky, varnish-impregnated cloth used to wipe tiny dust particles from surfaces. Store in a sealed glass container.

Pickstick
Used to lift dust and lint off a varnish finish before it dries. To make one, see page 111.

Steel wool
(grade 3/0 or 4/0)
Used for fine smoothing between coats of finish.

Cloth rags
Used for wiping and rubbing. Should be clean, lint-free cotton.

Capturing beauty with a clear finish. After smoothing the wood surface *(page 102)*, and bleaching *(page 106)*, filling *(page 107)*, sealing *(page 107)* or staining *(page 104)* if necessary, select the finish from the chart above that best suits the wood. To preserve the warm texture of mahogany, for example, use a penetrating finish *(page 109)*, which soaks into the wood and is easy to apply and touch up. On wood such as maple or cherry, you can ensure durability by applying a varnish finish *(page 110)*. For a soft sheen, choose satin-type; for a shiny surface, choose high-gloss. At left are some of the tools and supplies needed to apply a finish. For wiping on oil, or for waxing and polishing, you will need a supply of clean, lint-free rags. Apply varnish or shellac *(page 111)* with a paintbrush; spraying is best for lacquer *(page 112)*, since it dries extremely quickly.

Apply the finish outdoors. If you must work indoors, choose a dust-free, well-ventilated area; equip the room with a spark-proof exhaust fan. Take special care when spraying a finish indoors, since sprayed droplets can float for hours. Lay out newspapers to protect the work area. Wear long pants, a long-sleeved shirt, a shop apron and rubber gloves; wear a respirator if you are applying lacquer or working with a substantial amount of toxic solvent. Always check the effects of any finish by first applying a small test patch on an inconspicuous surface.

WIPING ON PENETRATING FINISH

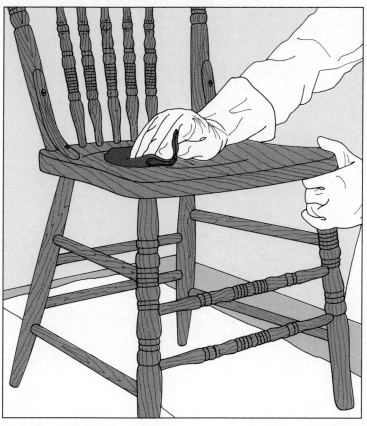

1 **Applying boiled linseed oil.** Products that soak into the wood rather than coating the surface are referred to as penetrating finishes. They give wood a natural appearance and texture while they protect it. Commercially prepared penetrating finishes are sold as Danish oil, teak oil or rubbing oil. But you can make your own from boiled linseed oil or tung oil. Penetrating finishes are all applied in much the same way; follow the manufacturer's instructions for variations. To give wood a classic rubbed finish with boiled linseed oil, first gently wipe the surface with a tack rag. Mix boiled linseed oil with an equal amount of turpentine. Pour the mixture onto a cotton cloth and spread it over the wood, working along the grain *(left)*. Wait 15 to 20 minutes for the oil to penetrate the wood, then reapply the oil to any dry spots. After another 15 to 20 minutes, wipe excess oil from the surface with a fresh cloth. Allow at least 24 hours for the oil to dry completely. To prevent used cloths from igniting spontaneously, soak them with water and put them in a sealed metal container, or hang them out to dry—do not pile them up. After the oil is dry, use grade 3/0 steel wool gently to rub each surface along the wood grain. Wipe with a tack rag and reapply the oil. Repeat as necessary to build up the sheen, then renew the finish once or twice a year, as required.

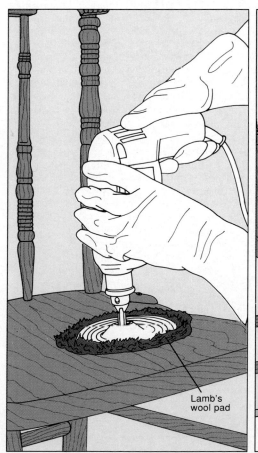

Lamb's wool pad

Paste wax

2 **Polishing for a high sheen.** To intensify highlights in a penetrating finish, use a cotton cloth to buff each surface vigorously in a circular motion, softening resins in the oil and smoothing the finish. Use a lamb's wool pad attached to a power drill to buff a large, flat surface *(far left)*; apply light pressure to guide the pad slowly along the wood grain. To smooth and protect the surface, rub gently along the grain using grade 4/0 steel wool lubricated with a small amount of paste wax or furniture polishing oil. Wipe the surface with a cotton cloth to remove the excess *(near left)*. Polish with a fresh cotton cloth, buffing vigorously in a circular motion. Clean the work area and safely store or dispose of all tools and supplies *(page 112)*.

BRUSHING ON VARNISH

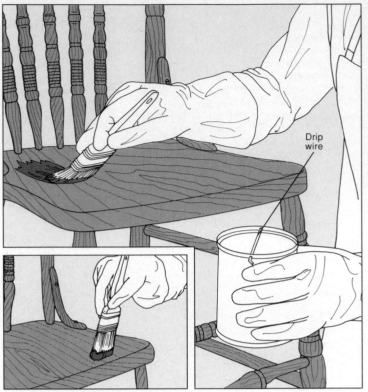

1 **Applying varnish.** First apply a coat of sealer, if necessary *(page 107)*. Prepare a wide-mouth metal or plastic container for the varnish by making a drip wire: Punch two holes at the top of the container, cut a piece of wire from an old hanger and thread the wire through the holes in the container. Gently rotate the unopened can of varnish to mix it without creating air bubbles. Pry off the lid and, taking care not to agitate the can, slowly pour a small amount of varnish into the container. Replace the lid immediately. If you are applying polyurethane varnish, be sure that the furniture surface is completely free of any silicone residue *(page 98)*. Follow the manufacturer's directions carefully, especially regarding the drying time between coats.

Load a stiff varnish brush by dipping it into the varnish, coating only one third the length of the bristles. Stroke the bristles against the drip wire to remove the excess. Varnish one horizontal surface at a time, propping the furniture when necessary. Apply the varnish in a flowing motion, along the wood grain and always in the same direction, using moderate pressure *(left)*. Stroke on the varnish in parallel passes, without overlapping it. Lift the brush at the end of each stroke to keep it from touching or dripping on an adjacent surface *(inset)*.

Drip wire

2 **Tipping off for an even coat.** As soon as one surface is coated, spread a thin layer of varnish lightly across the grain in long, sweeping passes, applying moderate pressure *(left)*. Lift the brush away from the edge at the end of each pass to keep from touching it. "Tip off," or level, the varnish immediately, using a brush that is nearly dry. Holding the brush almost perpendicular to the surface and brushing along the grain, pass the tips of the bristles gently over the varnish, softening brush marks and wiping out any air bubbles. Between coats, reseal unused varnish and store used brushes. Wrap brushes in aluminum foil or plastic food wrap and place them in the freezer, or suspend the brushes with the bristles submerged in mineral spirits, but not touching the bottom of the container.

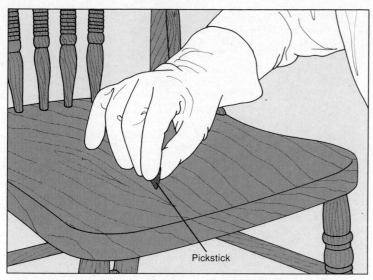

Pickstick

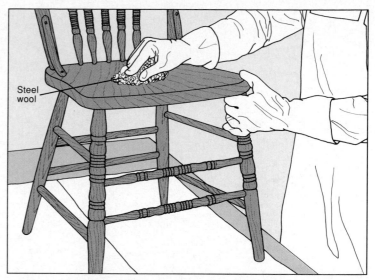

Steel
wool

3 **Picking out dust.** Use a homemade pickstick to lift out specks of dust or lint from the varnish before it dries. To make a pickstick, you need rosin, usually available in crushed form at a music store, a cotton swab, and varnish. Pour a small amount of varnish into a small can and set the can into a larger can of boiling water. Allow 10 minutes for the varnish to warm up, then add rosin (7 parts rosin to 1 part varnish) to the heated varnish, stirring until it dissolves. Let the mixture cool. Dip a cotton swab into the mixture, wet your thumb and fingers with water and pull off the end of the swab, rolling it into a pear-shaped point that is tacky but firm. To pick up dust or lint specks, lightly touch the pointed end of the pickstick to the surface and slowly lift the speck from the still-wet varnish *(above)*. An artist's brush or a toothpick can also be used for this purpose.

4 **Smoothing between applications.** When the varnish is dry, smooth the finish along the grain, using 4/0 steel wool *(above)* or super-fine sandpaper. Apply light pressure to dull the sheen slightly. Be careful not to sand through the layer of varnish. Clean each surface after smoothing by brushing, then wiping it with a tack rag. Repeat steps 1, 2 and 3 to reapply varnish as needed; apply at least two coats after the sealer. If you are applying polyurethane varnish, be sure to apply the second coat within the time specified by the manufacturer, or it will not adhere. Reseal unused varnish and clean the brushes *(page 112)*. Wax and buff the finish *(page 87)*, if desired.

APPLYING SHELLAC FOR A SATIN FINISH

Shellac

DENATURED
ALCOHOL

Denatured
alcohol

Thinning and applying shellac. Shellac is easy to apply, dries quickly and sands easily. It makes a good sealer *(page 107)*, but because it is not resistant to water, heat or alcohol, shellac is not a practical final finish for furniture that will receive a lot of wear and tear. Choose orange shellac to lend an amber hue to dark wood such as mahogany, walnut or butternut, or to wood that is darkly stained; use white shellac to provide a natural shade. Shellac is sold in a four-pound or five-pound "cut" (shellac resin dissolved in alcohol), which must be thinned with denatured alcohol for application. Thin a four-pound cut by mixing one part shellac with three parts denatured alcohol; thin a five-pound cut by mixing one part shellac with four parts denatured alcohol *(left)*. To thin shellac for use as a sealer, mix one part shellac with eight parts denatured alcohol. Stir slowly to avoid introducing air bubbles. Reseal the shellac and denatured alcohol when not in use. To apply shellac, use a paintbrush, loading no more than two thirds the length of the bristles. Brush in one direction, along the grain, lifting the brush at the end of each stroke. Do not backbrush over previously applied shellac, since it dries very quickly and rebrushing will striate the finish. Allow four hours for the surface to dry before applying another coat; apply at least three or four coats after the sealer. Let the final application of shellac dry for 12 hours before smoothing.

SPRAYING ON LACQUER

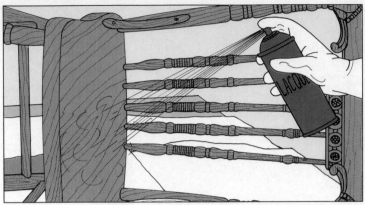

Spraying lacquer in smooth sweeps. Lacquer gives a hard, beautiful finish that resists impact, wear, water, heat, alcohol and mild acids. Lacquer can be brushed on, but it tends to leave stroke marks. Aerosol cans, although expensive, provide the most successful and practical way to apply lacquer. After sealing *(page 107)* and smoothing the wood, clean it thoroughly with a brush and a tack rag. Lacquer is highly flammable and emits toxic fumes; work outdoors, out of direct sunlight, and wear an organic vapor respirator to filter out harmful fumes. Read the manufacturer's instructions carefully. Shake the aerosol can vigorously to mix the lacquer, initially for at least two minutes, then periodically, between spray passes. Practice spraying the lacquer on scrap wood. Then, holding the can at a 30-degree angle, 12 to 14 inches from a vertical surface, spray along the wood grain from one edge to the other in a long, continuous sweep *(left, top)*. Repeat applications of lacquer in alternating directions, each pass overlapping half of the one preceding it. On turnings or other narrow surfaces, hold cardboard or scrap wood behind the surface to catch excess lacquer spray *(left, bottom)*. Let the lacquer dry for about 20 minutes, then smooth the surface gently and clean it with a tack rag. Apply four or five coats of lacquer, allowing the final application to dry for 12 hours before smoothing. To dispose of empty cans, press the nozzle to expel all gas propellant, then discard the cans without puncturing or burning them. Before storing a partly used can, turn it upside down and press the nozzle briefly to prevent the lacquer from clogging it. Clean up the work area and safely store or dispose of all tools and supplies *(below)*.

CLEANING UP

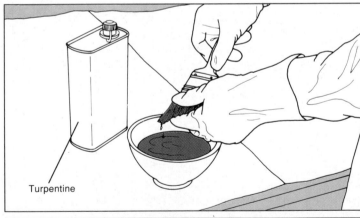

Turpentine

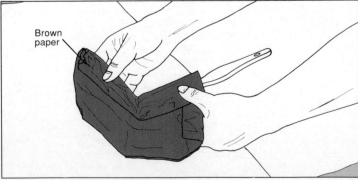

Brown paper

Cleaning and storing tools and supplies safely. Conduct a thorough cleanup immediately after each stage of refinishing—not only to prolong the life of your tools and supplies, but to ensure your own safety. Any stripper, solvent or finish is hazardous; always follow the manufacturer's directions and precautions. Reseal cans containing these products after each application, and store them away from sources of heat, sparks or flames and beyond the reach of children. If you transfer any material to a smaller can, transfer the label or recopy safety information onto the new label. Throw out empty cans, first releasing the gas propellant in aerosol cans. Clean tools after use, and store them in a locked tool box or hang them out of reach of children. Soak used newspapers and cloths in water and dispose of them in sealed metal containers to keep them from igniting spontaneously; start each new stage in the refinishing operation with a fresh supply. Store clean respirators in dustproof containers, and change the filter or cartridge regularly, according to the manufacturer's instructions.

To clean a brush after applying stain or finish, pour a small amount of the product's solvent into a shallow, wide-mouth container. Soak the bristles of the brush in the solvent then, wearing rubber gloves, squeeze out excess solvent *(left, top)*. Repeat until the bristles seem clean, then wash the bristles in mild detergent and warm water, rinse them well and dry them by blotting with a cotton cloth. Wrap the brush in a long strip of brown wrapping paper. Fold up the end of the paper over the brush, without bending the tips of the bristles *(left, bottom)*. Tie or tape the paper. Store the brush flat or hang it from the hole in its handle.

TOOLS & TECHNIQUES

This section introduces tools and techniques for furniture repair, including using a vise, cutting with handsaws, shaving and smoothing wood and handling power tools. Charts on sandpaper, wood fasteners and woodworking glues are presented for quick reference. A look at proper clamping methods and an inventory of common wood joints round off the chapter. Tools particular to repairing upholstery *(page 64)*, repairing furniture surfaces *(page 84)* and refinishing *(page 96)* are illustrated and described in their own chapters.

Buy the best-quality tools you can afford and treat them with kindness. Protect their cutting edges by checking wood for hidden nails and screws before you start to work. If a saw becomes dull, take it to a professional for resharpening or buy a replacement blade from a hardware store. Sharpen planes and chisels on a 250/1000 combination-grit whetstone *(page 118)* lubricated with water or light machine oil, according to the whetstone manufacturer's instructions. If a blade is badly chipped, you can have it reground professionally. Wipe wood resin and dirt from blades with a clean rag dipped in mineral spirits, and rub a few drops of light machine oil on the blades with a soft cloth to keep them rust-free. Follow the manufacturer's instructions to clean and lubricate power tools. Store tools on a shelf away from children, in a locked metal or plastic tool box, or hang them out of reach. Store a hand plane on its side to protect the blade from damage.

To protect the finish on a piece of furniture that needs repair, have on hand an old blanket to pad the floor or work table. Also handy are sheets of cardboard or cork to protect wood from the jaws of a vise, and scrap wood to use as clamping pads and hammering blocks.

Use grounded power tools in a dry area with a grounded outlet. When cutting or sanding wood, wear safety goggles to protect your eyes from sawdust and wear a dust mask to protect your lungs from particles. Work with toxic substances outside or in a well-ventilated area, and wear a canister respirator with the appropriate organic filter.

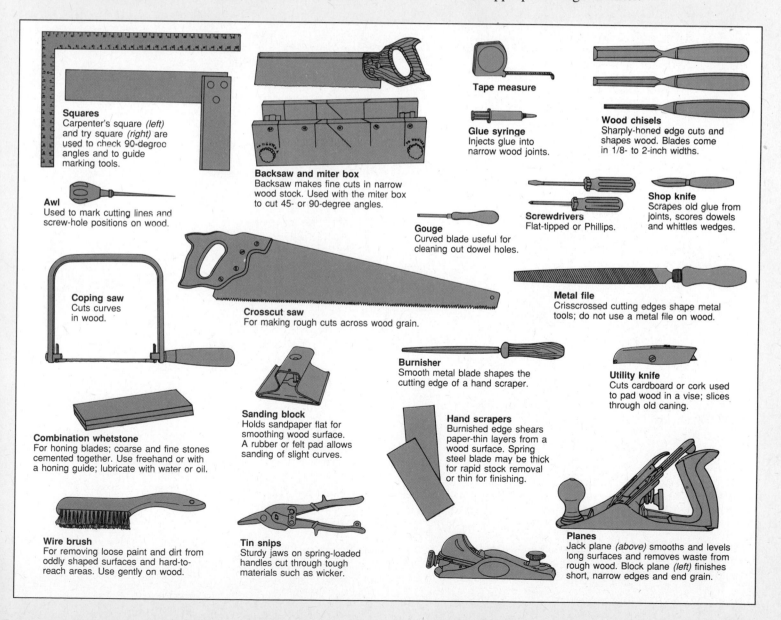

Squares
Carpenter's square *(left)* and try square *(right)* are used to check 90-degree angles and to guide marking tools.

Awl
Used to mark cutting lines and screw-hole positions on wood.

Backsaw and miter box
Backsaw makes fine cuts in narrow wood stock. Used with the miter box to cut 45- or 90-degree angles.

Gouge
Curved blade useful for cleaning out dowel holes.

Coping saw
Cuts curves in wood.

Crosscut saw
For making rough cuts across wood grain.

Combination whetstone
For honing blades; coarse and fine stones cemented together. Use freehand or with a honing guide; lubricate with water or oil.

Sanding block
Holds sandpaper flat for smoothing wood surface. A rubber or felt pad allows sanding of slight curves.

Wire brush
For removing loose paint and dirt from oddly shaped surfaces and hard-to-reach areas. Use gently on wood.

Tin snips
Sturdy jaws on spring-loaded handles cut through tough materials such as wicker.

Tape measure

Glue syringe
Injects glue into narrow wood joints.

Screwdrivers
Flat-tipped or Phillips.

Wood chisels
Sharply-honed edge cuts and shapes wood. Blades come in 1/8- to 2-inch widths.

Shop knife
Scrapes old glue from joints, scores dowels and whittles wedges.

Metal file
Crisscrossed cutting edges shape metal tools; do not use a metal file on wood.

Burnisher
Smooth metal blade shapes the cutting edge of a hand scraper.

Utility knife
Cuts cardboard or cork used to pad wood in a vise; slices through old caning.

Hand scrapers
Burnished edge shears paper-thin layers from a wood surface. Spring steel blade may be thick for rapid stock removal or thin for finishing.

Planes
Jack plane *(above)* smooths and levels long surfaces and removes waste from rough wood. Block plane *(left)* finishes short, narrow edges and end grain.

TOOLS FOR REPAIRING FURNITURE

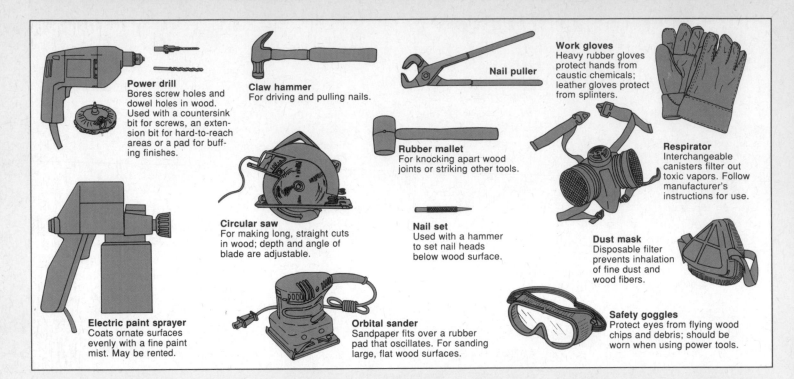

Power drill
Bores screw holes and dowel holes in wood. Used with a countersink bit for screws, an extension bit for hard-to-reach areas or a pad for buffing finishes.

Electric paint sprayer
Coats ornate surfaces evenly with a fine paint mist. May be rented.

Claw hammer
For driving and pulling nails.

Circular saw
For making long, straight cuts in wood; depth and angle of blade are adjustable.

Orbital sander
Sandpaper fits over a rubber pad that oscillates. For sanding large, flat wood surfaces.

Rubber mallet
For knocking apart wood joints or striking other tools.

Nail set
Used with a hammer to set nail heads below wood surface.

Nail puller

Work gloves
Heavy rubber gloves protect hands from caustic chemicals; leather gloves protect from splinters.

Respirator
Interchangeable canisters filter out toxic vapors. Follow manufacturer's instructions for use.

Dust mask
Disposable filter prevents inhalation of fine dust and wood fibers.

Safety goggles
Protect eyes from flying wood chips and debris; should be worn when using power tools.

SECURING WOOD IN A VISE

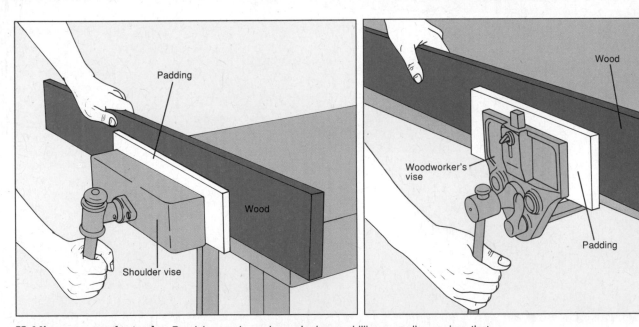

Padding

Wood

Shoulder vise

Woodworker's vise

Wood

Padding

Holding your work steady. Precision work, such as planing or drilling, usually requires that a wood furniture part be anchored in a vise. The shoulder vise *(above, left)* is built in to a woodworking bench; the woodworker's vise *(above, right)* is screwed onto a work table. To open the jaws of either vise, turn the handle counterclockwise. Fit the wood piece between the jaws in the desired position; insert wood, cardboard or cork padding to protect the wood surface from the jaws. Turn the handle clockwise to close the jaws of the vise against the wood, then tighten the handle an extra quarter turn. To release the piece from the vise, give a hard push on the vise handle with the heel of your hand.

CUTTING WOOD WITH A HANDSAW

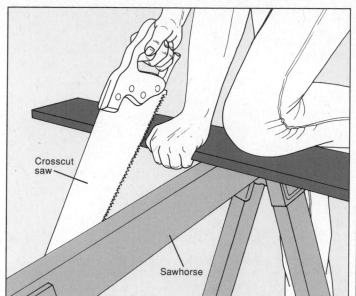

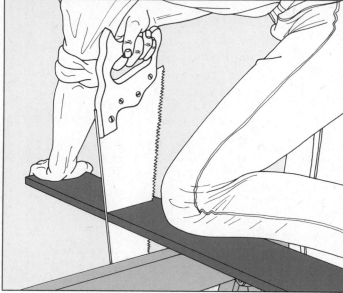

Cutting across the grain with a crosscut saw. A crosscut saw, which has about eight teeth per inch, is designed to cut quickly and roughly across a board at a 90-degree angle to the wood grain. Use an awl and a carpenter's square or try square to score a guideline on the board. Place the board across two sawhorses or on a work surface, with the waste end overhanging. Steady the board with one knee and hand; fold your thumb under your index finger. To start the cut in the edge of the board, hold the saw almost vertical, align your shoulder and arm with the line of the cut and draw the blade slowly toward you a few times. Once a notch is cut in the wood, lower the angle of the saw to about 45 degrees *(above, left)* and cut through the wood on the downstroke, until the blade is about 1 inch from the end of the cut. To finish the cut without splintering the wood, grip the waste end with one hand, hold the saw vertical *(above, right)* and use short up-and-down strokes.

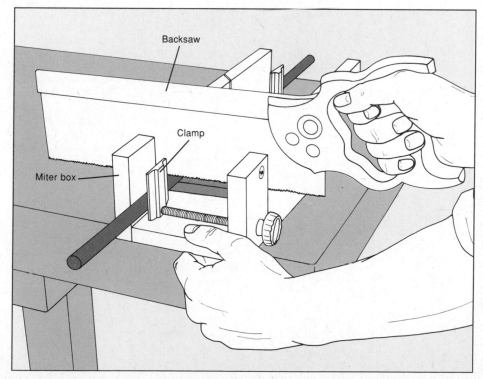

Using a backsaw for a smooth cut. The backsaw has about 13 teeth per inch and makes finer, cleaner cuts than the crosscut saw. It is often used with a miter box to cut at a precise 45- or 90-degree angle. Clamp the base of the miter box in a vise or hold it near the edge of a steady work surface. If the box is made of wood, cover the inside bottom with scrap wood to protect it from the bite of the saw. If the miter box has built-in clamps, clamp the wood in the box; otherwise, brace the wood against the back and bottom of the box with your hand, the finished side facing you. Slip the saw blade into the appropriate slot and grip the handle firmly, keeping your arm, shoulder and hip in line with the saw. Holding the blade level *(left),* start a notch by drawing the saw toward you a few times, then use long forward and backward strokes to cut the wood. Stop short of pulling the blade tip out of the front slot or butting the rear guide with the saw handle while cutting.

HANDLING A WOOD CHISEL

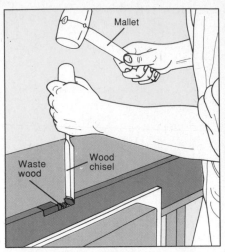
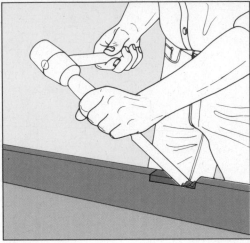
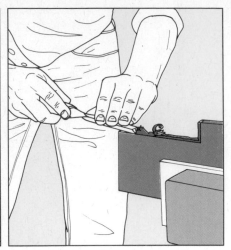

Notching and shaving wood with a chisel. When working with a chisel, always point the cutting edge away from your body and secure the material you are cutting in a vise. The method for using a chisel depends upon the cut being made. To make a deep cut along a scored outline, hold the chisel vertical, with the bevel facing the waste wood. Set the chisel tip against the outline and strike the handle with a mallet *(above, left)*. To pare off a thick layer of wood, hold the chisel at a 30-degree angle to the wood surface, bevel down, and strike the handle with a mallet *(above, center)*, lifting away short chips of wood. To smooth a wood surface, hold the chisel horizontal, bevel up, and use hand pressure only to make light strokes *(above, right)*, shaving away thin curls of wood.

WORKING WITH A HAND PLANE

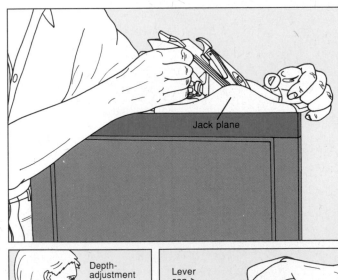
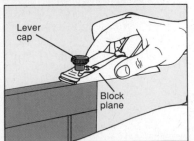

Trimming wood with two kinds of planes. A properly adjusted hand plane with a sharp blade provides a simple way to shave wood surfaces. The jack plane is used for heavy-duty leveling; the block plane trims smaller pieces of wood. The plane blade, or iron, is mounted in the plane at a set angle to the base. Its cutting depth and lateral position can be adjusted. To adjust the iron, hold the tool upside down and turn the depth-adjustment nut until the edge of the iron barely protrudes from the mouth of the plane *(bottom, far left)*. Push the lateral-adjustment lever from side to side until the iron edge is aligned squarely within the mouth. Test the plane on scrap wood; continue adjusting until you get the cut you want.

To use a jack plane, secure the wood piece in a vise and place the toe of the plane on the surface to be planed. Hold the front knob and the handle firmly and start the stroke, putting pressure on the toe. As you push the plane forward along the grain, shift the weight to the middle of the plane, then before the plane extends past the edge of the wood, transfer all pressure to the heel of the plane *(left, top)*, raising the plane from the surface in a smooth motion. When planing end grain, protect the corners of the wood from splintering by clamping a piece of waste wood to each end, or by lifting off before reaching the end, and planing the remainder in the opposite direction.

To level wood with a block plane, hold the plane in one hand, with the heel of the lever cap resting in the palm of your hand. Push the plane over the surface, putting more pressure on the toe *(bottom, near left)* and transfer the weight from the toe to the heel. As you finish each stroke, raise the plane from the surface in a smooth motion.

SMOOTHING A WOOD SURFACE

ABRASIVES

Sandpaper	Grit	Grade	Uses
Coarse	60 80	1/2 1/0 or 0	Sanding heavily coated surfaces; removes thick layers of paint, varnish or rust; levels deep depressions and scratches.
Medium	100 120	2/0 3/0	Sanding moderately coated surfaces; removes paint, varnish, rust; levels shallow depressions and scratches.
Fine	150 180	4/0 5/0	Final sanding of bare wood; light sanding of intermediate coats of paint.
Very fine	220 240	6/0 7/0	Light sanding of primer or sealer coats; final sanding before applying finish.
Extra fine	280 320	8/0 9/0	Removing fine particles and air bubbles from intermediate coats of finish.
Super fine	400	10/0	Final sanding before applying last coat of lacquer; reduces luster on final coats of varnish or enamel.

Steel wool	Grade	Uses
Very fine	2/0	Final removal of residue from chemical stripper; deglossing varnish or enamel.
Extra fine	3/0	Final smoothing of wood before applying finish; used with a lubricant for spot repairs.
Super fine	4/0	Applying rubbing stain, wax or oil; smoothing between finish coats; reducing luster on final coats of varnish or enamel.

Choosing an abrasive. Depending on its grade, sandpaper can be used to level a rough wood surface or to polish a finished one. The backing, which may or may not be paper, lists the type and size of the grit and the weight of the backing. For work on wood, choose sandpaper with a grit of garnet, aluminum oxide or silicon carbide. Garnet, reddish in color, is best for smoothing rough surfaces. It tends to wear quickly. Aluminum oxide is a tough synthetic, colored light grey to brown. Use it to sand rough to medium surfaces. Silicon carbide, also called wet-or-dry, has a waterproof backing that allows it to be used with water as a lubricant. It performs well in fine grades for polishing. When sanding wood, progress from coarser to finer grits. Use a soft-bristle brush or a tack rag *(page 102)* to remove sanding particles.

Steel wool comes in pads ranging from grade 1 to 4/0. Grades 2/0 and 4/0 are comparable to very fine and super fine sandpaper. Lubricate a 4/0 pad with furniture oil to polish a fine finish.

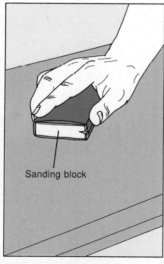

Evening surfaces with a sanding block. Sanding blocks are available at most hardware stores, but it is not difficult to make your own. Using a backsaw, cut a 1-by-4 wood block about 3 inches long. Saw a slot 1/8 inch deep along the center of one edge of the block. Sand away any sharp corners. Glue a piece of thick felt onto each face of the block. Cut a sheet of sandpaper large enough to wrap all the way around the block, plus 1/4 inch. Insert one edge of the sandpaper into the slot, fold the sheet around the block *(above, left)* and wrap the other end over the slot. To hold the sandpaper tight, staple the ends. Use the sanding block on flat surfaces, applying light pressure in short strokes parallel to the wood grain *(above, right)*.

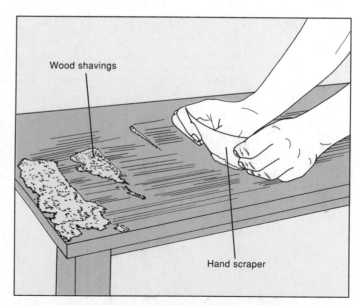

Shearing off a layer of wood. Burnish a hand scraper properly before using it *(page 118)*. Grip the scraper firmly with the fingers of both hands, placing your thumbs at the middle of the scraper. Bow the scraper slightly with your thumbs and tilt it forward. Push the scraper away from you along the wood grain, in long, continous strokes, producing fine wood shavings *(above)*. If you get fine sawdust instead, increase the angle of the blade.

SHARPENING CUTTING TOOLS

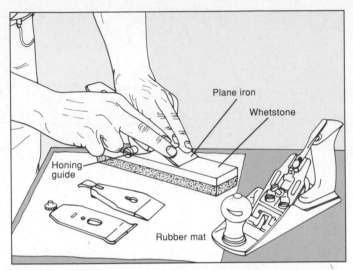

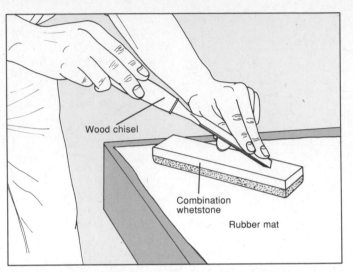

Honing a plane iron. Hone the plane iron before each use. Remove the cap screw with a screwdriver, then place the plane iron, bevel down, in a honing guide at the proper angle—between 25 and 30 degrees. Tighten the plane iron in the guide. Place a rubber mat beneath a combination whetstone to keep it from slipping and lubricate the whetstone with water or oil. Run the iron and guide along the coarser side of the whetstone several times, applying moderate pressure to the iron on the forward stroke *(above)*. To remove the metal burr that forms on the honed edge, flip the iron and guide, lay the iron flat on the stone and pull it along the length of the whetstone. Finally, polish the blade against the finer side of the stone.

Polishing the bevel of a chisel. When a chisel edge becomes nicked and dull, it will compress wood fibers rather than cut them. Sharpen a chisel on a whetstone before each use. Lubricate the whetstone. Hold the bevel of the chisel flat against the finer side of the whetstone. Using your body, rather than just wrist motion, push the chisel along the length of the stone, applying moderate pressure *(above)*. After any nicks have been honed from the edge, put a cutting edge on the bevel by tilting the handle slightly higher and using a circular motion. To remove the metal burr that forms on the edge, lay the chisel flat on the whetstone, bevel up, and pull the chisel toward you.

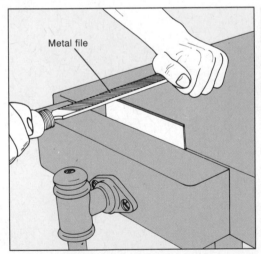

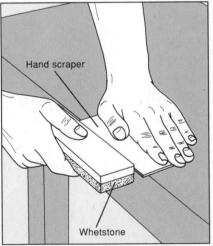

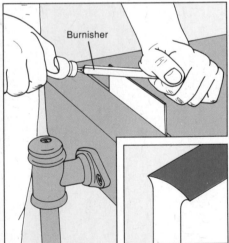

Filing, stoning and burnishing a hand scraper. To sharpen a hand scraper, you need a vise, a metal file, a whetstone and a hand burnisher. First, secure the hand scraper in the vise, long edge upward. Using moderate pressure, draw the file horizontally along the scraper edge a few times *(above, left)*. Flip the scraper over and file the other edge the same way. To remove serrations caused by the file, hold the scraper flat on a work surface with about 1/2 inch overhanging the edge and slide the finer side of a whetstone along both edges of the scraper several times *(above, center)*. Next, slide the whetstone back and forth on the flat sides of both edges to remove the metal burr. Secure the scraper in the vise again, and rub a burnisher over the flat sides of both edges. Then form the scraper hook *(inset)* by tilting the burnisher 10 to 15 degrees and passing it along one side of the scraper edge, then the other *(above, right)*. Burnish the opposite edge of the scraper the same way.

MAKING A STRAIGHT CUT WITH A CIRCULAR SAW

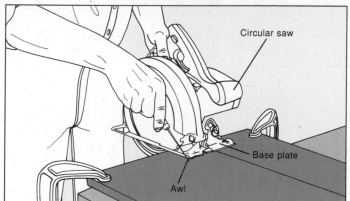

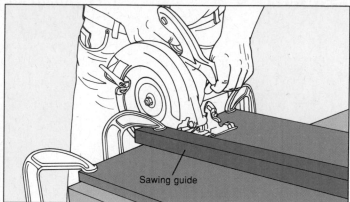

1 **Clamping and marking the piece.** Turn the piece of wood to be cut upside down, and use an awl and straightedge to mark a guideline for the cut. Raise the piece on four 2-by-4 boards: Place a board under each of the two side edges, and position a board along each side of the guideline, about 2 inches from it. Clamp the piece to the work surface near each corner. To mark a position line for the sawing guide (step 2), hold the saw against the end of the piece, lining up the notch in the base plate with the cutting guideline. Score a line with an awl along the edge of the base plate (above). Use the awl and a straightedge to extend this line the length of the piece, keeping it parallel to the cutting guideline.

2 **Cutting along the sawing guide.** Choose a straight 1-by-2 to serve as a sawing guide. Place it precisely along the position line and clamp it at each end. Set the depth of the saw blade to 1/2 inch more than the thickness of the piece. Position the base plate against the sawing guide, the blade about 1/2 inch from the wood. Turn on the saw and wait for the motor to reach full speed, then slowly push the blade into the wood (above). Push the saw steadily along the cutting guideline without forcing it, keeping the base plate against the sawing guide. If you cannot complete the cut in one run, do not try to start from the other end; rather, turn off the saw and reposition the piece without unclamping the sawing guide. Then insert the saw blade in the cut about 1/2 inch from where you left off, and complete the cut.

USING AN ORBITAL SANDER

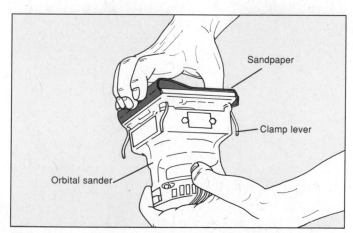

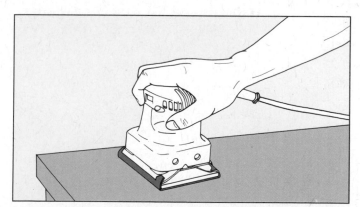

1 **Fitting sandpaper into the orbital sander.** Consult the chart on page 117 to choose the right sandpaper for the job. Use scissors to cut a piece of sandpaper to fit the pad of your orbital sander, or buy pre-cut orbital sander sheets. Pull the lever on each side of the sander to open the clamps. Fit one end of the sandpaper under one clamp (above) and close it. Pull the sandpaper tight against the pad and fit the other end under the opposite clamp.

2 **Smoothing a wood surface.** Grip the sander and turn it on, waiting for it to reach full speed before starting to sand. Starting near one corner of the surface to be sanded, guide the orbital sander along the wood grain (above) without pushing down on it. Lift the sander after each complete stroke. After sanding, dust the surface with a soft-bristle brush. If a finer finish is required, complete the job by hand with a sanding block.

WOOD FASTENERS

Flat-head wood screw
The most common screw for fastening wood, it can be countersunk below the wood surface and its head concealed with a wood plug or putty. Available in various lengths and diameters, indicated by number; made of steel, brass or other alloys.

Round-head wood screw
Fastens decorative hardware such as drawer pulls and handles. The round head is not countersunk. Available in various lengths and diameters, indicated by number; made of steel, brass or other alloys.

Oval-head wood screw
A decorative fastener for hardware. The underside of the screw head is countersunk and the oval top protrudes. Available in various lengths and diameters, indicated by number; made of steel, brass or other alloys.

Casing nail
Similar to a finishing nail. Has a tapered head that can be driven below the wood surface with a nail set. Sized by pennyweight, expressed by letter "d".

Wire brad
Smaller and thinner than a finishing nail, the brad has a tapered head that can be driven below the wood surface with a nail set. Available in lengths ranging from 3/8 to 1 1/2 inches.

Finishing nail
Has a small round head that can be driven below the wood surface with a nail set. Sized by pennyweight, expressed by letter "d".

Box nail
Has a wide, flat head that lies flush with wood surface; thin shank of nail is less likely to split wood than the common nail.

Hanger bolt
Made of steel with a machine-screw thread at one end and a wood-screw thread at the other end. Used with a corner bracket of metal or wood to join table legs to the apron.

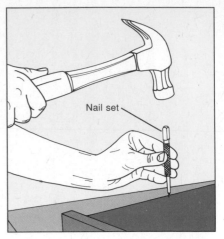

Using a nail set. To set the head of a finishing nail, casing nail or brad below the surface of the wood, first drive it in with a hammer until the head protrudes 1/8 inch. Choose a nail set with a tip slightly smaller than the nail head. Place the tip of the nail set on the head of the nail and tap the nail set with the hammer *(above)*, driving the head about 1/16 inch below the surface. Cover the nail head with wood putty, if desired.

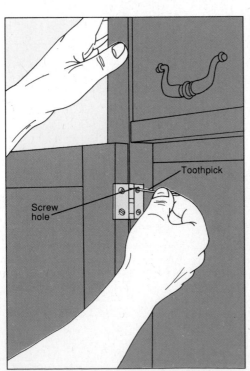

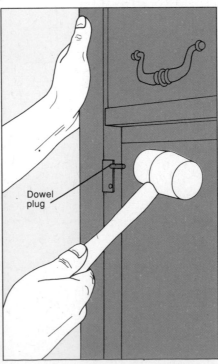

Building up a loose screw hole. To reseat a loose screw, insert toothpicks into the hole *(far left)* and break off their ends. Drive in a screw partway to position the toothpicks. Remove the screw and add glue to the hole, then drive the screw into place. For a badly enlarged screw hole, use a hardwood dowel to pack the hole. Fit a drill with a bit that matches the diameter of the dowel you will use (1/4 inch in narrow pieces of wood, 3/8 inch in wider pieces). Use masking tape to mark the drill bit to the depth of the screw hole. Bore straight into the hole, stopping when the masking tape touches the wood. Cut the dowel slightly longer than the depth of the hole, bevel one end slightly and score the sides with a shop knife or pliers. Coat the dowel and the inside of the hole with glue. Tap the dowel into the hole *(near left)*, trim it flush with a coping saw, then sand it smooth. Allow the glue to set for three to four hours, then drill the new screw hole into the dowel, using a drill bit slightly smaller than the diameter of the screw.

WOODWORKING GLUES

Glue	Characteristics
White glue	Made of polyvinyl acetate, white glue is a good all-purpose adhesive for indoor furniture. It sets in 30 minutes and takes about 24 hours to form a strong bond. White glue dries clear, but does not sand well. Because it has poor moisture resistance, it is not a good choice for repairing outdoor furniture.
Yellow glue	A favorite with woodworkers, yellow glue is thicker, slightly stronger and more moisture resistant than white glue. It sets in 30 minutes and cures completely in 24 hours. Yellow glue does not dry clear; excess should be wiped away while it is still wet.
Epoxy	The most versatile of adhesives, epoxy forms a strong bond, without clamps, on wood, glass and metal. Epoxy usually comes in two tubes: a resin and a hardener. Mix these two ingredients in equal proportions before applying the glue. Epoxy sets quickly and can be sanded. Because it is waterproof, it can be used on outdoor furniture. Wear gloves when mixing and applying epoxy, since it can cause skin irritation. Apply in a well-ventilated area.
Contact cement	This is a good choice for gluing large surfaces that receive little stress, such as veneers and plastic laminates. Apply contact cement to both surfaces, then let it set for five minutes before bringing the surfaces in contact. Mating surfaces must be positioned precisely, since mistakes in alignment cannot be corrected. Apply in a well-ventilated area.
Instant glue	Made of cyanoacrylate and sold under several brand names, this adhesive will bond virtually anything. A couple of drops flow freely into hairline cracks between wood and other materials to form an instant bond without clamping. Since instant glue bonds in less than 10 seconds, wear rubber gloves when applying the glue to prevent accidentally bonding skin.

Choosing the right glue. Glues vary in strength, water and temperature resistance, gap-filling ability, toxicity and drying times. Use the chart at left to help you choose the right glue for the job. In general, most furniture repairs can be handled with white or yellow glue. Yellow glue, also called woodworker's glue, is generally preferred to white, since it sands better and has higher heat and moisture resistance. Applied to tight, clean-fitting joints and properly clamped *(page 122)*, these glues dry to produce a bond stronger than the wood itself.

Other adhesives are used for more specialized jobs. Epoxy contains a resin and a hardener, and bonds wood and just about everything else. Contact cement is mainly used to bond thin, flexible materials to a flat surface. It is flammable and toxic, and takes a steady hand to mate the surfaces properly. Instant glue can bond a multitude of substances, including skin, in less than 10 seconds, and should be handled with great caution.

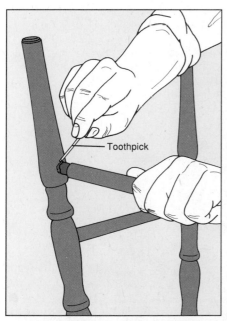

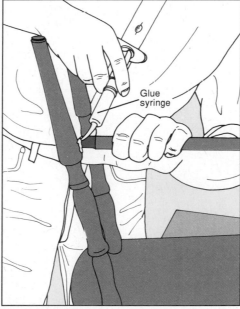
Glue syringe

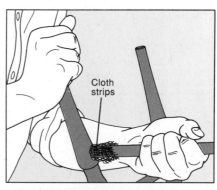
Cloth strips

Building up an ill-fitting joint.
Many glue joints fail because a dowel has been whittled down or a tenon has shrunk and the surfaces do not fit snugly. One way to build up a dowel or tenon is to coat it with glue, wrap it with thread, then wait for the glue to dry before regluing the joint. Another method is to wrap the dowel with cloth. Cut two strips of cheesecloth 3 inches by 1 1/2 inches, and spread a thin layer of white or yellow glue on the dowel or tenon. Lay a cheesecloth strip across the end of the dowel and press the cloth ends against the dowel. Lay the second strip over the first, forming a cross. Coat the cheesecloth with white or yellow glue. Fit the joint together *(above)*, trim off the excess cloth with a utility knife and clamp the joint *(page 123)*.

Sticking with glue. Apply glue to a clean, dry surface: Scrape away dried glue and wipe or vacuum away sawdust and wood chips. If the wood surfaces are perfectly smooth, score them lightly with a shop knife or the serrated jaws of pliers. Glue should be applied in a thin, even layer to both gluing surfaces. One method is to drip a few drops of glue from the bottle and work it into and around the joint with a toothpick *(above, left)* or an ice-cream stick. To force glue into tight corners, use a glue syringe, available at hardware stores, or an old hypodermic syringe with the needle removed. Take out the plunger to load the glue syringe with white or yellow glue. Push the long, thin tube of the injector directly into the joint, or into a 1/16-inch hole drilled into the joint for this purpose, and depress the plunger slightly *(above, right)*. Wiggle the joint to distribute the glue, then clamp it *(page 122)*.

Toothpick

CLAMPING FOR A SOUND JOINT

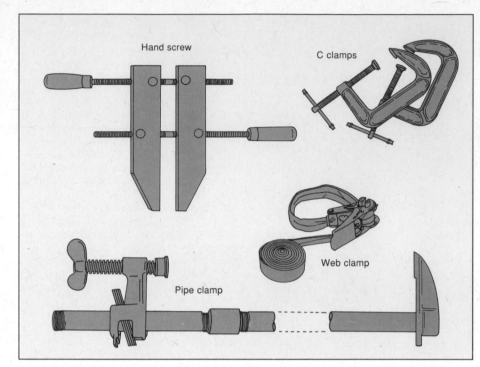

Good clamping practices. Clamps hold a joint in position while the glue sets. At left are four useful clamps for furniture repair. The C clamp serves for most small jobs. The versatile hand screw can do the job of a C clamp, but also adjusts to clamp non-parallel surfaces. The pipe clamp can be long or short, depending on the length of pipe used. The web clamp or band clamp encircles oddly shaped pieces and pulls them together. When applying a clamp, pad its jaws to protect the wood finish from the bite of the clamp; cardboard or cork can be wrapped around fine wood turnings or curves. To distribute clamping pressure, pad with strips of wood that stretch from clamp to clamp. Insert waxed paper between the joint and the pad to avoid gluing the pad to the wood. Tighten the clamp just enough to hold the pieces together. An even, continuous bead of glue escaping from the joint indicates proper clamping pressure; too much pressure can force out too much glue and "starve" the joint.

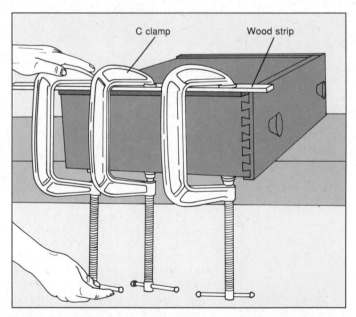

Using C clamps. C clamps can close a crack, secure work to a work surface and hold cutting guides in position. When clamping a freshly glued joint, position the clamp as close to the joint as possible, and insert wood pads beneath the clamp jaws. For larger areas use several clamps, evenly spaced, and add a wood strip to spread the pressure evenly. Use a C clamp of the appropriate size for the job; small repairs in a large clamp can throw the joint out of alignment. Turn the screw of the C clamp clockwise by hand *(above)* until the work is held snugly, then give an extra quarter turn. When using more than one clamp, tighten them alternately to maintain even pressure on the joint.

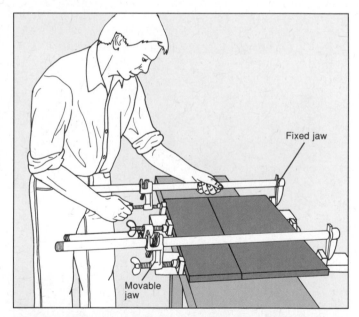

Securing wide pieces with pipe clamps. Handy for spanning table tops, the pipe clamp consists of a pair of jaw fittings attached to a 3/4-inch pipe of any length. To apply this clamp, fit the fixed jaw of the clamp against one edge of the work, then press the spring mechanism on the movable jaw and shift it until the shoe rests against the opposite edge. Hold the pipe in one hand while turning the screw handle until the shoe is snug *(above)*, then give an extra quarter turn. When using more than one pipe clamp, tighten them alternately to maintain even pressure on the joint. Position three pipe clamps as shown above: Raise the work on 2-by-4s covered with waxed paper and run the center clamp beneath it to equalize the pressure exerted by the two top clamps.

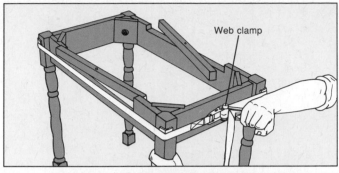

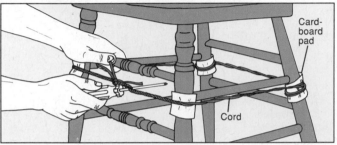

Pulling it together with a web clamp. The cinching action of the web clamp makes it useful for encircling irregular shapes and binding several joints at once. To apply this clamp, thread the web through the center of the ratchet, loop it around the piece being clamped and pull the excess web through the slot. Fit pieces of cardboard under the web where it contacts the wood to protect its finish, then crank the clamp taut *(left, top)*. Crank the handle by hand or, in some models, tighten the clamp with a screwdriver.

A homemade tourniquet clamp of non-stretching cord can take the place of a commercial web clamp. To apply a tourniquet to chair legs, as shown here, wrap a piece of cardboard around each leg near the joints being glued and secure it with masking tape. To keep the cord from slipping, wrap it once around each rear leg, then bring it around the front legs and pull it taut. Knot the ends together. Slip a screwdriver, a length of dowel or a sturdy stick through the doubled cord and twist it to tighten the cord *(left, bottom)*. Wedge the screwdriver against the foot rail to prevent the cord from unwinding.

WOOD JOINTS

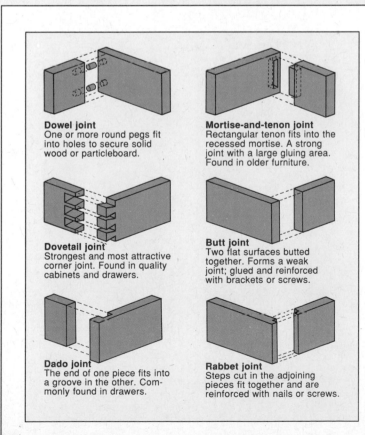

Dowel joint
One or more round pegs fit into holes to secure solid wood or particleboard.

Mortise-and-tenon joint
Rectangular tenon fits into the recessed mortise. A strong joint with a large gluing area. Found in older furniture.

Dovetail joint
Strongest and most attractive corner joint. Found in quality cabinets and drawers.

Butt joint
Two flat surfaces butted together. Forms a weak joint; glued and reinforced with brackets or screws.

Dado joint
The end of one piece fits into a groove in the other. Commonly found in drawers.

Rabbet joint
Steps cut in the adjoining pieces fit together and are reinforced with nails or screws.

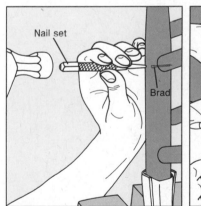

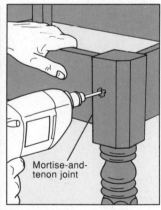

Removing locking fasteners. Chair and table joints are often reinforced by hidden fasteners. A small dimple in the wood near a joint indicates a brad. To remove it, position a small nail set over the brad and strike the nail set with a hammer *(above, left)*, forcing the brad head through one part of the joint into the second part. If the tip of the brad pokes through the other side of the joint, use pliers to pull it out. If a dowel locks the joint, try tapping it out with a mallet and a smaller dowel. If the dowel is glued in place, drill it out. Fit a drill with a bit that is slightly smaller in diameter than the dowel. Use an awl to punch a starting hole in the end of the dowel and drill straight into the dowel *(above, right)*, stopping about half-way through. To prevent splintering caused by a drill-bit exit hole, position the drill on the other end of the dowel, if it is exposed, and drill out that half. Blow sawdust out of the hole.

REBUILDING A BROKEN DOWEL JOINT

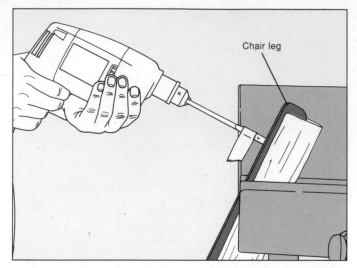

Chair leg

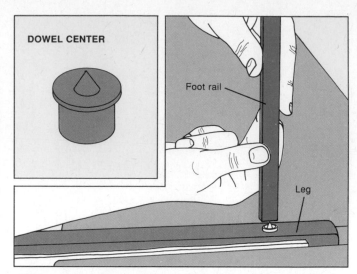

DOWEL CENTER

Foot rail

Leg

1 **Drilling into a broken dowel.** A dowel joint may break, leaving the dowel stuck in the hole. To repair the joint, drill a hole through the center of the broken dowel and install a new dowel. Secure the piece (in this case a chair leg) in a vise, padding its finish. Select a drill bit of the same diameter as the replacement dowel and wrap masking tape around the bit 7/8 inch from the end. Drill straight into the broken dowel *(above)*, stopping when the tape touches the wood. Blow out the sawdust.

2 **Using a dowel center to mark the drilling point.** A dowel center *(inset)* helps to align a dowel joint precisely. Reposition the leg in the vise so that the dowel hole faces upward, then insert the dowel center, point up, into the dowel hole. Use sandpaper to smooth rough edges from the adjoining piece (in this case, a foot rail). Mark the drilling point for the foot rail by lining up the two parts and pressing them together *(above)*. The dowel center will leave a position mark in the foot rail.

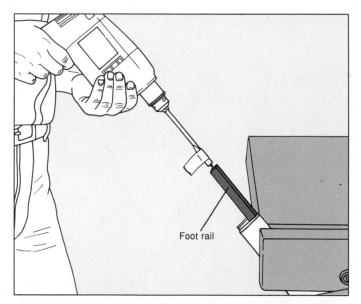

Foot rail

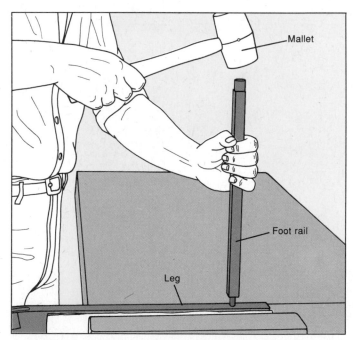

Mallet

Foot rail

Leg

3 **Drilling the dowel hole.** Release the leg from the vise and set it aside. Secure the foot rail in the vise, padding its finish. Use an awl to punch a drill starting point at the dowel center position mark. Using the same drill bit as in step 1, bore straight into the foot rail at the mark *(above)*, stopping when the tape touches the wood. Release the foot rail and tap out the sawdust. Cut a dowel of matching diameter 1 1/2 inches long, and bevel both ends slightly with coarse sandpaper. To allow excess glue and air to escape as the dowel is forced into the hole, score the dowel by drawing it through the serrated jaws of pliers.

4 **Fitting the joint together.** Secure the leg in the vise again. Spread white or yellow glue on the dowel and in the new dowel holes, then with a mallet tap the dowel into the hole in the leg. Slip the hole in the foot rail onto the dowel and tap it in place *(above)*. Remove the leg from the vise. Reassemble the chair and clamp the joint with a web clamp or tourniquet *(page 123)*. Wipe away excess glue with a clean, damp cloth. Release the clamp after 24 hours.

REBUILDING A BROKEN MORTISE-AND-TENON JOINT

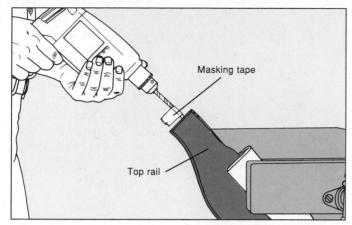

Masking tape

Top rail

1 **Drilling into the tenon.** If the tenon is badly damaged, cut it off and rebuild the joint with hardwood dowels. To begin, secure in a vise the part with the broken tenon (in this case, the top rail of a chair). Use a backsaw to cut the tenon flush with the wood surface and smooth it with medium-grit sandpaper. Use an awl to punch two drill position marks in the tenon, about 1 inch apart. Fit a power drill with a bit that matches the diameter of the dowel you will use (a 1/4-inch dowel for small joints, a 3/8-inch dowel for large joints). Wrap masking tape around the drill bit 7/8 inch from the end and bore a dowel hole straight into the top rail at each position mark *(above)*, stopping when the tape touches the wood.

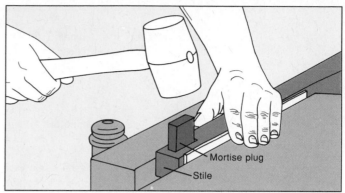

Mortise plug

Stile

2 **Plugging the mortise.** Release the top rail from the vise. Secure the mortised part (in this case, the back stile of the chair) in the vise, mortise facing upward. Use a chisel to clean out any remains of the broken tenon. Measure the length, width and depth of the mortise and use a backsaw and miter box *(page 115)* to cut a hardwood plug to fit. Bevel one end of the plug with medium-grit sandpaper and score lines on the sides of the plug to allow glue to flow around it evenly. Spread a thin layer of white or yellow glue inside the mortise and on the sides of the plug. Knock the plug into the mortise with a rubber mallet *(above)*. Wipe away excess glue with a clean, damp cloth. Let the glue set for three to four hours, then smooth the plug flush with medium-grit sandpaper.

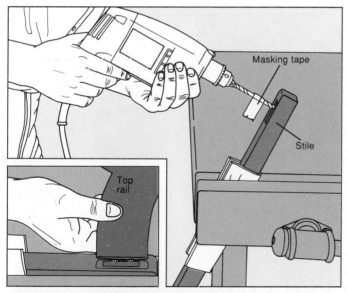

Masking tape

Stile

Top rail

3 **Drilling holes in the plugged mortise.** To make sure that the two pieces fit together properly, insert a dowel center *(page 124)* into each drilled hole in the top rail, the point facing upward. Align the two pieces in proper relation to each other *(inset)* and press them together. The dowel centers will leave position marks in the mortise plug. Use an awl to punch drill starting holes at the marks. With the taped bit you used in step 1, bore a hole straight into the top rail at each mark *(above)*, stopping when the tape touches the wood.

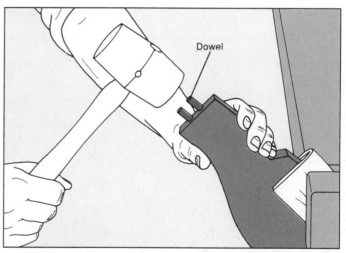

Dowel

4 **Assembling the joint.** Cut two dowels 1 1/2 inches long and bevel both ends slightly with coarse sandpaper. To allow excess glue and air to escape as the dowel is forced into the hole, score each dowel by drawing it through the serrated jaws of pliers. Secure the top rail in the vise. Spread white or yellow glue on one end of each new dowel and in each new hole in the top rail then, with a mallet, tap the dowels into the top rail *(above)*. Spread glue on the dowels and in the dowel holes in the mortise plug, then align the back stile with the top rail and tap the dowels into the holes. Remove the top rail from the vise. Reassemble the chair and clamp the joint with a pipe clamp *(page 123)*. Wipe away excess glue with a clean, damp cloth. Release the clamp after 24 hours.

INDEX

Page references in *italics* indicate an illustration of the subject mentioned. Page references in **bold** indicate a Troubleshooting Guide for the subject mentioned.

ACKNOWLEDGMENTS

The editors wish to thank the following:
Ann Babin, Ottawa, Ont.; Canadian Centre for Occupational Health and
Safety, Ottawa, Ont.; Russell Caplette, Kennebunk, Maine; Louis Gleicher,
New York Marble Works, Inc., New York, N.Y.; Neeraj Gupta, Association
of Specialists in Cleaning and Restoration, Falls Church, Va.; Gene and
Katie Hamilton, St. Michaels, Md.; Janet Hauser, Hauser Furniture, San
Diego, Calif.; Michael J. Hrtschan, Tradition Furniture Refinishing, Montreal,
Que.; John Kilby, W.H. Kilby and Co. Ltd., Toronto, Ont.; Tony Kudelko,
Weber Furniture Service Inc., Chicago, Ill.; Karl Kunkel, Professional
Upholsterer Magazine, High Point, N.C.; Roger Landreville, Atelier Roger
Landreville, Montreal, Que.; Lothar Loacker, Williams All Seasons, Highland
Park, Ill.; Gordon Macpherson, Montreal, Que.; Dr. Michael McCann, Center
for Safety in the Arts, New York, N.Y.; Jim McGill, Atelier Jim, Montreal,
Que.; Paul McGoldrick, Pianoforte, Montreal, Que.; Carlo Monaco, Tremco
Ltd., Toronto, Ont.; Fred Montgomery, Baystate Restoration, Brockton,
Mass.; Quebec Poison Control Centre, Sainte-Foy, Que.

The following persons also assisted in the preparation of this book:
Marie-Claire Amiot, Claude Bordeleau, Serge Paré, Gilles Proulx,
Natalie Watanabe and Billy Wisse.

Typeset on Texet Live Image Publishing System.